Collective Action in the European Union

D1344660

A key explanation for the development of European integration concerns the actions and perspectives of private and public interests. But if interests face great problems in working together at the European level, their ability to contribute to European integration is questionable.

Collective Action in the European Union is the first ever systematic investigation of collective action issues at the EU level itself. Bringing together an impressive array of EU and interest group scholars to investigate a key issue in European political economy, this study considers whether collective action is driven at the European transnational level by rational, utility maximising behaviour, or whether explanations couched in social terms are more convincing. The first chapters identify and address wider issues in transnational collective action. Later chapters apply these issues to specific domains, such as business, the professions, consumers, and environmental interests. Many of these chapters introduce fresh empirical evidence, including original surveys of the constituency of Euro groups and of national groups who operate at the European level.

The volume adds a rich tapestry of issues to the literature on collective action and presents some striking conclusions, including: that under certain conditions collective action is not problematic at the EU level; that a proliferation of new organisational formats has occurred; and that the European institutions are heavily involved in the group formation and maintenance process.

Justin Greenwood is the Jean Monnet, and University, Professor of European Public Policy at the Robert Gordon University, Aberdeen.

Mark Aspinwall is Lecturer in Politics at the University of Durham.

Collective Action in the European Union

Interests and the new politics of associability

Edited by
Justin Greenwood and
Mark Aspinwall

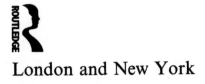

London and New York

First published 1998
by Routledge
11 New Fetter Lane, London EC4P 4EE

Simultaneously published in the USA and Canada
by Routledge
29 West 35th Street, New York, NY 10001

Typeset in Times by Pure Tech India Ltd, Pondicherry
Printed and bound in Great Britain by Creative Print and Design (Wales),
Ebbw Vale

British Library Cataloguing in Publication Data
A catalogue record for this book is available from the British Library

Library of Congress Cataloging in Publication Data
A catalogue record for this book is available from the Library of Congress

ISBN 0–415–15974–1 (hbk)
ISBN 0–415–15975–X (pbk)

Contents

Figures

Tables

List of contributors

Mark Aspinwall Mark Aspinwall is Lecturer in Politics at the University of Durham. His research interests are in European integration, and comparative political economy in western Europe. He is the author of *Moveable Feast: Pressure Group Conflict and the European Community Shipping Policy* (1995).

Maria Green Cowles Maria Green Cowles, Assistant Professor, University of North Carolina at Charlotte, has published articles in the *Journal of Common Market Studies, the Journal of European Public Policy* and *German Politics and Society*. She is currently completing a book entitled *The Politics of Big Business in the European Union*.

Laura Cram Laura Cram is Jean Monnet Fellow in European Public Policy at the University of Strathclyde. She is author of a number of articles on EU institutions and European integration and of *EU policy-making: Conceptual Lenses and the European Integration Process* (Routledge, 1997).

Justin Greenwood Justin Greenwood is Jean Monnet, and University, Professor of European Public Policy at the Robert Gordon University, Aberdeen. He is the author of *Representing Interests in the European Union* (1997), editor of the *European Casebook on Business Alliances* (1995), and coeditor of *Organised Interests and the European Community* (1992).

Grant Jordan Grant Jordan is Professor of Politics at the University of Aberdeen. His recent work on interest groups includes a forthcoming book (coauthored with William Maloney), *Protest Business: Mobilising Campaign Groups*. His interest in public policy is reflected in *The British Administrative System* (1994) and (as coeditor with Barry O'Toole) *Next Steps: Improving Management in Government?* (1995).

Niels Christian Sidenius Niels Christian Sidenius, Associate Professor in Political Science at the University of Aarhus, at present Dean, Faculty of Social Sciences, University of Aarhus. Research interests include industrial politics, business–government relations, interest associations, and EU policy making.

Ruth Webster Ruth Webster is currently undertaking a doctoral thesis at the Robert Gordon University, Aberdeen. Her research focuses on the patters of interaction between interests operating within the European environmental arena.

Alasdair R. Young Alasdair R. Young is a DPhil candidate at the Sussex European Institute. He recently completed, with Helen Wallace, an Economic and Social Research Council funded project on balancing public and private interests in EC regulatory policy making. A coedited volume is forthcoming and a coauthored book is in progress.

Acknowledgements

The contributors wish to gratefully acknowledge the financial support of the British Academy and the Carnegie Trust for the research on which a number of chapters are based, and the support of the British Academy and the European Consortium for Political Research, which enabled the contributors to meet together on two occasions.

The editors particularly wish to thank Lara Stancich for her assistance with the final editorial stages of this collection, and to both Linda Strangward and Lara Stancich for research assistance with the survey data presented in Chapter 1.

Abbreviations and acronyms

ACEA	Association of European Automobile Constructors
AmCham	American Chamber of Commerce
ANEC	European Association for the Coordination of Consumer Representation in Standardisation
BDI	Bundesverband der Deutschen Industrie
BEUC	European Consumers' Organisation
CA	Consumers' Association
CAP	Common Agricultural Policy
CBI	Confederation of British Industry
CCBE	Council of Bars and Law Societies of the European Community
CCC	Consumers Consultative Council
CEC	Confédération Européenne des Cadres
CEFIC	European Chemical Industry Council
CEG	Consumers in Europe Group
CEN	European Standards Committee
CENELEC	European Electro-technical Standards Committee
CEO	Chief Executive Officer
CI	Consumers International
CIFE	Council of Industrial Federations
CNE	Climate Network Europe
COFACE	Confederation of Family Organisations in the European Community
COREPER	Committee of Permanent Representatives
EAIC	European–American Industrial Council
ECAS	Euro Citizen Action Service
ECCA	European Campaign for Clean Air
ECFTU	European Confederation of Free Trade Unions
ECO	European Community Office of BirdLife International

ECOSA	European Consumer Safety Association
EEB	European Environmental Bureau
EEC	European Economic Community
EEG	European Enterprise Group
EFAH	European Forum for the Arts and Heritage
EFPIA	European Federation of Pharmaceutical Industry Associations
EFTA	European Free Trade Area
EFTA CCC	Consumer Consultative Council of the EFTA Secretariat
EMAS	Eco-Management and Audit Scheme
ENER-G8	A group of major energy-intensive manufacturing firms
EO/IFCTU	European Organisation of the International Federation of Christian Trade Unions
EO/WCL	European Organisation of the World Confederation of Labour
EPE	European Partners for the Environment
EPHA	European Public Health Alliance
ERT	European Round Table of Industrialists
ESNBA	European Secretariat of National Biotechnology Associations
ESPRIT	European Strategic Programme for Research and Development in Information Technology
ETSI	European Telecommunications Standards Institute
ETUC	European Trade Union Confederation
EU	European Union
EU Committee	EU Committee of the American Chamber of Commerce
EUROCADRES	Council of European Professional and Managerial Staff
EURO COOP	European Community of Consumer Cooperatives
EURO-C	Consumer Unit of the European Trade Union Confederation
EuroCommerce	European Federation of Retailing and Distribution
EUROFER	European Confederation of Iron and Steel Industries
EUROFIET	European Regional Organisation of the International Federation of Commercial,

	Clerical, Professional & Technical Employees
EWOS	European Workshop for Open Systems
FEANI	Fédération Européenne d'Associations Nationales d'Ingénieurs
FGSD	First General Systems Directive
FoEE	Friends of the Earth Europe
FoEI	Friends of the Earth International
GPSD	General Product and Safety Directive
Groupe des Présidents	Groupe des Présidents des Grandes Entreprises Européennes
ICA	International Cooperative Alliance
ICFTU	International Confederation of Free Trade Unions
ICRT	International Communications Round Table
ICT	Information and Communication Technology
IEC	International Electro-technical Committee
IEIC	European Inter-regional Institute for Consumer Affairs
IFCTU	International Federation of Christian Trade Unions
IGC	Inter-Governmental Conference
IOCU	International Organisation of Consumers Unions
ISO	International Standards Organisation
ISCO	International Standard Classification of Occupations
IUFO	International Union of Family Organisations
NCC	National Consumer Council
NFCG	National Federation of Consumer Groups
NFUS	National Farmers' Union Scotland
NGO(s)	non governmental organisation(s)
OECD	Organisation for Economic Co-operation and Development
OEEC	Organisation for European Economic Co-operation

PAC	Political Action Committees
REEN	European Third Sector Training Network
RSPB	Royal Society for the Protection of Birds
SAGB	Senior Advisory Group Biotechnology
SECO	European Secretariat for Coordination in Standardisation
SEM	Single European Market
SEPLIS	European Secretariat of the Liberal, Independent and Social Professions
SGSD	Second General Systems Directive
T&E	European Federation for Transport and Environment
TABD	Transatlantic Business Dialogue
TUC	Trades Union Congress
UASG	UNICE Advisory and Support Group
UEAPME	European Association of Craft, Small and Medium-Sized Enterprises
UN	United Nations
UN-ECE	United Nations Economic Commission for Europe
UFC	Union Fédéral des Conse
UNICE	Union of Industrial and Employers' Confederations of Europe
WCL	World Confederation of Labour
WWF	World Wide Fund for Nature

European Union Directorates-General

DG I	External Economic Relations
DG IA	External Political Relations
TFE	Enlargement Task Force
DG II	Economic and Financial Affairs
DG III	Industry
DG IV	Competition
DG V	Employment, Industrial Relations and Social Affairs
DG VI	Agriculture
DG VII	Transport
DG VIII	Development
DG IX	Personnel and Administration
DG X	Information, Communication, Culture, Audiovisual
DG XI	Environment, Nuclear Safety and Civil Protection
DG XII	Science, Research and Development Joint Research Centre
DG XIII	Telecommunications, Information Market and Exploitation of Research
DG XIV	Fisheries
DG XV	Internal Market and Financial Services
DG XVI	Regional Policies and Cohesion
DG XVII	Energy
DG XVIII	Credit and Investments
DG XIX	Budgets
DG XX	Financial Control
DG XXI	Customs and Indirect Taxation
DG XXII	Education, Training and Youth
DG XXIII	Enterprise Policy, Distributive Trades, Tourism and Cooperatives
DG XXIV	Consumer Policy and Health Protection

1 Conceptualising collective action in the European Union

An introduction

Mark Aspinwall and Justin Greenwood

The representation of interests in the European Union (EU) is undergoing rapid transformation. Private interests at the EU level have come to embody a significant force in European politics, affecting the way agendas are shaped and legislation is made. Approximately 693 formal EU-level interest groups have been formed, with more coming into existence every year, although there is no consensus on the precise number (a recent Commission database of 700 groups was released in consultative form in the hope that it would stimulate further information about other groups). Even less well known is the number of groups that have failed.

The European tradition of interest representation differs from practice in the United States. American politics has been steeped in pluralist representation from its inception. Some observers of American political life have marvelled at the number of civic associations, as Alexis de Tocqueville did in his book *Democracy in America* (1946); more recent observers have lamented the apparent decline in civic associability (Putnam, 1995). But there has always been a focus within the American polity on both the pluralist nature of civic voice and its relevance to political life.

Modern European states, on the other hand, have a tradition of strong political parties or administrative elites, insulating them (at least relative to America) from particularist private demands. This does not mean that private interests are impotent, but that they exist within an established framework that is usually less conducive to disruption by new interests and is usually restricted to fewer access points. However, the addition of a new 'polity' – the European Union – has added uncertainty to some of these established systems. The juxtaposition of discrete national systems of interest representation within a supranational system where varying degrees of authority are vested (depending on the policy area) raises fascinating new questions about the logic of collective action. How does the interaction of interests at the European level affect the established patterns of representation nationally? What is the motivation for EU collective action, and what shape does it take? A new opportunity structure has presented itself, challenging conventional European state–society relations, and the contributors to this volume have addressed the implications associated with that change.

Brussels shares some striking similarities with Washington. The structure of decision making in the EU lends itself to interest articulation in much the same manner as the federal government does in Washington. Divided institutions, fragmented and occasionally warring directorates within the Commission, many points of access within the institutions – all these provide opportunities for interest groups to feed the policy making process.

But there are clear differences between the EU and the US as well. At the EU level, territorial interests, rather than functional or ideological ones, have always been predominant. It is the peculiar nature of EU decision making that the Council of Ministers, representing the member states, has the final say over most legislation. The European Parliament, site of nascent pan European political parties, has only recently qualified as a contender for real influence, though that has changed with every revision of the Treaty of Rome. It is now beginning to attract interest activity as a result of what has been termed its conditional agenda setting power (Tsebelis, 1994).

The European Commission is the main forum to which private interests are attracted. The Commission estimated in 1992 that 'there are approximately 3,000 special interest groups of varying types in Brussels' (Secretariat of the European Commission, 1992: 4). Whilst this now appears to have been something of an overestimate, what is undisputed is the growth of interest representation in the EU (Butt Philip, 1985; Greenwood, 1997), and the way in which the lack of Commission resources creates opportunities for private interests (Metcalfe, 1992). Using information from the two principal directory sources available at the time, the 1995 European Public Affairs Directory (Landmarks Publications, 1994) and the 1992 Directory of European Associations (European Commission, 1992), a team of researchers at the Robert Gordon University in Aberdeen,[1] UK, compiled, in 1995, a list of 693 European-level interest groups, which perhaps more accurately reflects the population concerned with EU affairs. This population includes both formal and informal organisations which are created to address matters relating to the European Union. They include large and small businesses, consumers,

Table 1.1 European-level interest groups surveyed, November 1995–February 1996

Category	Group population (& number of questionnaires distributed)	Number of questionnaires returned	Response rate %*
Business	439	265	60
Consumer	6	5	83
Union	18	10	55
Professions	69	31	45
Public interest	147	83	56
Other	14	8	57
Unclassifiable		3	
TOTAL	693	405	58

* All percentages used in tables throughout are rounded up or down to the nearest whole per cent

environmentalists, other public interest groups, labour unions, and professional groups, but exclude territorial offices of regional and local authorities. This population was surveyed between November 1995 and February 1996. The sample, and the response rates obtained, are described in Table 1.1.[2]

Business groups thus predominate, accounting for 63 per cent of all those composited from the two Directories; 66 per cent (251) of all Euro groups (of both federated and direct membership type) were established prior to 1980, suggesting that the formation of such groups is not a relatively recent phenomenon in response to the single market. However, there are some significant differences between the categories of groups in periods of formation. Thus, whilst public interest groups account for 21 per cent of all Euro groups, a much higher proportion of these (69 per cent – 44 groups) were formed after the launch of the single market. This phenomenon can be attributed both to the enhanced competencies of the EU and to the activities of the European institutions themselves in developing networks with public interest groups (Chapter 3). Some 59 per cent of public interest groups are in receipt of European funding, while at the lower end of the scale only 4 per cent of groups representing the professions are in receipt of such help. Indeed, of interest is that the highest concentration of Euro groups to be found in the Brussels district are public interest groups (82 per cent – 110 groups), whereas only 36 per cent of groups (25 groups) representing the professions are based in Brussels, factors which are explained in Chapter 3 and Chapter 8 by reference to the institutional incentives provided by the EU, and to the historical relationship between individual member states and social groups.

As for the resources of Euro groups, some 55 per cent (155 groups) have a turnover exceeding 100,000 ECU. A higher than average 63 per cent (40) of public interest groups have such a turnover, compared with 53 per cent (92) of business groups. Similarly, while one-third of all groups (34 per cent – 138 groups) have five or more staff, the highest proportion of these (45 per cent – 38 groups) are public interest groups, compared with 28 per cent of business groups (i.e. 72 groups). A number of public interest groups in Brussels are policy offices of wider international movements (such as Amnesty International, Friends of the Earth, Greenpeace, and the World Wide Fund for Nature), each employing more than 100 staff world-wide. These groups are more concentrated than are the more specialised and numerous business groups, such as those in the oil industry, which has an entire trade association wholly devoted to environmental issues. Thus, the large size and budgets of the public interest groups are due to their concentration and the fact that many of them are in receipt of external funding.

As the number of groups has increased, so has the number of formats, adding complexity to the political environment. Interests are organised at the European level in a variety of ways, including direct membership, federations of national associations, and *ad hoc* networks (Tables 1.2 and 1.3).

Two-thirds of Euro groups are federated structures, that is, associations of associations, with the remainder consisting of direct membership outlets; 18 per cent (i.e. 73 groups) of Euro groups include other Euro groups in their membership. This indicates a significant degree of formal networking between groups, and a mechanism for the dissemination and socialisation of information and ideas. There are fewer direct membership organisations for the professions than for

Table 1.2 Principal[3] types of Euro group: federated or direct membership

Principal Type of Group	Number	%
Association of other associations	268	66
Direct membership – individuals	33	8
Direct membership – firms	104	26
TOTAL	405	100

[3] *See Notes at Chapter end.*

Table 1.3 Principal types of Euro group: federated or direct membership, by business, public interest, professions

	Business		Public Interest		Professions	
Principal type of group	N	%	N	%	N	%
Association of other associations	175	66	52	63	26	84
Direct membership: individuals	6	2	18	22	4	13
Direct membership: firms	79	30	9	11	0	0
Direct membership: individuals and firms	5	2	4	5	1	3
TOTAL	265	100	83	100	31	100

public interest or business groups, whilst membership organisations comprising individuals are principally to be found amongst public interest groups. As is argued later in this chapter, the type of Euro group may influence the pattern of incentive structures for associability.

One of the most significant issues facing these organised interests is the shifting balance of power among European institutions. Qualified majority voting, extended in both the Single European Act (SEA) in 1986 and the Treaty on European Union (TEU) in 1992, robbed the member states of veto power in some economic areas. Moreover, a new codecision procedure was created in the TEU, which gives the European Parliament a greater role in decision making and for the first time the ability to reject legislation that the Council favours. These institutional changes have strengthened (albeit moderately) functional and ideological interests at the expense of territorial interests, and helped to underpin the importance of non state actors in the policy making process; the rising numbers of these actors reinforces their impact in Brussels.

In addition, in the past ten years the EU has been given new competencies in areas such as consumer, social and environmental policy, and could by the end of the decade have powers over monetary policy and a single currency as well. This growth of authority has created the conditions for a parallel growth in interest representation as the need for information on complex regional economic issues becomes more urgent, and the opportunities to influence EU legislation spreads to new policy areas. These political changes have given organised interests new opportunities. New institutional balances of power, increased competence for the supranational level, changing state–society relationships, increased global economic transactions, more complexity and uncertainty – all these have raised the stakes for European actors.

At the same time, this is a story about European integration, and this collection deviates from the stale functional–territorial debate over the process of integration. Instead, it combines two fields of political science – European integration and collective action – in order to gain new insights on both. It bridges the gap between the large body of literature that has accumulated on European interest representation, and theories of collective action, which have focused primarily on national level association. It addresses the specific issues that firms, individuals and other actors face in organising at the European level, and in turn what this means for the process of integration, for institutional change, and for the evolution of member state politics.

The contributors to this book show that European-level actors are organising for the purpose of achieving collective political goals, rather than to take advantage of selective material incentives. Indeed, this volume shows that collective action cannot simply be thought of in terms of actors responding to the presence of particular stimuli; uncertainty, lack of information, and creative propagation of new symbols and allegiances by the supranational institutions (as Chapters 2 and 3 demonstrate) have led to new constituencies even without specific and identifiable incentives.

The immediate purpose of this chapter is to address the question: why associate at the European level? Much less attention will be devoted here to the equally interesting questions: why create the group in the first place; why stay associated; why inter group coalitions form; and why choose particular group formats. Although the contributions in this study do look at these questions, the main purpose here is to devise a relatively parsimonious conceptual framework to answer the principal questions: why associate? and, how is associability achieved?

The authors include those whose work has concentrated on the context and agency of European institutions (Cram, Chapter 3 of this volume); on the activities of sectoral interests at the EU level (Cowles in Chapter 5; Greenwood, Chapter 6; Webster, Chapter 8; and Young in Chapter 7), on collective action theory more generally (Jordan in Chapter 2), and on a specific country context (Sidenius in Chapter 4). The result is a distinctive contribution to the literature that adds to our understanding of both collective action questions and European integration.

ACCOUNTING FOR COLLECTIVE ACTION AT THE EU LEVEL

Why do various actors join Euro groups? Have they organised collectively in order to gain information, influence policy, because there is pressure to do so within an industry, or for non material reasons? What is the role of selective material incentives? Political pluralism, identity, activism, the desire for social change – these might explain some collective action, but can we seriously believe that business groups are forming for reasons other than economic ones? More to the point, can the political be separated from the economic?

Under Olsonian assumptions (Olson, 1971) (see Chapter 2, Jordan's discussion of Olson) one would expect a broad consumer organisation made up of individuals to face greater problems of collective action than a small group of very large businesses. One would also expect a federation of national associations to face different calculations of self-interest and rationality than direct membership organisations. Rational choice collective action theory has been applied with greatest reward within a homogenous political environment, where actors do not need to think about entering new cultural and political landscapes. The presence of multiple vertical levels – substate, national, EU level – and various new horizontal political environments (other member states), makes membership decisions much more complex and blurs the distinction between action and outcome.

The principal focus for these Euro groups is the supranational institutions of the European Union, particularly the European Commission. What is on offer in Brussels – the putative shorthand for these institutions? Brussels is where the agenda is shaped in those policy areas where the EU has competence. Commission proposals have their genesis and decisions are made here. Interests seek influence over regulation and enablement, measures for integration, promotion, and funding. Information which helps shape this agenda is traded for influence – European institutions need information from private actors; in turn, these actors are in a position to shape the outcome of the debate. Without voice there is no influence. Survey data bear out this obvious but important fact (Tables 1.4–1.9).

Of significance in Table 1.4, therefore, is the very limited extent to which hard, material, economic types of incentives such as discounts and access to services are provided by Euro groups. Apart from representing members' interests in Europe, the membership services of access for members to EU working parties, information

Table 1.4 Membership services provided by a sample of Euro groups

Service	Number	%
Representing members' interests in Europe	382	94
Access for members to EU advisory committees, working parties, etc.	254	63
Information newsletters	279	69
Advice services	250	62
Discounts with suppliers	14	3
Membership discounts to join other organisations	9	2
Access to business services	39	10
Access to legal services	62	15
Access to public affairs consultants on preferential terms	14	3

newsletters, and advice services, are provided by approximately two-thirds of Euro groups. These are analysed by domain in Table 1.5.

There appear to be some important differences between the domains in the membership services provided, particularly in the provision of the services identified as common in Table 1.4. Thus, access to EU working parties is less commonly provided for members by public interest groups than by those representing business and the professions, whereas the reverse is true in the case of information

Table 1.5 Membership services provided by a sample of Euro groups: business, public interest, professions

Service	Business N	Business %	Public Interest N	Public Interest %	Professions N	Professions %
Representing members' interests in Europe	260	98	70	84	29	94
Access to EU advisory committees, working parties, etc.	179	68	37	45	19	61
Information newsletters	170	64	70	84	22	71
Advice services	170	64	52	63	12	39
Discounts with suppliers	10	4	4	5	0	0
Membership discounts of other organisations	3	1	4	5	2	6
Access to business services	25	9	8	10	4	13
Access to legal services	46	17	8	10	5	16
Access to public affairs consultants on favourable terms	10	3	3	4	0	0
Number responses	265		83		31	

Table 1.6 Types of associational format by membership services provided

Membership service	Federated membership		Direct membership	
	N	*%*	*N*	*%*
Access for members to sit on EU advisory committees, working parties, etc.	179	*67*	84	*61*
Information newsletters	170	*64*	104	*76*
Advice services	170	*64*	92	*67*
Access to business services	25	*9*	19	*14*
Access to legal services	46	*17*	28	*20*
Total number of respondents	265	100	137	100

newsletters. Advice services are far less commonly provided by groups representing the professions, reflecting the generally lower level of resourcing of these groups.

Table 1.6 provides a limited degree of evidence for different membership rationalities applying between federated and direct membership types of Euro groups. Apart from access to EU working parties, direct membership groups tend to provide more of each of the incentives in Table 1.6 than do federated structures, although the differences are small.

Of interest from Table 1.7 is the importance attached by groups themselves to the provision of information as a membership incentive, ranking joint first alongside the more obvious 'representing members' interests in Europe'. This is examined by domain in Table 1.8.

Some significant differences are evident in Table 1.8. Apart from the small numbers involved in the category 'providing members with access to discounts on goods and services', the majority of the most commonly provided membership services were less often ranked as important by public interest groups. It is possible that this reflects the

Table 1.7 Factors rated *1* or *2* in importance (scale 1–5) of a sample of Euro groups

Factor	Number	%
Representing members' general interests in Europe	316	*85*
Access to EU working parties, etc.	160	*53*
Providing members with information on EU Issues	298	*84*
Providing members with access to services	119	*45*
Providing members with access to discounts on goods and services	12	*6*

Table 1.8 Factors rated *1* or *2* in importance (scale 1–5) of a sample of Euro groups: business, public interest, professions

	Business		Public Interest		Professions	
Factor	N	%	N	%	N	%
Representing members' general interests in Europe	220	89	48	67	25	89
Access to EU working parties, etc.	125	60	17	31	10	50
Providing members with information on EU issues	205	88	50	70	21	78
Providing members with access to services	77	44	23	43	11	55
Providing members with access to discounts on goods and services	4	3	7	17	1	7

position of some public interest groups as policy offices of wider international organisations, rather than membership organisations *per se*. Once again, access to EU working parties seems to be much less important to public interest groups than to others. Business groups, interestingly, were more likely to rank most of the commonly provided membership services as important. Once again, the importance of information as a membership incentive is emphasised by this table.

Table 1.9 shows that specific incentives tend to be of equivalent importance both for recruiting and sustaining membership. There was

Table 1.9 Factors rated by a sample of Euro groups as among the two most important in encouraging affiliation, and sustaining membership, of their own organisation

Factor	Recruiting Members	Sustaining Members
Representing members' general interests in Europe	252	239
Providing members with access to services	44	45
Providing members with information on European issues	171	167
Providing access to discounts for members on goods and services	2	3
Providing members with access to EU committees, etc.	31	30
Miscellaneous factors	75	70
Total cases	288	281

no significant difference between domains in terms of the importance of incentives.

Thus, respondents overwhelmingly indicated that information and influence were the primary reasons for both encouraging and sustaining membership of Euro groups. One indicator of this is the growing number of informal networks which have emerged in recent years to satisfy demand for networking, gossip, news, views and interpretations; one such example of this is the EU Committee of the British Chamber of Commerce, with its regular programme of breakfast meetings with keynote speakers. Information is returned to private interests as well, in the form of intelligence about political and economic developments. Selective incentives to entice group formation sometimes exist, such as Commission funding for core group operations and development or the provision of professional services by large groups to members. However, evidence suggests the preponderant reasons for association in Brussels are influence and information.

MODELLING COLLECTIVE ACTION

We now turn our attention to modelling collective action in the EU. This entails the identification of three sets of variables, and a consideration of the hypotheses they may generate. The dependent variable is collective action; the independent variables are the incentives necessary to induce collective action; the intervening variables are the contexts through which these incentives are assimilated. We treat each in turn below.

Defining and differentiating collective action

Collective action is defined here as 'the investment of resources by individuals or organisations and the bringing together of these individuals or organisations in the collective pursuit of a common interest, which may result in selective or collective benefits' (the seminal statement on the distinction between these benefits is given by Olson). It is important that actors invest resources (such as time or money) in this pursuit; without this level of commitment, it is not possible to describe their action as collective. Equally, they must be brought together in the sense of belonging to a movement and gaining membership of an organisation, regardless of how formal the organisation. This again signals a commitment to an ongoing effort, irrespective of the motive for membership. An example that would fall outside this definition is the American case of a contribution to a political action committee, where the contribution is akin to a market transaction – a particular product is chosen and paid for. This definition is not always easy to apply in practice. As we hinted above, organisations may be highly informal and *ad hoc* in nature. While federations of national associations and direct membership groups are well known types, recent years have witnessed the growth of collective structures in Europe which are not formal groups, but rather platforms, coalitions, and alliances linking different types of interests in various degrees of permanence. Thus, the forms of collective action range from formal groups (at one end of the spectrum) to 'disorganised collective action', such as *ad hoc* alliances (at the other end). Groups may begin life as relatively informal networks or clubs, before progressing to a more formalised arrangement. Alternatively, they may begin as formal groups.

Informal groups have emerged primarily around large firms, and range from visible groups with a loose organisation, to privately organised *ad hoc* dining clubs. Some are issue based, others are built around sectors, while others are cross sectoral. Some are open membership structures, sometimes initiated by the European institutions, while others are more exclusive clusters of a select number of firms. Some are developing into more recognisable and formal Euro groups, whereas others are transient, or are likely to remain, by design, as informal meeting points (see Chapter 5 on the changing nature of business interest representation in Europe). These informal groups have become fashionable in recent years as the interests within them find such structures valuable; as Cram has suggested, cooperation in one type of structure can lead to collaboration elsewhere (Cram, 1995a). But equally, such structures can lead to the foundation of similar forums by outsiders who witness their effectiveness, or who seek to find ways of responding to their exclusion. In turn, this illustrates how the presence of collective structures, and participation within them, can influence the behaviour of private interest actors themselves.

At the more visible end of the spectrum are an increasing number of round tables, such as those which have sprung up in information technology and banking. Some round tables have become formal groups, while others are a semi permanent form of dialogue between firms. Other visible structures include issue alliances, which, as in the case of computer software patents, arise because of the inability of sector-wide groups to accommodate the competing interests concerned (Pijnenburg, 1996). An example of another type of issue structure from the IT sector illustrates Cram's point about how participation in the European institutions can yield cooperation. That is, collaboration within the CEN/CENELEC framework facilitated the creation of the European Workshop for Open Systems (EWOS) in 1987 as a means of drafting standards (Greenwood and Cram, 1996).

Other visible groups have emerged along cross sectoral, multi-issue lines. The European Business Agenda (formerly Business in Europe) group, a Brussels-based group comprising a handful of large British firms arising from a select dinner event, has sought to influence the behaviour of the British government towards Europe and towards the Intergovernmental Conference which began in early 1996. The group has no formal secretariat, is kept deliberately small and informal, and operates primarily through interpersonal exchanges between a group of friends based in Brussels. Such features mean that group members can exchange gossip freely about developments in Brussels without problems of accountability, and work very quickly together as issues demand. Because of the nature of the group and its focus upon high politics areas, it is not a lobbying organisation, but operates more at the level of ideas and information.

The less visible groups also span the sectoral, and cross sectoral, dimensions. One example of the latter is provided by the Ravenstein group (Cowles, 1994; Coen, 1995), an elite, dining club group of government affairs directors operating from Brussels, where individuals meet and talk informally. Multinational firms in the IT sector from Europe and the USA meet as a wholly private organisation without a formal structure or budget, and with a temporary rotating chair. Members are invited by a particular company to a lunch meeting at which a topic will be presented followed by a discussion, and consideration of the latest rumours.

There are now a plethora of these kinds of structures encompassing a variety of interest domains. As Alasdair Young describes in Chapter 7, European and national consumer groups have developed elaborate structures for coordinating their participation in the European standards bodies. Moreover, Ruth Webster points out in Chapter 8 that the Group of Seven major European environmental organisations has been adept at informal collaboration on a variety of issues. Other forms of organisation include caucuses of firms seeking to provide a particular direction to the activities of a particular interest group. They can provide important 'think tank' capacities and ideas leadership, as well as providing a 'short and unclogged' information channel and socialisation network for members (Pijnenburg, 1996: 27). Their exclusive and informal nature, together with their networking roles, raises interesting questions of collective action. They provide flexibility for firms to respond to the unpredictability of the European business environment, whether they act as issue networks, information and socialisation networks, ideas forums, or quick response mechanisms. They can enhance identity and interest cohesion, and carry few risks of a loss of autonomy that might arise from compromising positions through Euro groups (Cram, 1995a; Pijnenburg, 1996).

While transient groups may in some cases fit the definition of collective action as set out above, it is important that members have common interests in the collective structure, and that these interests are not one-off events or temporarily coinciding desires. Common interests do not perish with the passing of a discrete event or issue; they also survive the change in formats discussed above. Therefore, *ad hoc* meetings between different types of interests called in response to external stimuli, such as a meeting between car manufacturers and consumer groups to discuss entrenched differences between car safety standards, would not be sufficiently permanent to fit the definition of collective action.

Defining collective action broadly enough to include a variety of different groups raises an important point: the very structure of these groups (apart from the incentives they provide) may affect the membership decision. When firms, for example, may choose between several competing forums (such as federations of national associations, direct firm membership associations, and others), their perceptions of the efficacy of these forums will be important to their membership decisions. Which brings us to the second set of variables.

Membership incentives

A number of incentives induce latent group members to take collective action at the European level. These include the pursuit of information and influence, the availability of external funding, social status, the desire to act responsibly, among many others. Some of them may emanate from the group itself; others may be external. But they need to be ordered in a theoretically coherent way. In order to make sense of these incentives, we have arranged them in a matrix, adopted from rationalist, pluralist, and commitment perspectives on collective action (see Figure 1.1).

The matrix adopts (with alterations) the incentive distinctions raised by Olson (1971) and by Clark and Wilson (1961). Horizontally, the matrix represents a division between selective and collective incentives. Selective incentives are those promising a benefit specifically for

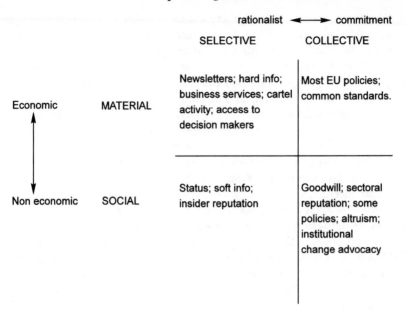

Figure 1.1 Typology of incentives

the joiner; collective incentives suggest that the benefits will apply to both members and non members. One of Olson's most important (and controversial) contributions to the literature was the assertion that actors would, in most cases, only join groups if selective incentives were made available. These incentives would reward them for the contribution of their resources, and would be available to them alone (see Jordan, Chapter 2; for other critiques, see amongst others, Moe, 1980; Dunleavy, 1991; Schlozman *et al.*, 1995; Walker, 1983; Marsh, 1976; Sabatier and McLaughlin, 1990; Jordan *et al.*, 1994). Any collective goods which emerged because of the existence of the group would be by-products, secondary to the provision of selective incentives.

The importance of this contribution for our purposes is the distinction between selective and collective incentives. The former are expected to appeal to those making a rational, self-interested choice about the best means to enhance their well-being. The latter (we adopt the language of Sabatier and McLaughlin, 1990; Sabatier, 1992) are expected to appeal to those committed to some notion of the greater good. While commitment seems to be important for the creation and maintenance of some large groups of individual members, it can plausibly be attributed as a general motivating factor for all collective action in which the incentive to join is not strictly selective. In other words, even among small groups of businesses, a commitment to the goals of the group would be essential for those who see the primary attraction as the creation of a collective good. This differentiation is slightly problematic in practice, as we discuss shortly, but it represents a reasonably attractive first cut on the distinction between personalised (or selective) incentives and collective incentives (often perceived by those advocating them as being in the public interest).

Vertically, the matrix represents a division between material and social incentives. Material incentives are those bringing direct and indirect economic gain; social incentives imply a less tangible gain, such as status or personal gratification. The image is one of hard versus soft incentives. Here we adapt the typology of Clark and Wilson (1961), who distinguished between material, solidary, and purposive incentives to reflect the different stimuli individuals respond to – from remunerative and economic to social and psychological. Some of the latter rewards, falling into the purposive category, were considered ideological or issue-based, and did not provide tangible benefits. However, we do not distinguish between solidary and purposive incentives, but group them together under the social rubric, on the grounds that the more meaningful distinction is that between economic and social incentives. The latter case involves those which attract members who believe in advancing public goods of a non economic nature.

In the EU, material selective incentives are those providing specific targeted goods to group members, such as newsletters and business services. It includes what we term hard information, that is information which promises a specific material reward. These are contained in the upper left box. It may also include access to decision makers where this provides a tangible economic benefit to the participant. Material collective incentives (in the upper right box) are also economic, but once provided apply to all members of the latent population. These include most common policies and industry standards, and more particularly the ability to exert influence on the decision making process leading to the adoption of these policies or standards. In this case, access to decision makers would be for the purpose of collective, rather than selective, goods.

Social selective incentives (in the lower left box) provide specific targeted social goods to potential members, including the status associated with European political activity. In addition, soft information falls within this category. This refers to the sort of information available to insiders, such as rumours and advance knowledge, that does not have an immediate and obvious economic payoff. Moreover, certain actors may derive a unique benefit from having a reputation as insiders, and this would fall within the social selective category. Likewise, firms may wish to gain a reputation as good corporate citizens, which may cause them to participate in a group effort. Individuals also derive personal satisfaction from contributing to what they view as a noble cause; this personal satisfaction is a social selective incentive.

Social collective incentives (in the lower right box) refer to non economic benefits accruing to the public as a whole. These include altruistic incentives and the desire to change institutional decision making mechanisms. Social collective incentives also include promoting the reputation of an entire sector through flag waving or good corporate citizen activities, although such actions may also have underlying material motivations. Finally, social collective incentives might prompt participation by those wishing to contribute to certain policies of a normative, justice oriented nature, such as anti racist or pro human rights pronouncements by the EU institutions.

While this neat division of incentives into a matrix is helpful as an explanatory device it is somewhat misleading. In reality, incentive types are not discrete and it is difficult to distinguish between selective and collective incentives, and between material and social incentives. For example, a protectionist industrial policy benefiting producers at the expense of taxpayers and consumers would represent a collective good to some and a collective bad to others. In other words it would be a partial collective good, which means that it is also a partial selective good. Likewise, social incentives such as status or insider access to soft information and institutions may easily be translated into influence, meaning that the lure of material gains may be an end-product of such access.

Environmental policies also straddle the line between material and social. To some, a tough environmental policy represents the protection of all citizens from the externalities of industrial activity. To others, it is a material burden to the costs of production, and might attract interests on those grounds. In addition, the sense of satisfaction from supporting a good cause, even if it does not materially benefit the individual, may be considered a selective return on investment (Moe, 1980). Therefore, it is more useful to think of these incentives as existing along a continuum, from material to social on one side, and from selective to collective on the other.

This framework of incentives is a self-consciously positivist approach, which assumes the existence of clear signals to which potential group members respond. However, in addition to the existence of these incentive signals, it would appear that there are perceptual issues at work affecting the way actors process them; we believe that the way they are perceived by actors depends on several specific features of the incentives: their exhaustibility; their tangibility; and their fungibility.

The exhaustibility of an incentive refers to the extent to which additional group members subtract from the supply of the incentive. For example, the availability of EU funding for research projects or for regional development is finite; therefore, one would expect early claimants to have a superior case, and this ought to spur interested parties to action. On the other hand, incentives such as altruism, status, or selective membership benefits like insurance discounts are presumably less subject to being exhausted. This gives actors the assurance that the incentives will continue to be available, and thus gives them an open decision horizon.

The tangibility of the incentives refers to how obvious or clear they are. Many incentives, such as influence or informal information gathering capabilities, are not clearly defined ahead of the group joining decision and therefore cannot be assessed with certainty before the actor joins the group. Indeed, the perception of missing out on something, almost irrespective of the reality, may be an important membership incentive. This lack of knowledge places many potential group members in an area of great uncertainty and could in theory cause them to react in very different ways. Firms and other business organisations, as well as labour and consumer groups which are interested in preparing for the single market, may feel the need to minimise surprises (McLaughlin and Jordan, 1993; see also Chapter 2) in this uncertain environment by taking collective action at the European level. This is so because there is a perception that the opening of markets has brought with it considerable risk and opportunity, and to cope with this, economic actors need information about political and economic conditions (Vipond, 1995), ranging from information about politics and markets, to network information such as the strategies and behaviour of competitors, or simply gossip.

The uncertainty associated with incentives such as influence or information has led some to the conclusion that economic interests often join Euro groups in order to alleviate the costs of non membership (McLaughlin and Jordan, 1993; Greenwood and Cram, 1996). In other words, it is the fear of losing out that drives membership decisions in the face of vague and ill-defined incentives, rather than the wish to take advantage of specific benefits. However, distinguishing the cost of staying out from the benefit of being in may in practice be difficult. Actors may indeed interpret the incentive signals by reference to what they have to gain or lose, but more crucially, it is the specific benefits themselves, or the thought that such benefits might possibly exist (information and influence most importantly) that ultimately attract members to groups, even when they are of varying clarity and certainty. In other words, it is not simply the fear of losing out that may drive membership decisions, but the fear of losing something that may benefit the group member. Latent group members respond to these incentives (whether positive or negative) in different ways. Some may attempt to perform a hard cost–benefit analysis. Others, in a climate of uncertainty, may attempt to limit the damage of non membership (as a kind of insurance of policy). Finally, there are organisations, particularly those which are themselves associations, where there may be a generally supportive culture towards affiliation; some two-thirds of Euro groups are federations of national associations (see also Chapter 4).

The fungibility of incentives refers to whether they are available in more than one place. For example, if cheap insurance was being offered by a Euro group as an enticement to potential members, but was also available locally, the strength of the incentive would be reduced. This probably explains why incentives unique to the European level are so important in attracting members to Euro groups. Throughout Euro groups, for example, information provision was ranked as important by 84 per cent, while representing members' interests in Europe was ranked as important by 85 per cent. Moreover, traditional selective material incentives such as discounts on goods and services ranks very low as an incentive at the EU level, reflecting the fact that these services are available elsewhere. In Denmark, as Niels Sidenius explains in Chapter 4, national associations have various routes they can choose from to engage in political activity, of which one is EU-level collective action. EU action may or may not be the most feasible route taken – depending on a variety of other factors – but the existence of alternative means of satisfying goals is important.

The context of membership decisions

The third aspect of the model involves spelling out the intervening variables which influence the processing of specific incentives by actors and ultimately the outcome of EU collective action decisions.

We suggest there are four specific intervening variables, each operating at a different level of analysis. They are the type of unit (individual, firm, and so on), the state context, the EU institutional environment, and the global or extra-regional environment. Variations in each of these intervening variables lead actors to interpret and process group membership stimuli in specific ways, leading to different outcomes.

Type of unit

Many different types of actors have chosen to associate in Brussels – individuals, firms, trade unions, environmental and other public interest groups, associations of the professions, governmental bodies, and others. Can we categorise collective action decisions based upon the characteristics of these actors? In other words, with a given set of incentives, do actor-types emerge in regular and predictable patterns? We believe so. The features of the unit making the collective action decision – size, function, and organisational characteristics – will colour its decision. The organisational nature of the unit (individual, firm, chamber of commerce, industry federation, national association, regional association, and so forth) as well as its goals and decision making abilities, will be important to determining the level of collective action.

At one end of the spectrum are units with an efficient decision making ability, clearly defined objectives, and sufficient resources to support the cost of membership. At the other end are looser units (such as social movements) with a less efficient decision making apparatus, ill-defined policy aims, and perhaps lower levels of resources. The segregation of the dues-paying part of the organisation from the part of the organisation making the membership decision may also affect the decision.

Actors are faced with different membership calculations depending upon the organisational context from which they start. The decision to join a direct membership organisation may be a relatively straightforward one for a monolithic actor; on the other hand, when national associations consider whether to join a European federation (which make up two-thirds of all Euro groups), the input of constituent members will be diluted. In this case the relevant actor is the national association itself. The leadership of national associations may manipulate membership decisions to create the necessary consensus for joining a Euro group, particularly where 'epistemic communities' have formed among leadership elites or leaders perceive their career paths to be enhanced by European membership. National associations might also believe that they would be unable to serve their members' interests without membership of a European federation; even where benefits appear marginal, therefore, national groups risk being undermined by a failure to join. Although these factors would appear to push national associations to membership (the contributions by Jordan, Young and Sidenius show a clear bias in favour of group joining by national associations), it is important to recognise that decisions depend on the desires of leaders and members, and on the level of democracy in the organisation, among other things.

Moreover, the fact that there are organisational differences between units even within the same industry provides scope for different capabilities for association. For example, firms may be represented by dedicated national sectoral associations, or alternatively by broader national chambers of commerce. The latter represent a wider range of interests and therefore tend to have less well-defined objectives and aims. As Ruth Webster points out in her contribution, organisational differences between the hierarchical Greenpeace and the grassroots approach of Friends of the Earth leads to differences in their propensity to take collective action. Consumer groups, likewise, have different traditions at the EU level (see Chapter 7). Indeed, different groups arose at the EU level because of the different traditions of consumer representation in Europe. As Young explains in Chapter 7, rather than accommodate different traditions within a single Euro group, multiple consumer groups were created to give voice to them.

Our research suggests that the most effective European groups in terms of attracting members tend to be those in business sectors characterised by a relatively high degree of concentration with only a limited number of potential members; where the firms are multinational and bring with them experience of operating in a variety of regulatory environments and collective structures; and where sectoral definition is marked, limiting the danger of competition from members in other sectors whose interests diverge (Aspinwall, 1995a; Greenwood, 1995a). Thus, one of the most effective actors at the European level is the European Federation of Pharmaceutical Industry Associations (EFPIA), while some of the least effective are tourism related interests. Pharmaceutical firms find the issues very similar no matter what the territorial operating environment – governments seek to attract them because of their earning capacity, but worry about medicine prices, selling standards, and safety. The shared challenges faced by pharmaceutical companies have created a habit of cooperation in international forums beyond the European Union, and it has not been hard to reproduce this at the European level (Greenwood, 1995b). Interestingly, however, Sidenius shows that trade unions in Denmark are the most Europeanised (in respect of Euro group membership) of the national associations there – even more than business – which questions assumptions of greater general business mobility.

State context

Within EU member states there are cultural, historical, ideological, and geographical factors that offer constraints or opportunities for private interest associability across borders. Particular institutional patterns of policy making affect the aptitude of state interests to organise transnationally, as Justin Greenwood shows in his account of the professions in this book. In hierarchical, state dominated systems, interests tend not to develop transnational (EU level) strategies as readily as in more open, liberal polities. Recent comparative research has demonstrated that a broad divide separates northern and southern member states, with southern states exhibiting characteristics of hierarchy and statism that make it more difficult for interests to engage in cross national group formation (Pagoulatos, 1996; Kosmidis, 1996; Josselin, 1996; Aspinwall, 1995a; for a comparative study of Italian regions, see Putnam, 1993).

The factors that are predicted to make the state context particularly important are the degree of state administrative autonomy from private actors and the level of state control of the economy. Historical patterns of close working relationships between state administrative elites and producers have cemented a hierarchical interaction that undermines incentives for European-level collective action. This is augmented where state economic control is high. Some states have chosen to cede public authority to the market; others have retained control through public ownership, subsidies, and other means (although the EU is causing a convergence in approaches in some areas). Again, state economic control affects the prospects for EU collective action among private interests, reducing the incentives in specific areas where state control is high. This is one reason why southern consumer organisations have been less involved in the Brussels process than northern ones (Sidjanski, 1989). Geography also plays a role here: groups from southern member states often find it harder to find the resources and time to be involved in Brussels activities simply because of the distance.

However, these broad state-level generalisations mask important sectoral differences. In Greece, for example, the experiences of the banking, telecommunications and shipping sectors have varied widely (Pagoulatos, 1996; Kosmidis, 1996; Bredima-Savopolou and Tzoannos, 1990). In banking and telecommunications, where international competition has not been the norm, interests are oriented toward state protection, seeking exceptions to EU requirements for liberalisation. In shipping, which is highly internationalised, industry groups are active at the EU level and in other international organisations. Moreover, there is evidence (particularly among large firms – see Chapter 5) that the national patterns of association began to break down under the influence of both globalisation and institutional change in the EU.

EU institutional context

Following a now familiar neo institutionalist logic that institutions condition social action (March and Olsen, 1989; Steinmo, Thelen, and Longstreth, 1992; Bulmer, 1994a) a third prediction is that the European institutional environment affects the potential for collective action. Adapting Hall's definition (1986: 19), this contextual variable asserts that supranational institutions provide formal rules, compliance procedures, and standard operating practices that structure the relationship between individuals in various units of the polity and economy. There are several ways that EU institutions may condition the incentives of private interests regarding collective action.

First is the constitutionality of the sector, or the authority of the supranational institutions. Where authority exists (and as policy output accumulates), we predict a growth in collective action, since interested private actors would be likely to respond (and indeed might be asked to respond by the Commission). Clearly, the stakes are raised in policy areas which fall within the remit of the EU institutions, and we expect to see greater collective action among interests affected by EU activity. Virtually all the contributions here confirmed this rather common-sensical notion in their findings.

There are many ways the EU institutions exercise authority, including drafting proposals, making decisions, implementing and enforcing decisions, and allocating funding. In addition, there are now many policy areas over which the EU exercises authority. One of the most obvious is the single market, which has fostered large firm collaboration through a wave of mergers, acquisitions, takeovers and strategic alliances (Jacquemin and Wright, 1994). As firms began to find their 'national champion' status under threat, so the need for membership of Euro groups intensified, both because of the uncertainties presented by the European market, and because of the need to seek 'Euro champion' status for particular industries at the European level. For instance, a Danish firm seeking to bid for a public procurement contract in Portugal for the first time needs some degree of intelligence about market and labour market conditions. While the Euro group may not be the principal source of its information, it does present the chance to network and gather impressions or points of view. Similarly, firms may be able to obtain reassurance for their Europe-wide market strategies by networking or witnessing the behaviour of other firms in Euro groups.

The emphasis in the above sections has been on working through examples from the field of business. But outside of business contexts, many of the same pressures for group membership arise. Among subnational governments, for instance, there is a great desire to gain from structural funds. The impression of competition between regions and localities for structural fund assistance is illusory because of the role of member states as gatekeepers of applications, and the ability of member states to gain from their own regions receiving structural fund award status (Greenwood, Levy and Stewart, 1995). Dense and varied networks of regional and local authorities at the European level can be observed, with high levels of collaboration, including arrangements between neighbouring authorities to pool resources by dividing membership of Euro groups and sharing the benefits between them. In social fields, opportunities to obtain Euro gold, to swap know-how, to take advantage of new possibilities to network, and to respond to the Commission's attempts to build transnational networks (including the availability of expenses to attend meetings) means that, once again, EU competence – or intervention – may lead to collective action.

Supranational institutional competence has grown with every revision of the Treaty of Rome, and it is tempting to see important new sources of attraction for private interests, particularly in the economic sphere. However, the 'shoot where the ducks are' logic of supranational collective action is bounded by the continuing relevance of state authorities, as we saw in the previous section. The ducks are in more than one place; where states retain authority and competence, interests will have less reason to organise at the European level. Moreover, the virtual completion of the single market, the important role member state governments play in implementing and enforcing European rules, and the ascendance of subsidiarity as a principle of policy making all point to the continuing relevance of member state authority.

Second, supranational institutions condition collective action by providing multiple access and veto points for information and influence on the part of interests. Divided institutions, fragmented policy competencies within each of the institutions, the lack of a large and well-resourced bureaucracy, and a tradition of relative openness to input all create a potential vacuum to be filled by private interests. In biotechnology, for example, different groups have formed different relationships with the European institutions, partly as a response to the fragmentation of policy competencies. Four Commission services are involved in biotechnology: DG III, DG VI, DG XI, and DG XII. Of these, DG XI, with competence in environmental policy, is partly isolated. Nonetheless, DG XI and the small firm group in biotechnology, the European Secretariat of National Biotechnology Associations (ESNBA), (until merger in 1996) developed a mutually supportive relationship as a response to their respective marginalisation, to the extent that officials from DG XI attended board meetings of the ESNBA. The large firm group in biotechnology (until merger with ESNBA), the Senior Advisory Group Biotechnology (SAGB), once refused to attend meetings with DG XI on the grounds that ESNBA has been invited. Here, SAGB enjoyed a much closer relationship with the other Commission services, and in particular DG III (Greenwood and Ronit, 1995).

Third, following the traditional pluralist argument, countervailing interests may be encouraged by the perceived success of one set of interests (whether to add nuance to the position of other groups or oppose them fully). Thus, small businesses may associate in response to the action of large firms; likewise, consumer, labour, and environmental groups may decide to take action in response to business interest representation. In transport, industrial consumer groups organised rapidly in the 1980s (particularly in aviation, road, and maritime sectors). This occurred in the wake of the Single European Act as the perception among consumers grew that a policy network detrimental to their interests was hardening between DG VII and carrier groups. In these ways, the EU institutions alter the political–economic environment (and the perception of interests) such that the scope of collective interest is focused more sharply on Brussels.

Finally, the agency role of the supranational institutions plays a very important part in attracting interests to the European level. Institutions matter even where they do not have authority, as Laura Cram points out in Chapter 3. The Commission in particular has become an agent of change in its repeated efforts to achieve policy linkage, create new symbols, identify problems and solutions, and attract new interests (Cram, 1995b; Bulmer, 1994a; Lindberg and Campbell, 1991). In addition to the Commission, the European Court has acted to promote a European *acquis*. The activism of the supranational institutions is limited by political expediency, but nonetheless they play a role in creating the institutional context which determines the incentive structure for interests.

The external environment

Our last intervening variable looks at the influence of the global political economy – and particularly market and regulatory structures – upon decisions by European actors to associate at the European level. Simply put, market and regulatory convergence in a broad multilateral context may prompt collective response, but not in a way confined to the EU (see Cerny, 1995, for a discussion of how globalisation affects state provision of public goods). Conversely, divergences may preclude transnational cooperation at any level.

This approach has its intellectual roots in the functionalism of David Mitrany (1944), who argued that incremental functional transfer of authority to global bodies would have the desired effect of taking responsibility for governance of technical issues away from nation states, thereby drawing the allegiance of civil society to a higher level of authority (see also Taylor, 1983). Haas (1958) developed this into a theory of European integration, arguing famously (among other things) that interest allegiance would be drawn inexorably to the European level. However, by the 1970s he had concluded that extra-regional effects could have unintended and ambiguous consequences. In one of the most succinct and telling statements on this issue he asserted that external influence could have two effects: [either] 'it may result in the deliberate encapsulation of the regional entity, and its separation from the rest of the world' [or] 'it may result in the watering down of regional commitments in favour of tighter links with global and extra-regional entities' (Haas, 1975: 33).

The existence of global functional regimes has a dual effect upon private interests. First, it draws their allegiance away from Brussels to a higher level and may, if EU member states have agreed to the rules of these regimes, rob the EU of authority. An example is airline safety, where the International Civil Aviation Organisation has for several decades been the repository of political legitimacy. Second, regime norms exercise a harmonising influence on market actors, because their principles and rules encourage behavioural adjustment toward permissible practices (see Greenwood, 1995b, on pharmaceuticals).

These areas tend to be technical and non redistributive, but they do present an obstacle to purely regional collective action.

In addition, there are strong global market forces encouraging a convergence of views among economic actors. The growth of foreign direct investment, trade, common management and production processes, and the spread of liberal ideas of deregulation and privatisation, have all changed the basic calculus of cross border collective action (Cerny, 1995; Aspinwall, 1995b). Among some private actors, these changes may spur advocacy for the purposes of promoting greater standardisation in markets. Other actors, however, will resist the greater competition these changes imply, and will forgo collective action in favour of an entrenchment of the privileged state–producer relationship.

The effect of the product cycle is predicted to have a motivating influence on interests. Firms acting in defence of the *status quo* may respond to different sets of incentives than those trying to bring about change. Thus, interests in older smokestack industries, particularly those in decline, will advocate different types of action (protection, for example) than interests in newer industries (research and development funding, for example). Moreover, firms in the early stages of the product cycle may have a greater propensity to compete as they cluster around rival technologies and seek endorsement of industry standards; this occurred in biotechnology healthcare, with market concentration occurring later as small firms which produced significant technological developments were taken over or were the target of partnership initiatives with larger firms, or dropped out of the market altogether. On the other hand, firms in the later stages of the product cycle may need to work at the European or national levels in response to threats from new competitors. European shipping companies as well as steel and cement producers facing competition from the Far East and Eastern and Central Europe are an example of the latter. Indeed, collaboration in these industries has been so close that a number of firms have been fined by the European Commission for anti competitive behaviour.

Collective action of a nature encouraged by global economic change need not necessarily be limited to the European level. By definition, these changes affect economic interests beyond the borders of Europe (Bressand, 1990), which is why environmental interests were organised on a broad international basis before creating groups at the EU level, as Webster points out. On the other hand, European interests may be encouraged to associate in order to advocate a distinctly regional solution (Sandholtz and Zysman, 1989; Cowles, 1995b), or to take advantage of funds or market opportunities provided by EU integration (Harvey, 1995). One example is the telecommunications industry, where rapid technological change and deregulation have combined to open national borders to competition and prompted alliances between national telecoms operators, including those outside the EU. While this does not rob the EU of a mandate in telecoms policy, it does colour the risks and opportunities faced by market actors, and thus the incentives for collective action. A very different example is provided by the market for many agricultural products, which (apart from trade liberalisation) is less prone to globalising forces. This fact means that far less scope for transnational common advocacy exists between European agricultural producers and those outside the EU.

The relevance of context

Clearly these contextual scenarios are not mutually exclusive. Agricultural producers, by their nature, are tied more directly to state and regional authorities, and it is not simply the fact that technological change and foreign direct investment have failed to reach them that precludes global political alliances. EU competence is strong in this field.

To take another example, inefficient steel producers in several EU states are affected by conflicting forces which confuse the calculus of collective action for them (Grunert, 1987). They have for long periods enjoyed cosseted status, subsidised by the state and selling in protected markets. This scenario would be enough to predict that collective action would be difficult to achieve. But the early competence of the European Coal and Steel Community, the authority of the EEC over state aid, the new competition from emerging markets, and the opening of internal markets, have together created a situation where steel interests have one of the longest and closest histories of European-level associability. Indeed, EUROFER (European Confederation of Iron and Steel Industries) has historically been one of the best resourced of all European federations. Protectionism in national markets is therefore not a sufficient condition to predict associability.

In a number of sectors (including textiles, steel, chemicals, agriculture), the opening of Eastern and Central Europe, with its cheaper products, has presented a new challenge to Western European producers and a rationale to work in Brussels against open borders with the east. Deregulation and privatisation have combined to encourage rationalisation, cost cutting, and greater competition, which may encourage either an EU-level response or an attempt to seek state protection.

CONCLUSION

This chapter has tried to portray in a relatively parsimonious way how actors across the European Union come to grips with the dizzyingly complex array of factors leading to a possible decision to join a Euro group. Adapting incentive-types from earlier theorists, we suggest that a continuum of selective–collective and (cross-cutting that) material–social incentives emanate signals to latent members. These signals may be perceived in a relatively straightforward manner, or they may be unclear and vague.

We have also attempted to establish the contextual environment within which various units respond to incentives for European-level collective action. Latent members process those signals and decide whether to join based upon a variety of factors operating at different levels of analysis, including the nature of the actor, the state context from which it emerges, the European institutional context (which varies according to policy area and over time), and the external environment. The fact that there are multiple vertical polities, extending from substate authorities (in some countries) to member state governments to the EU level; and also multiple horizontal polities (member states) with cultural and institutional idiosyncrasies, complicates matters for the theorist. For the potential group member, these vertical and horizontal complications add transaction costs not normally found in group-joining decisions. Political differentiation, organisational distance, potential uncertainty about leaders across boundaries, and language and communication problems all add complexities to the logic of collective action, and this increases with the number of latent polities.

How might these contextual issues affect the membership decision? There are two potential ways. First, they may weed out the unsophisticated, under-resourced potential members of groups, who believe the distance and uncertainty of potential rewards not to be worth the investment. Second, they may, if group leaders are successful in exploiting these transaction costs and uncertainties, lead to increased membership of Euro groups.

The contributions which follow, in their various ways, address the issues put forward in this framework. The chapters by Grant Jordan and Laura Cram explore the issue of incentives, often finding that incentives are unclear, ambiguous, or constructed by the supranational institutions. Niels Sidenius focuses on collective action within one of the member states (Denmark), where state–society relations should affect all actors identically. The next four chapters look at actors within particular domains. Even within these domains, there are differences between actor-types, as Ruth Webster (environmental groups, Chapter 8) and Alasdair Young (consumer groups, Chapter 7) point out. Among big business, as Maria Green Cowles (Chapter 5) shows, key changes are taking place which suggest that firms are becoming more proactive, more oriented to specific policy issues, and motivated by influence peddling rather than information seeking.

Finally, as Justin Greenwood suggests (Chapter 6), the importance of historical relationships between the state and social groups, such as the professions, has hindered the creation of EU-level advocacy groups and meant that national associations have continued to support national regulation.

NOTES

1 The survey team comprised Justin Greenwood, Linda Strangward, Lara Stancich and Mark Aspinwall. The authors wish to record their thanks to Linda and Lara for their impressive research assistance with the survey. A publication detailing the full survey results is forthcoming, coauthored by the entire research team.
2 Since the survey was undertaken, another directory has been published, listing over 1500 groups; they include consultancies and law firms which are outside the scope of this study (Butt Philip and Gray, 1996).
3 It is recognised that some Euro groups comprise both associations and firms, or both firms and individuals. Many also have a second, associate tier of membership. However, virtually all Euro groups can be categorised as principally federative or direct membership in structure.

2 What drives associability at the European level?
The limits of the utilitarian explanation

Grant Jordan

WHAT IS THE PROBLEM?

This chapter focuses particularly on the emergence of business groups, which are widely seen as being dominant both numerically and politically in the EU arena (see Aspinwall and Greenwood in Chapter 1). The chapter initially accepts the proposition that there is a collective action issue to be addressed. Why do firms join together in an attempt to secure an outcome that may be enjoyed by the 'selfish' firm without the investment of effort or resources? Why not free ride?[1]

The scale of participation in policy influencing European organisations apparently challenges the academic assumption that much interest group participation is irrational. This chapter reviews a range of different explanations that attempt to explain away the apparent inconsistency between predictions of the difficulty of mobilising collective action and the empirical proliferation of such activity. Two main types of explanation for collective action at the European level are introduced. The first is essentially material self interest, but the second is that a general, and perhaps ideological, collective good motivation underpins even business membership. Initially however the paper discusses the work of Mancur Olson, which underlines that the mobilising of participation is generally a problem for collective action bodies – and that of Claus Offe, who sees it as less problematic for business than for other types of groups.

These preliminary comments imply a problem that may not exist in the minds of real life individuals or companies and their staffs. The academic literature is fixated by the logical possibility that any firm or individual would seek to save resources by not supporting a collective effort. This perhaps unrealistic assumption about the decision process creates an equally unrealistic literature of explanation. In trying to account for membership, the tendency is to map ever more complex decision processes involving a broader set of incentives until the parcel of incentives seems sufficient to account for the observed level of membership. Yet it may be that empirically membership is a decision that is often not carefully considered; and in over-complicating the account of the process we are misportraying it. The attempt to be comprehensive serves to camouflage basically simple rule of thumb decisions.

Discussions with group organisers in a number of sectors suggests that they are often simply not 'hung up' on potential free riding in the way that economists assume. Several factors can be identified that offset the free riding temptation, but to an extent we may be looking for a remedy for something that group organisers do not see as needing fixing. This is very different from saying that organisers are not concerned about membership: that is vital. The point is that they do not see the reason for non membership as deliberate cost based free riding. It is more likely, in their view, that they are combating ignorance of the group,[2] a failure to connect support for the goals with the need to give financial support,[3] or dissent from the goals of the group,[4] or suspicion of the efficacy of the group.[5]

The final part of the chapter argues that the issue of group mobilisation at the European level may not in fact be one of collective action. It suggests that the phenomenon of seeking to influence the political environment in Europe lacks the distinguishing characteristic of collective action (that is, problems in mobilising members). If businesses or other organisations have made a prior decision to attempt to influence the environment in which they operate, then participation within Euro groups is a rational (even economically rational) means to that end. This is even more the case for national groups operating in supranational organisations. Participation is then a means to advance the interests of the national grouping. In these circumstances, not operating in the wider organisation, whose goals you support when there is an opportunity to do so, that is as sensible as free riding the launch of a lifeboat on a sinking ship.

Hirschman (1982: 78) noted that there was inconsistency between Olson's 'triumphant theory and the recalcitrant practice'. He noted that, 'Mancur Olson proclaimed the impossibility of collective action for large groups at the precise moment [1965] when the Western world was about to be all but engulfed by an unprecedented wave of public movements, marches, protests, strikes and ideologies'. Group proliferation – notwithstanding the Olson prediction – has been a European-level phenomenon (see Chapter 1).

Though the proliferation of collective bodies pursuing policy influence in Brussels suggested that Olson has been contradicted and groups are far more successful at combating free rider tendencies than he thought, at another level – the lack of resourcing and political weakness of most of these bodies – his thesis may appear to have partial success. However, it is the thrust of this chapter that the weakness of the collective action bodies does not result from Olson-type free riding by self-regarding firms or individuals, but because potential participants wish to preserve their own autonomy. They are not so much economising as choosing different strategies.

The multiplicity of levels

A difficulty encountered in this topic concerns the complication caused by the different levels at which relevant activity can be taken. Thus some empirical material introduced refers to the decisions made by firms about membership in their relevant national sectoral trade body; other discussion concerns individual firm participation in a national-level umbrella group for business or commerce; or discusses the participation of the firm directly at European level on its own account, or how the company interest is indirectly advanced at European level by a national organisation. Yet other discussions are about the interaction of national associations in a European federation; while yet others are about the direct participation of firms in European institutions or about the participation in European decisions within a club of similarly placed industrial competitors. All these different sorts of activity are about the general theme of the representation of interests, but these different collective action problems require different solutions. Wilson (1991), for example, found that in the US narrow trade associations seemed more successful in mobilising potential membership than did general purpose business organisations. Groups have differentiated levels of success in recruitment in different parts of their markets. Bigger businesses seem more likely to join than smaller – though in principle the smaller might find the services more valuable (May and McHugh, cited in Grant, 1993: 106; Plotke, cited in Petracca, 1992).

BEFORE OLSON

In political science almost everything is debatable: certainty is unusual. Yet in interest group studies the history can be starkly divided into pre and post 1965 – that of the pre Olson and post Olson worlds.

It is a weakness of the literature on lobbying at the European level that the Olson contribution is rarely discussed.[6] In the broader field of interest groups even those who disagree with his conclusions recognise the logical power of the central argument. Olson discredited the inevitable growth of interest groups theme that is sometimes found in the Euro literature.

Before the impact of Olson the leading authority in the explanation of membership was David Truman (1951). His work is empirically rich, intellectually sophisticated and most often dismissed (as it often is) by those who have not read it. However, important though it is, the Truman approach failed completely to anticipate the Olson criticism. Truman argued that conflict was commonplace in society, and then assumed that groups were the more or less automatic consequence of these lines of conflict. He assumed that groups were an important phenomenon in all societies and therefore the emergence of groups was taken for granted. As they were viewed as endemic[7] the issue of their emergence was not an obvious problem. Truman asserted that man is a social animal and that with rare exceptions man is always found in association with other men. Indeed he cited Dewey's claim that 'associated activity needs no explanation, things are made that way' (1927: 151 quoted in Truman, 1951: 14).[8] Truman said that the 'Robinson Crusoe hypothesis that members are best conceived of as isolated units is inadequate psychology as well as unfashionable economics' (Truman, 1951: 14).

Olson (1965, 1971 edn: 1) revolutionised the discussion of interest group participation so that it was dominated by a conception of individual rationality. He said that:

> It is often taken for granted, at least where economic objectives are involved, that groups of individuals with common interests usually attempt to further those common interests... if the members of some group have a common interest or objective, and if they would all be better off if that objective were achieved, it has been thought to follow logically that the individuals in the group would, if they were rational and self-interested, act to achieve that objective.
>
> (Olson, 1965, 1971 edn: 1)

This assumption he rejected. Instead his starting point was that potential members of a group will not join unless their contribution secures advantages above and beyond what they can share if they free ride. He argued that, 'just as a state cannot support itself by volunteers' contributions or by selling its basic services on the market, neither can other large organisations support themselves without providing some sanction, or some attraction, distinct from the public good itself, that will lead individuals to help bear the burdens of maintaining an organization'. He concluded that the distinguishing feature of significant lobbying organisations was that, 'these groups are also organized as a by-product for some *other* purpose' (Olson, 1971: 15–16, 132: quoted in Marsh, 1976: 258; emphasis in original).

THE OLSON WATERSHED

Olson in 1965 provided a powerful image of the decision about participation that undermined the Truman proposition about a natural, even inevitable, emergence of groups to reflect shared interests. In Olson's account the potential participant is seen as making an economically rational calculation about his/her/its best interests. The expectation is that if there is not a net benefit (benefit less cost) then the potential contributor will free ride. In *The Logic of Collective Action* Olson argued that collective action was problematic and not the 'natural' response to shared concerns. He suggested:

> But it is *not* in fact true that the idea that groups will act in their self-interest follows logically from the premise of rational self-interested behavior. It does *not* follow, because all of the individuals in a group would gain if they achieved their group objective, that they would act to achieve that objective, even if they were all rational and self-interested. Indeed, unless the number of individuals in a group is quite small, or unless there is coercion or some other special device... *rational, self-interested individuals will not act to achieve their common or group interests.*
>
> (Olson, 1971: 2; emphasis in original)

Olson (1971: 2) argued that potential members of a group will not act unless 'some separate incentive, distinct from the achievement of the common or group interest, is offered to the members individually on the condition that they help bear the costs or burdens involved in the achievement of the group objectives'. In other words membership contributions which fund the pursuit of collective objectives are made because the rational member obtains selectively non collective rewards obtainable only by those in membership. This book addresses the question of why members give support to business groups. Even if groups can usefully further business causes, the thrust of the Olson argument is that this is not in itself a sufficient reason for self-interested firms to support them.

The fundamental implication of the Olson thesis was that collective mobilisation would be far more difficult than pluralist thought or group theory assumed. He argued that 'the common view that groups of individuals with common interests tend to further those common interests appears to have little if any merit' (1971: 2). Hardin (1982: 42) observed that post Olson, 'one who wishes to understand how a particular group succeeds in cooperative action for collective benefit can no longer merely assume that the group's success is rationally motivated in the sense that individual actions can be rationally motivated'. For Olson, the assumption was that in considering the incentives that did induce membership, non material factors were largely irrelevant. Therefore group membership was crucially underpinned by the offering of selective (usually material) incentives available only to those in membership.

THE OFFE EXPLANATION: BUT IS THE BUSINESS MOBILISATION PROBLEM REALLY EASIER?

There is probably more written on mobilising public interest and other non public groups than on business groups. This is perhaps for two reasons. Firstly, there has apparently been a particular escalation in the numbers of non business groups – though this point is subject to some counter argument. Secondly, non business groups seem to have a more difficult mobilisation problem. Olson argued that the logic for small groups (the scale of many business groups) made their organisation easier – and it is assumed that business groups will have a range of material economic incentives available. Put simply, it is assumed that a business group will have more selective benefits to offer than, for example, Amnesty International; and that the issues implicit in mobilising a comparatively narrow set of businesses are much less difficult than in generating the mass memberships of public interest groups. The public interest group, in this light, seems more 'free rideable' because it has few selective and / or material incentives to offer. The Olson argument was that the mobilisation problems faced by business and non business groups were different – and there was an advantage to business in this non symmetry.[9]

The basic Olson position is accepted by others, most influentially Offe (1985), who saw collective action as particularly difficult for labour organisations, and less so for associations of business firms as they reflected a utilitarian logic. Offe's main proposition was that successful trades unions needed to be able to mobilise effective sanctions and that this involved the active participation of the individual members. He claims that on the other hand business groups are different because they themselves carry only a limited sanctioning potential whereas the decisive source of power remains with the individual firm and its strategic choices. He concluded that the consequence was that the problem of creating and maintaining unity among members is considerably less serious for business associations than for unions. In maintaining that there is a collective action problem to explain, one has in passing to prove that there is a difficulty for business groups.

Offe's influential argument accepted that there was a unity problem in business organisations, but that for business there was a comparatively easy reconciliation of internal divergences (Offe, 1985: 189). Offe may be correct when observing that 'the proportion of actual members to eligible members is regularly much higher in business associations than in unions' (*ibid.*: 191), but his explanation of this (unproven) 'fact' may be wrong: the explanation may not lie with the two factors that he identifies.[10] Contrary to Offe, this chapter argues that membership of business organisations is distinguished by its lack of immediate self-interest. In noting the relative success of group mobilisation Offe may have the right answer – for the wrong reason.

This is not to restore an assumption that there are not distinctive problems for business and other groups. Offe quotes Lindblom's observation that 'by some unthinking habit, many (interest group) works treat all interest groups as though on the same plane, and, in particular, they treat labour, business and farm groups as though operating at some parity with each other' (*ibid.*: 175). However, even if one accepts that step of the argument that business is different, it does not follow that Offe correctly sketches the differences.

Offe starts by noting the similarities – at a level of generality – between labour and business groups. He says that there is voluntary membership (usually), a more or less bureaucratic structure of decision making, dependence on material and motivational resources, efforts to change their respective environments into more favourable ones, and so forth. However, he then claims that there are important differences between the types of organisation. He suggests workers are inherently atomised in their relations with each other even though they need to associate to respond to the inherently integrated nature of capital.

He says that the union problem is in part in trying to determine an optimal package of demands from the labour side: how much in wages can be traded off for increased work satisfaction? He claims that the capitalist firms have a much simpler task as all the relevant questions can be reduced to the measuring rod of money. Moreover, the business problem need not be settled collectively but by authority. It can be argued however that this considerably over-simplifies the nature of capitalism with its conflict between firms, management and shareholders, areas of investment within the company, and so on. These claims by Offe seem to both raise problems that are in practice of limited importance to unions and neglect all kinds of tensions within the business world.

Offe asserts that the power relationship between the individual worker and the capitalist favours the latter. This seems highly probable, but the argument he constructs on this non contentious base is less persuasive. He goes on to say that superior power also means superior ability to defend and reproduce power: 'The powerful are fewer in number, are [less[11]] likely to be divided among themselves, have a clearer view of what they want to defend, and have larger resources for organized action, all of which imply that they are likely to succeed in recreating the initial (power) situation' (Offe, 1985: 182). He argues that an association of the powerless can only succeed by 'changing the standards according to which these costs are subjectively estimated within their own collectivity' (*ibid.*: 183). He says that these associations need to form a collective identity which will change perceptions of the costs. So the argument is that business mobilisation is essentially utilitarian and self-interested, but the motivation for mobilisation of the powerless is different and rests on non utilitarian thinking. This is the case, he asserts, even if the union only deals in utilitarian issues such as increasing wage rates. In a key passage he says:

> No union can function for a day in the absence of some rudimentary notions held by the members that being a member is of value in itself, that the individual organization costs must not be calculated in a utilitarian manner but have to be accepted as necessary sacrifices, and that each member is legitimately required to practise solidarity and discipline, and other norms of a non-utilitarian kind. The logic of collective action of the relatively powerless differs from that of the relatively powerful in that the former implies a paradox that is absent from the latter – the paradox that interests can only be met to the extent that they are partly redefined.
>
> (Offe, 1985: 183)

This is a stylish and elegant argument. Unfortunately it is contradicted by the available empirical evidence: there does not seem to be a strong utilitarian basis for business group membership. Instead Offe's account of the collective action of the powerless in non business groups sounds rather similar to conclusions by others about business mobilisation. Plotke treated business mobilisation as a 'political project'. He (in Petracca, 1992: 175) has noted that:

> political efforts by business cannot be explained solely in terms of strategic calculation aimed at realizing economic interests. Rather, such political efforts are conceived and pursued when economic phenomena are interpreted in the light of normative political and cultural commitments. This is a process, which entails shaping political identities.
>
> (Plotke, in Petracca, 1992: 175)

Offe claims there are two mechanisms that facilitate a comparatively easy and non contradictory reconciliation of internal divergences in business organisation (1985: 189). Offe's first component of his argument of the relative ease of business mobilisation is the greater potential for business groups to offer by-products to maintain internal integration (by this he appears to mean selective incentives). He specifically notes that these are particularly important for small firms, which are, he says, more dependent than large ones for services or private goods.[12] He argues that 'to become (and to remain) a member of a business association that provides access to such services becomes almost imperative in those (frequent) cases where no alternative access to such services exists' (*ibid.*: 189). This argument is that small companies, at least, join interest associations because it is in their self-interest to do so as they receive services (for example advice and information) not available elsewhere (*ibid.*: 189).

Offe, apparently determined to find strategic advantage for business groups over labour, argues that when unions do offer selective services such as book clubs, travel services, legal advice, insurance, they provide only minor advantages over the services that can be provided in the market place outside of union membership. There is then in his account an assumption that the selective incentives available from business are inherently more valuable to the constituents than in the non business cases.

Offe appears to have decided *a priori* that business groups are more influential in policy making than unions, but if it is true that business may hold some privileged position in policy making it is not the case that in all respects they must be at an advantage. It is possible that in the specific area of mobilising collective organisations then the business group is as handicapped as any other – or, at least, that its reasons for relative success might not be those advanced by Offe. Even if business groups are mobilised in disproportionate numbers, the crude assumption that the numerical preponderance of business groups in any listing of policy participants is an indicator of business power may be wrong. The creation of a group is often the response to a perceived lack of influence, not a sign of influence. Secondly, the proliferation of business viewpoints can lead to disputes within the business camp and the undermining of the authority of the business case. A British business group professional, Mark Boleat, has written (1994: 46) 'there is nothing worse than having two or three competing trade associations which, as if by some invisible law, seem to spend much of their time attacking each other's views and jostling for position'. In a very different sort of comment from that made by Offe in his 'first principle' arguments, Connelly (1992: 160) noted that environmental and consumer groups were at an advantage because they 'seldom submit the wording of a draft representation for approval to their membership; the latter (business groups) are often constrained in precisely that respect, resulting in a bland formulation – seeking to reconcile the often conflicting interests of their membership in crucial matters of detail'.

Offe's second argument about the relative ease of business group mobilisation was that the achievement of the goals of business groups did not require solidarity or a willingness to act among the membership. He says that thus there is no tension for the business cases between the 'privatistic' motivation pandered to by selective material incentives and the organisational aims. On the labour side however, he suggests that ultimately members have to act collectively if the union is to be effective and that private motivations are somehow in conflict with this. He says that far from the business association requiring the active participation of the member, the organisation does not interfere with, or in any way attempt to regulate, what remains within the range of decision making of the individual firm. He says 'the obligations and commitments that the individual firm takes upon itself are quite marginal and thus less likely to involve any disincentive to join' (*ibid.*: 190).[13] He argues that business groups do not depend on their sanctions on the cooperation of members, and that 'the rank and file members appear to be the top executives of unions as far as sanctions are concerned; while some sanctioning potential of business and employers' associations resides with the organizations' executives alone' (*ibid.*: 184–5)

Offe's argument is built on a claim that 'in order to succeed in accomplishing stated interests, an organization must be able to mobilize sanctions. The strike is the ultimate sanction that unions can mobilize' (*ibid.*: 184) However, the currency of effective influence is not necessarily derived from the strike weapon. If in fact unions have influence for more subtle reasons such as the possession of information or a desire for legitimacy by policy makers, then the issue for unions and their members may not be significantly different from that for business groups and their members. Indeed given the power of votes held by union membership the unions might be less dependent on coordinated group action by members than business groups: political parties have to assume that union members can vote in ways that reflect their union interests.

Offe says that the leadership in even bureaucratic unions is less able to use sanctions at its own discretion than do business leaders. He says that whatever sanctioning potential there is in workers' associations becomes effective only through their organised members and explicitly coordinated action (*ibid.*: 185). But why do authors writing on business associations discuss the power of cooperation rather than sanctions? Boleat (1994: 43), then Director General of the Association of British Insurers, contrasts the popular image of hard hitting vocal trade associations with the reality that the effective trade associations work quietly, and with, rather than against, the government. 'There is one school of thought that equates representational work with insulting the Government and intimidating MPs and Ministers with letters. This approach will, in most cases, be counter productive' (Boleat, 1994: 44).

Offe claims that the limited range of interests processed by the (business) association and the fact that these can 'relatively easily be decided upon on the basis of quantitative criteria of costs and returns' leads to greater membership. This repeats the implication that a membership is a sort of good value purchase: there are identifiable and quantifiable selective benefits from membership. Do such cost/benefit considerations in fact underpin the level of association at the European level? An equally convincing first principles argument might be that businesses are characteristically in competition with each other and that this might make cooperation difficult.

However, the thrust of this chapter is that the explanation might not be exclusively – or even principally – for the reasons set out by Offe. If the joining question is expanded to 'what is in it, and for whom, in what arrangements?' this signals that different forms of collective association may be providing different rewards for different parties, and indeed different participants can be getting different rewards out of the same organisation. All participants need not be following an identical logic.

Given that companies are found (apparently) supporting collective action within the institutions of the EU – and the Offe explanation is unconvincing – the need is for an explanation to counter Olson's free riding prediction and better fit with practice. Here two lines of argument are advanced. The first package of 'explanations' reviewed accepts that companies – notwithstanding the general rationality of free riding – find particular and selectively rewarding benefits in membership. These reasons are more or less in line with the Olsonian interpretation. They accept a utilitarian, pragmatic and self-interested case for group membership. The second set of arguments accepts that membership is still rational, but expands the range of incentives and rewards that are seen as relevant. The explanations are not utilitarian or economically rational in a narrow sense.

UTILITARIAN ACCOUNTS

Doing valued things more cheaply

As noted in the first section there are a range of ways of attempting to influence outcomes in Europe. Why would a profit maximising company expend resources in any of these avenues? The Olson/Offe expectation for business groups is that what counts are selective (material) incentives only obtainable through membership. Despite the general scepticism in this chapter about the overall adequacy of that explanation there are some such factors and selective material incentives are part of the explanation.

Companies can find membership rewarding (literally) in several ways. The company might find out some information at an earlier date through membership. This might be commercially valuable and in itself justify membership. Such information could be obtainable without membership of a collective body: it could be secured in-house or bought in from a commercial political monitoring consultancy. But it might simply be cheaper to join a collective organisation that pools resources in an intra-trade club. So one characteristic of a collective group that potentially acts as a material incentive is where it acts as an information gathering device which can do certain tasks more economically (for example follow and summarise debates, keep press cuttings, give early alert of proposed policy changes, and so on). This sort of advantage is simply secured more cost effectively (overheads are spread through the membership) and simply through group membership. Joining a group obviates the need to think about gathering such information – and incurring the transaction costs of looking for other ways of getting the same information.

Participation in collective action arrangements in this light is simply a choice to secure cooperatively something that one wishes because this reduces the cost. Any lobbying aspect of collective action is funded as the by-product of memberships, which are centrally based on the availability of selective material advantages such as the securing of information. If the group can provide valued benefits cost effectively, then membership is rational in Olson's terms and indeed free riding would be irrational.

At face value this bulk buying of information is a good reason for membership of some European-level body, but it might be easy to over-estimate its importance. Such information is often obtainable from governments (but a certain political sophistication might be needed to access this) or from national groups. Moreover, there certainly are instances where large companies with their own in-house political scanning operations will be in group membership without any need for group help; indeed on occasion the firm will alert the group about developments rather than vice versa.

Member firms, especially large sophisticated firms, are not much impressed by these sorts of utilitarian incentives. Marsh's respondents in the CBI emphasised that a great deal of the information was available elsewhere from government departments or sectoral trade associations. But the Marsh (and Grant) data very clearly show that different sizes of companies had different reasons for joining the CBI. While none of the thirty-one large (1,000 plus employees) joined for services as the main reason, seventeen out of the twenty-two small companies (fewer than 200 employees) cited services as the main factor. In fact twenty-three of the thirty-one large companies said that services were not at all important.

The cheap buy need not only be information and in national-level collective organisations the selective incentive might be help with governmental documentation (for example, grant applications), hand holding in pay negotiations, or cheap insurance. But it is difficult to think of credible examples at the Euro level where the group can supply something that is not available from a government agency – and indeed even available national-level data place less stress on this sort of incentive than might be imagined from first principles. For one thing the sort of company that is large enough to be concerned at European-level developments is probably large enough to do its own good deals on insurance and other aspects. Again the Marsh (British) survey gave good illustrations: 'The CBI (Confederation of British Industry) has a limited staff and it is unlikely that they could provide us with any information or services that we couldn't generate more easily within our organization' (1976: 262). There is little reason to imagine that the Euro environment is different and that Euro organisations are more service oriented.

Doing valued things: entering the closed shop

Another sort of membership that Olson recognised as rational was where there were advantages only for members: one example was the trades union closed shop, where employment was only available to members. This near coercive-type membership can be found in the business sector. Membership of the Society of Motor Manufacturers and Traders was *de facto* compulsory for manufacturers as participation in the important annual motor show was restricted to members (Marsh, 1976: 263). This is certainly an explanation that meets both Olson's and Offe's understanding of group membership, but it may well be an unusual rather than typical feature.

Doing valued things: cost effective policy change?

A different, but still essentially self-interested, type of goal from membership is where a firm recognises that it could seek policy change by its efforts and from its own resources, but joining forces with other affected organisations spreads the costs. So again the broad idea is that something that is valued is better secured through collective action. Indeed 'DIY' lobbying is even more free rideable than group lobbying to the extent that the firm can simply decide to do nothing and hope to be the beneficiary of the efforts of others.[14] When the British government wanted to impose VAT on takeaway foods then the major fast food chains could indeed have free ridden the industry initiative – but they participated on the basis that the collective effort shared costs and increased the probability of a successful outcome. Not participating in the collective effort might imply an even more expensive own-account activity. The collective effort was a means to secure self-interested ends by cheaper methods. In that climate the realistic alternative to membership was not so much free riding as self financing.

Unless the outcome is truly zero sum (say the allocation of one factory to a particular site) then the company investing resources in an organisation to improve the business political environment is helping itself as well as helping the industry. Certainly this is free rideable, but Olson concedes that the position of a company that is one of a small number of potential members is different from that of the public interest groups, where the chances of the membership of any extra individual is very unlikely to be pivotal.

Sidenius (1994: 10) points to the existence of company networks (such as the European Enterprise Group or the IT Round Table) as a form of collective action. The issue of free riding does not seem very relevant in this kind of context. The participants see the main goal as maximising policy change (or defence) and not minimising costs: they are prepared to invest with the main focus being the defence/ promotion of the sector. If a large problem is identified in a sector, the pressing matter for the constituent firms is likely to be how to abate the damage/grab the opportunity. In that situation the operative question is: does the likely group lobbying expenditure look sensible in terms of the prospective benefit to the industry (which the particip- ating firm will share)? The free riding firm will ask quite another question: 'can we obtain benefits without contributing?'

Doing valued things: collective is better?

The previous point assumes that membership is about attaining some desired goal (policy change) more cheaply or more effectively (the group might give the firm an early warning of change). There are however other benefits (at least in theory) that are perhaps not obtain- able at all without collective action and can only be provided through collective means. It is not that the group delivers cheaply, but that only the group can deliver. Some aspects of policy change for the collective good might fit into this heading. Some changes may only be possible if there is collective action and the individual firm could not secure them acting unilaterally. If the firm values these outcomes, it recognises that they cannot be provided without supporting a broader group. Of course this is an area of potential free riding in which the company can calculate that others will contribute to the provision of the facilities to secure change and it can save the subscription.[15] However, there is a difference between free riding something in the expectation that others will obtain it and so allow the effort to be free ridden, and free riding which strikes directly at the probability of provision because it is the success of collective organisation that will produce success. To free ride in these circumstances would be counter productive. Logically the activity is free rideable, but it might not be very sensible as the risks of free riding in this context seem particularly clear.

The sort of reward that seems deliverable only (or at least most probably) through collective action is where sectors have possibilities of access to decision processes only through collective conduits. The culture of the European policy making institutions – with preferences both practical and ideological – arguably encourages collective action. Policy makers undoubtedly benefit from the policy making simplification that results from dealing with coherent, representative, well-informed, effective, collective groups: the group can marshal arguments and determine priorities in a way that is useful for policy makers. This makes negotiation simpler.

There are also claims in the literature that EU decision makers have a preference for consultation via groups as this is more 'European' (Pryce, 1973; Grant, 1989; Greenwood, 1997). Therefore, because of the preferences of the bureaucracy, collective action can produce a level of access and influence that is qualitatively different from that available through own-account lobbying. This perspective predicts that successful outcomes from collective group lobbying are much less likely from the sum of individual firms' lobbying – even if they all sought identical ends and acting separately they invested as much or more in terms of resources as did the group. So a collective effort produces something qualitatively better than the aggregation of own-account efforts. But though this explanation assumes that membership is pursued for material and self-interested lines, strict and short term self-interest would still inhibit membership.

Collective organisations can therefore claim the unique selling point (USP) that they can secure a better collective outcome for all. These benefits (at least in theory) are perhaps not obtainable at all without collective action and can only be provided through collective means. This, though, creates the collective action problem for the group: how to inhibit an individual rationality, which would impair the collective outcome. Just because collective action provides superior results states rather than solves Olson's major point. However, the core argument that there is something not available if there is widespread free riding is a disincentive to free riding.

This, however, assumes some kind of restrictive consultation by policy makers in favour of collective units: in practice decision makers might not be so discriminating as this suggests. It might make ideological and practical sense for policy makers to restrict access exclusively to Euro groups but in practice they are not so choosy – and that weakens the idea that collective is the only option.

Steering the group

Above we have seen that firms join groups because it can be advantageous for them in pursuing their 'selfish' needs (see under 'Cost effective policy charge') or that they are prepared to pay disproportionately for collective lobbying because they still calculate they will be particularly advantaged by collective outcomes/rewards that are more likely to be delivered via collective activity (see under 'Doing valued things: collective is better?').

A slightly different proposition is that more importantly from the company view than the costs that might be saved by free riding are the costs that could be incurred if the policy agreed by the group and the EU did not fit the requirements of the firm to the maximum feasible extent. What we saw above assumed that the firm wanted the same as the rest of the industry; an inducement to membership is that free riding is neglecting a chance to determine the nature of the collective good that is being sought. In practice the group can develop a variety of demands that in general might be seen as collective, but might be antithetical to the interests of particular firms. The so-called collective goals are not uncontroversial, fixed or self-selecting. Participation in the group allows the company to veto decisions about priorities or to get wider backing for its own priorities.

The wish to have a group shopping list that matches the company interest as closely as possible has been the factor that has pushed the creation of direct membership associations at the Euro level. The club better fits the firms' agendas. There are tensions within collective arrangements between the attractions of large organisations which can aggregate financial contributions, claim increased legitimacy – as against the possible cost of irrelevance, policy blandness and loss of focus. Smaller, more focused direct member groups can offer a tighter link between the members and the agenda adopted.

Wearing the group disguise

If we accept that Euro groups have a potential for easier access (see under 'Doing valued things: collective is better?' above), one reason for not free riding is that the group can be used as an umbrella under which firms can advance arguments that are perhaps more of a private that a general nature. Presented as group agenda items, they are less likely to be dismissed by policy makers as self-interested pleading. This is a variant on the steering proposition: it assumes that the firm can establish its own objectives and seek to further them in the policy process by presenting them as points of general applicability. This is not so difficult as it might seem once it is recognised that large organisations typically have sectoral and issue working parties where a firm can act in the shell of the group. They are then in the position of apparently representing the group – but with ambitions that suit their own firm.

Collective insurance: the prudent participator

An argument not set out by Olson, but which might justify corporate memberships is that whereas the costs are (broadly) known, the potential benefits are unknown. The firm cannot make a cost–benefit analysis because the benefits are unknown (and probably unknowable as they are in the future) – but might conclude that it is worth paying insurance just in case the costs of non membership are large. Membership might be prudent – even if not demonstrably economically rational. Free riding might be imprudent. Participation on a prudential basis might arise just in case the membership (and the resources it would give the group) were pivotal in terms of collective gains. It could be prudent in case it produced an early warning of something that might be crucial to the particular company. It could be prudent in the sense that one might want to be around within the organisation in case one had to act defensively to stop the group adopting a line that did not suit the prudent participator. In all these kinds of dimensions the important point is that the potential member cannot know the future costs of non membership – and hence thinks it sensible to purchase the insurance of membership.

The classic sort of public choice perspective was set out by McLean:

> a government can give import protection to all firms in the textile industry. It cannot practically give protection only to firms which are members of the Textile (Keep Out Foreigners) Industry Association. If the policy involves some indivisible element, potential members of every lobby are tempted to free-ride. If some of them do free-ride, the good is under-provided; if all of them free-ride, the good is not provided at all.
>
> (McLean, 1991: 63)

There are some assumptions in this standard presentation that may be at odds with day-to-day reality. It assumes that the level of provision is related to the scale of the lobbying, and that reduced lobbying leads to reduced supply of the good. In fact the good is lumpy and the potential free rider cannot assume that free riding will give a marginally reduced good; there may be no good at all. The free riding perspective assumes that the free rider has confidence about the consequences of inaction but they cannot confidently assume that if they free ride others will not notice.

Adam Smith's discussion of prudence (as opposed to self-interest) in the *Theory of Moral Sentiments* suggests that self-interest is more sensible as part of a wider framework of common concerns. He said that individuals were primarily concerned with security. This could lead them to preferences above immediate self-interest. As Axelrod (1984) has pointed out cooperation is not a one-off matter. Therefore companies might join in matters where they have no direct motivation or stake because they will be investing in the possible collaboration of others in the future. So behaviour that is not strictly economically rational can be reasonable. Cyert and March (1963) argued that one had to reject a one-dimensional profit maximization interpretation of firms. In the light of the inherent uncertainty involved they saw cooperation in business groups as worthwhile:

> Our studies indicate a quite different strategy on the part of organizations. Organizations avoid uncertainty. (1) They avoid the requirements that they correctly anticipate events in the distant future...(2) They avoid the requirement that they anticipate future reactions of other parts of their environment by arranging a *negotiated environment*. They impose plans, standard operating procedures, industry tradition, and uncertainty absorbing contracts on that environment.
>
> (Cyert and March, 1963: 120; emphasis in original)

In terms of collective action they argued:

> In the case of competitors, one of the conspicuous means of control is through the establishment of industry-wide conventional practices.... We do not mean to imply that firms necessarily enter into collusive agreements in the legal sense; our impression is that ordinarily they do not, but they do not need to do so to achieve the same objective of stability in competitive practices.
>
> (Cyert and March, 1963: 120)

Intra-group networking

A firm that free rides can lose out on the informal advantages of business opportunities that can arise from trading within the club. Some kinds of associate member status is available in many trade associations, where businesses which hope to sell to or buy from the particular trade are allowed a peripheral status that allows them access to the core membership while making a financial contribution to the group. This is, in effect, a selective advantage that is not open to the free rider. This point can be broadened to cover a range of benefits that firms might discover by participation. They might discover about technical breakthroughs, possible takeover opportunities; they might find senior managers they can attract, and so on. Being inside the group might produce selective rewards that are almost accidental and certainly are difficult to map out in advance, but these serendipitous rewards are not available unless the entry ticket is purchased.

Exploitation of the great by the small

These arguments generally support the idea that free riding in the real world is not necessarily sensible even if it is a logical possibility. Olson sets out several propositions that mean that free riding is not inevitable (these are particularly relevant for organisations of firms as opposed to public interest groups). His main explanation is that collective lobbying is a by-product of participation in the group for selective material reasons. A more technical argument he offers is the exploitation of the great by the small. Olson claims that 'logic' of membership is distinct for smaller (in terms of the constituency to be organised) bodies. In these (more likely to be groups organising firms than the larger potential numbers of public interest group members) the larger members may bear disproportionate loads:

> in a very small group, where each member gets a substantial portion of the total gain simply because there are few others in the group, a collective good can often be provided by the voluntary, self interested actions of members of the group.
>
> (Olson, 1971: 34)

He argues that the rewards for some companies are so strong that they will bear the full costs (or at least a disproportionate share) of the cost in these small organisations (Olson 1971: 28).[16] After all there can be a huge gap between costs and benefits. Even a five million pound cost of a lobbying operation would be negligible in a context that some lobbying on tax or other matters might yield benefits in the scale of hundreds of millions.

Olson anticipated that for the big companies it is better to subsidise the participation of others, because the enhanced legitimacy of the group with a broad range of members means that policy change is more likely. But this argument sees the large firms as acting selfishly not altruistically in this subsidising. They are bearing a disproportionate part of the costs because they see the project as worthwhile for themselves not because they feel obligations to smaller firms. Grant (1993 edn: 107) suggests that the larger businesses might knowingly subsidise the provision of services which are of more use to smaller members, in the belief that the participation of the smaller bodies enhances the political credibility of the group. The textbook example of this subsidisation phenomenon is Howard Hughes purchasing a television station to show western films all night so that he could watch them. While he bore the total cost others could benefit as a side effect.

Imperfect information

Olson also allows that the firm could join if it had an exaggerated sense of the impact of its own contribution. Jordan and Maloney (1997) stress the way in which group organisers can manipulate perceptions of the impact of individual subscriptions. Green and Shapiro (1994: 29) note that rational choice theorists typically move on to imperfect information models as a line of defence. This is perhaps a credible argument in terms of a public interest group, where perhaps only 5 per cent of the potential membership is recruited. It looks less credible when it is applied to business groups, which can often mobilise in excess of 90 per cent of their available clientele. Firms are unlikely to be in membership because of some exaggerated notion about the pivotality or political efficacy of their contribution.

Cartel making

In terms of logic, one attraction that might exist in firms working together is the opportunity this gives to the participating firms to fix prices. At least at the anecdotal level this seems to be a serious concern to Euro officials and needs attention. If done in a deliberate way this is illegal, but there may be informal ways relating to sharing views about what is going to happen to raw material prices, inflation, regulation, and so on, that mean that companies can collectively understand pressures on their pricing without deliberate price fixing.

Increasing the cost of non membership

One sort of rationality is for a firm to look at the costs involved and select the cheapest strategy in terms of its own expenditure, but there might be an industry-wide rationality that gives different conclusions. Thus if the oil industry as a whole gave government the impression that it was environmentally reliable then licences might be awarded in more environmentally sensitive areas. So what is rational for one company (a simple matter of deep sea dumping) might in the medium term be costly for the industry by harming the overall reputation of the industry.

As Olson shows, in situations with small numbers of potential participants the self-interested decision maker can see the immediate consequences for harming the overall industry case – of which they are part. Therefore in areas with small numbers of participants, actions are visible. Moreover, the point about a political process is that the other affected participants can intrude in the calculation process of the individual – bluntly or indirectly pointing to adverse consequences of a decision that is too short-sightedly selfish. The adverse impact on relations with others in the sector (with bottom line costs in terms of contracts, reciprocal support) is a factor in leading the firm to use a broad rather than a narrow interpretation of economic rationality. So one way in which free riding can be dealt with is through peer group pressure within the relevant potential membership. The mainstream explanation in Olson terms is that membership is induced by reducing the cost of membership by the selective allocation of benefits: there is logically another factor pushing potential participants into joining – if the cost of staying out is made uncomfortable.

THE 'SOCIAL' MEMBER

Though the previous section has advanced a number of different explanations of why membership might be self-interestedly adopted, another class of factors seems to be needed. Udehn (1996: 260) notes that Jon Elster is one of the important theorists who has deserted the attempt to explain membership simply in utilitarian terms. Of Elster's work he says: 'if economic man will not cooperate, or only conditionally, large scale cooperation can only be explained by invoking sociological man'. Elster sees the membership decision as resting on mixed motivations. Udehn (1996: 275) also draws attention to Knoke's test on the role of different sorts of incentives and his conclusion that 'the empirical literature on organisational incentives is a steady accumulation of findings that refute Olson's emphasis on selective goods as essential for collective action' (Knoke, 1990: 313).

The previous section tried to reconcile an apparently irrational (in Olson's terms) membership decision by incorporating into that decision a variety of factors that can make the decision economically rational. The following factors accept that the basis for the joining decision is other than an economic imperative.

Securing the collective good / avoiding collective bads

Empirical work has shown that individuals are far readier to claim that they contribute to the securing of collective goods than Olson supposed. For example a study of members of the Scottish National Farmers Union (NFUS) found that 70.6 per cent of members agreed that the fact that the NFUS represents farmers at government and EC level was 'very important'. (a further 16.6 per cent said 'important'). Though the incentive of cheap insurance was rated very important by 26.5 per cent of members, overall collective goals seemed much more important than selective material incentives (Jordan and Maloney, 1997).

Logically a firm can free ride collective bads just as it can free ride collective goods, but groups seem to find collective bads more effective in recruiting terms. Marsh (1976: 261) discovered that many of his respondents denied that services were an important reason for joining the CBI. These arguments generally support the idea that free riding in the real world is not necessarily sensible.

A major source for material on the assessment of the appeal of different incentives is Moe (1980). Though starting from an economic self-interest perspective he acknowledges that studies of small groups and larger voluntary associations have consistently suggested values other than economic self-interest are often important determinants of individual behaviour. He thus drops the assumption that individuals are economically self-interested and accepts incentives such as altruism, belief in a cause or ideology, loyalty, beliefs about right and wrong, camaraderie, friendship, love, acceptance, security, status, prestige, power, religious beliefs, racial prejudice (1980: 113). Relevantly for the (later) Offe argument, Moe points out that 'businessmen may believe strongly in free enterprise or individualism as social ideologies, not simply as rationalisations justifying their personal economic gain. (they)...may place much higher values on group goals than their own economic situations seem to call for'.[17] He argues:

> economic selective incentives are important member inducements ...on the other hand data...suggest that there also exists a rational basis for politically motivated membership. To begin

with, most members believe that their individual contributions do make a difference for their group's political success or failure... In addition to widespread perceptions of efficacy, there appears to be a purposive dimension of member involvement: many individuals indicate that a feeling of responsibility or obligation is an important consideration in their decision to maintain membership.

(Moe, 1980: 205–7)

However, even given the conventional wisdom that business groups are more dependent on collective incentives than Offe or Olson expected, the results of the survey reported in Chapter 1 are still unexpected in the degree of support that seemed to be given to general sectoral representation. This showed that whereas 69 per cent of public interest groups rated 'representing members' general interests' 1 or 2 on a scale through to 5 in terms of importance, such a figure rose to 89 per cent for both business and professional groups. Furthermore – though by a small margin – public interest groups appeared to be rated higher in terms of providing services and discounts and services.

A good corporate citizen

Partly membership can stem from an ethical duty to be a good corporate citizen: membership is what respectable firms do. It is not a high cost matter in terms of corporate budgets and therefore it might be seen as safer to go with the flow than make a decision to leave. From fragmentary evidence it looks like membership decisions are routine – unless there is an unusual event such as the arrival of new management looking for a quick turn around of the balance sheet – where cancelling subscriptions give an instant saving with no short term consequences.

This is compatible with the point in the previous section: that one participates to look like the other respectable firms. It also has self-interested implications. Reputation is a virtue that one can invest in. In the context of other sorts of groups this sort of consideration might be covered by Salisbury's notion of expressive benefit as an incentive. This sort of membership does not rest on the probability of group success but on the satisfaction of joining: it is thus free rider proof. Marsh (1976) establishes that among large firms collective incentives seem more relevant than selective in inducing membership. A survey of a British agricultural group by Jordan and Maloney in 1993 found that 72 per cent of National Farmers Union Scotland members agreed that 'all members of the farming industry have a duty to support the NFUS' was important or very important. An equity ethic has been identified (Marwell and Ames, 1979).

Collective irrationality or business ideology?

A slightly different interpretation of the good corporate citizen phenomenon is that businessmen are not representing their firms in making their membership decisions but the business elite. Thus decisions that are not in the strict self-interest of the firm make sense as the investment of the business elite in business prosperity. As well as a general support for business proposition there is the more personal factor that in the medium term businessmen might move post and it is sensible to keep the industry healthy.

Moe's evidence seemed to strongly suggest that 60–70 per cent of the members of the five different business groups he studied thought that individual contributions do make a difference to group success or failure (1980: 207) (Moe makes the important point that group leaders actively attempt to persuade members that this is the case). There appears to be an accumulation of evidence that support for the ends of business groups is as non utilitarian as that for the non business groups that Offe suggested. Marsh quotes one interviewee:

> If the CBI didn't exist we would need to create it. We want someone to stand up and talk for industry. The CBI knows what industry thinks because their channels of information are good... They may not always directly influence policy but they make sure government knows the bounds within which they can work in the industrial sphere.
>
> (Marsh, 1976: 264)

Affordability: whose budget?

The Olson approach assumes that firms can calculate benefits. It also assumes that companies are sensitive to the costs. However, very little is known about how decisions within organisations are made. The part of the organisation that obtains benefits may be different from the part that bears the costs, and hence the decision to join can be made without serious sense of cost/benefit. The benefits of membership may be spread through different parts of the member organisation. How is a membership retention decision made?

What appears most improbable is that firms make a careful annual calculation. As argued earlier it is in fact very difficult to enter any guess about benefits. In fact an important decision may not be about membership but level of activity. An active membership might be significantly more expensive than a minimum membership. In terms of travel and particularly executive time, organisations that seek to influence group policy are likely to have costs greatly in excess of the subscription.

Lucky rabbit's foot?

If membership is a response to difficult and unpredictable environments then a response that is somewhere between an insurance policy and a lucky rabbit's foot might be understandable. If enough other organisations do it the potential member does not have to make his own calculation but can join in on a 'me too' basis.

Individuals as decision makers: incentives at the personal level

There may be benefits to individuals in the companies that are distinct from those for the company. Some enjoy the social programmes. Others will be able to canvass for jobs. Knowing more about the industry as a whole might increase their marketability. Participation within collective organisations is presented by Olson as a burden but individuals might perceive the meetings as a relief from other aspects of business life. Marsh (1976: 261) quotes one CBI activist as attending because 'one of the problems of small firms is the intense loneliness of management'. Others conceded that there were benefits in terms of business opportunities or career development. A gold chain syndrome has been identified in which companies are active because their leaders enjoy the personal prominence that this gives them.

OR WAS OLSON RIGHT: THE UNDER-FED EURO FED?

Olson may not have foreseen the number of Euro-level organisations, but the fact remains that there is a paradox about the proliferation of groups. They may be numerous but they may be seen as weak. The logic that sees the formation of groups does not seem to push members to create powerful organisations. Powerful organisations would have extensive independent research and lobbying resources, a capacity to make binding agreements between the group and the Commission. In fact we do not have good data on the relative capacities of groups and their main constituents, but many Euro organisations do tend to a tokenistic presence. As reported in Chapter 1, survey data indicate that 65 per cent of all groups have four or fewer staff – rising to 74 per cent for business groups. It might be that several of the arguments sketched out above work without the need for a powerful organisation. There is a sense that the collective effort is the 'just in case' arrangement. If the subscription is relatively cheap it might be worth pursuing, but companies clearly want to retain control of their own representation and are also likely to act directly. Companies compete as well as cooperate.

Membership of business associations is likely to be different depending on the niche occupied by the group and the scale of the member company, but it appears that membership conceived of as a cost–benefit investment appears unusual. Grant and Marsh (1977: 46) recorded that the director of a large member company of the CBI told them: 'we make minimal use of CBI services. We don't remain members for that reason. Large firms know most things that the CBI could tell us ... Indeed the CBI sometimes comes to us for information'.

Olson presents the issue as being whether or not the membership cost is worthwhile. A different, but perhaps more realistic, issue for companies is whether the costs of active participation are worthwhile. The active company may, when allowing for executive time, travel, be making an investment much greater than the subscription. So the choice is not just about the cost of membership but about the type of membership that is to be pursued.

Business groups may exist but they may exist at a tokenistic level. Some membership is to ensure that the association does not take up a position unhelpful to the member. This aspect has already been suggested under the heading of steering the group. This section develops that point to note that a negative style of membership is unlikely to assist the development of an activist association.

Another explanation for organisational weakness has been set out by Camerra-Rowe. She (1995: 3) has drawn attention to the easy exit of firms from collective institutions to show that the impact of exit is stronger for associations in highly concentrated economic sectors with large component firms. Paradoxically, associations of individually powerful firms may end up being less effective than those associations of companies in more fragmented areas where the loss of any constituent is less serious. As she points out (1995: 14) this trend to weakness is exacerbated if the large actors also have different markets. This was the case in the automobile industry, where some firms like Daimler Benz and BMW saw advantage in open competition but Fiat, Renault and Peugeot did most of their business in protected home markets, which they wished to preserve. Camerra-Rowe concludes (1995: 15): 'despite being members of the same sector, the range of common interests was narrowed significantly by differences in market position and regulatory relations'.[18] The Camerra-Rowe paradox appears to be that an organisation which consists of individually influential members is weakened by the fact that these members can credibly defect and act on their own. For Camerra-Rowe the threat to collective action in small groups of big players is not free riding, but where the participants are free to act unilaterally. Non membership is not the same as free riding. Thus she argues that an individualistic, self-reliant strategy can lead to a firm winning concessions from the Commission as a result of own-account lobbying (*ibid.*, 6). This is very different from free riding and in the short term may be more expensive than collective action. And since the possibility of unilateralism tends to produce a policy constipation whereby there is a veto of anything but lowest common denominator policies, this requires that companies are organised to act on their own, exacerbating the tendency.

IS THIS A COLLECTIVE ACTION PROBLEM? AN ANALOGY

This section looks at two forms of what have hitherto been accepted aspects of the collective action phenomenon. First, it looks at the federation of national federations. If we are interested in explaining the (numerical) 'success' of federations of national organisations then the way in which these bodies are characterised may be vital. In the US a debate has emerged about collective action via political action committees (PACs). But as Gray and Lowery (1997) suggest, that debate may be ill-founded in assuming as it does that PACs 'are entirely new organisations established from scratch'. They suggest that PAC creation is a second order decision about how to pursue collective action: that much of the collective action problem will have been solved by the time the PAC issue is ripe. To change the metaphor, we have to be careful not to see everything as a nail just because we have the collective action problem hammer in our hands. Schlozman and Tierney (1986: 278) found that 90 per cent of the 3,000 groups they surveyed in the US entered into coalitions: acting together is normal for groups that want to secure political ends.

Following the Gray and Lowery point it can be argued that the creation of Euro Feds is a means to pursue collective action rather than a matter of deciding on collective action. We need to be sure that we are answering the correct examination question. As presented by Gray and Lowery the creation of PACs is part of an arms race among competing viewpoints. Each viewpoint will use a multiplicity of channels but a collective Euro group will be one of the tactics that can be utilised. If we assume that there are national-level collective bodies faced with attempting to secure influence at European level, there are several reasons why they would wish to enter a federated body. Brussels might be very important in terms of the policy field.

As sketched out above there may well be differential access to the European-level body on the grounds of a Euro ideology among officials. There may be a recognition that the industry as a whole benefits from collective action, and some off-setting considerations that reduce the likelihood of free riding. But this is to begin to ask the question of 'why would one act at the European level' rather than 'why associate? The implication of Gray and Lowery is that not all organisations would associate at this level – this is confined to those who have made a prior decision to get in the lobbying game. And studying the full population of organisations that might engage in lobbying when examining these, the actual issue of European action will inevitably confound very different types of decisions offered at the two tiers.

In this perspective we are dealing with a 'how' rather than a 'why' matter. Gray and Lowery present the notion of density-driven competition for access – the crowded room phenomenon. They say that as more interests are mobilised then more elaborate and thorough means of lobbying are needed. So Euro lobbying is part of a general inflation in the game: it is necessary to do this to keep one's position relative to competitors. The value of an extra channel increases when there is competition. The core idea seems to be that participation is more likely than free riding because the firm has decided that it wants to lobby. The issue is how can it best influence the game rather than can it save the entry price.

If the essence of the collective action issue is the difficulty in overcoming the free rider tendency then it does not in any practical sense arise for the second sort of arrangement discussed in this section – the direct member business club or umbrella organisations of organisations. In these arrangements the priority for the participating firms is again the opportunity to try to improve their working environment. If there is a tendency to free ride then the counter argument is captured by Olson's discussion of the group with few members. But it is probably not necessary to invoke an argument of that sophistication. If an organisation seeks to attain some important end then it is likely to enter with some enthusiasm into any alliance that helps it secure this. The free riding tactic is unlikely to even occur to a normal decision maker in these circumstances. Attempting to control one's risks positively is more pressing than the resting one's future in the possibility that the same ends can result from the activities of others. As Sidenius points out in Chapter 4 a tradition of associability at the national level is more than likely to be reflected at the international level. Similarly the participants discussed by Webster in Chapter 8 of groups involved in collective action on the environment are seeking to act – not seeking to benefit passively from the action of others.

CONCLUSION: THE FIELD OF DREAMS: BRINGING TRUMAN BACK IN

This perspective assumes that there are participants who want to secure certain ends: that they exist – with this motivation – carries with it the tendency to participate privately or collectively. Their overriding drive is to obtain influence rather than conservation of economic resources. If an EU with a clear policy role emerges in a world with these politically motivated policy participants, then the latter will be more likely to act than free ride. This is a sort of Truman-like argument of the inevitability of interest group behaviour, but it is amended in one important way. It does not assume that all individuals or organisations are driven to participate politically and collectively. It assumes however that some kinds of organisation are created with a need to attempt to influence outcomes. Firms which are dependent on political decisions or organisations set up nationally to exert influence are primed to act collectively at a European level. The 'collective problem' is about mobilisation: why do the potential participants not free ride? However, to get the organisations being discussed here to act cooperatively is not a problem: they will act through whatever channel they can find. For them the issue is not whether they should act or free ride: a proclivity to act is designed in. For such bodies the EU is an irresistible target. Provide the collective umbrella and they will be attracted: 'Build it and they will come'.

NOTES

1 The incentives operating in the decision about public interest groups are set out by Jordan and Maloney (1996).
2 One is not free riding a group whose aims one would support if informed about them, if the group has not effectively advertised itself and presented as a joining opportunity.
3 If one has an environmental group's badge on the car, and supports its general goals without sending a contribution, one is unlikely to be free

riding, but *de facto* acting as if one is free riding because the group has not successfully managed to connect the pro group predisposition with the follow through need for financial support.

4 One is not free riding an environmental group – even if it asserts it is acting in the public interest – if one sees its policies as infringing one's preferred life style.

5 Thus if one is not a member of the Association of University Teachers in the UK the explanation might not be free riding, but a decision to punish the group for glaring lack of success.

6 An important exception is shown by Sidenius (1994).

7 'In all these situations the fairly observant citizen sees various groups slugging it out with one another in pursuit of advantages from Government' (Truman, 1951: 11).

8 Olson gives examples of this belief in the 'ubiquitous and inevitable' nature of groups from Laski, Aristotle, Mosca, Simmel, Bentley and others (Olson, 1971: 17).

9 Part of the asymmetry may result from the nature of the demands that the respective interests are pursuing. It is difficult to think of things that the unions might wish of the political system that are not inherently controversial or are going to be subject to counter proposals from other groups. Boleat (1994) writes of how trade associations should expect to have 90 per cent of their contacts with civil servants not ministers. The trade association can have many issues of interest such as export support, product safety, where the subject might not be politically sensitive: this seems less probable for a trade union. Boleat notes that the real work in trade associations is not the high profile political lobbying, media work and so on, but, rather, the painstaking work to ensure that the government does understand the industry and that policy measures, when implemented, will have their desired effect.

10 In the introduction he did refer to the 'admittedly speculative manner' of the discussion (Offe, 1985: 6).

11 'Less is missing in the original but the context suggests it is a proof reading omission.

12 The small is different line is also advanced by Wilson, 1973; Moe, 1980 (Sidenius, 1994: 4)

13 He also argues that business associations have an advantage, because 'the totality of interests of members arises as an issue for the association are smaller for business associations than unions'. He says that there are hardly any of the ' "central life interests" of workers that do not appear, at least potentially, on the agenda of unions'. It is difficult to recognise that claim about the limited nature of the agenda of a business group as being a force leading to greater rather than less membership (1985: 190).

14 Strangely it is considered irrational by Olson to contribute to securing the common good, but it is not thought irrational for a company to work individually. Why is it not thought irrational to employ a lobbying consultancy?

15 More pessimistically they can assume that there will be too few contributions to secure change, but in this scenario it would be a waste of time for them to contribute.

16 It is not clear how small is to be interpreted but he treats the UN as a small organisation (Olson 1971: 36).

17 Udehn (1996: 211) notes Olson's comment that 'the adherence to a moral code that demands the sacrifices needed to obtain a collective good therefore need not contradict any of the analysis in this study; indeed, this analysis shows the need for such a moral code or for some other selective incentive' (1971: 61n and 160n). This concession that a moral code might be relevant is not further explored by Olson.

18 She also points out that as Daimler has other interests – electronics, insurance, marketing, there was no single trade association to represent this mix and for this reason the company was pushed to own-account lobbying.

3 The EU institutions and collective action
Constructing a European interest?

Laura Cram

It should be noted that the values and preferences of political actors are not exogenous to political institutions but develop within these institutions. The endogeneity of preferences is a major problem for theories of politics that picture action stemming from prior preferences.

(March and Olsen, 1989: 41)

In the late 1950s, Ernst Haas (1958: 4), in *The Uniting of Europe*, described Western Europe as a 'living laboratory' for the study of collective action between states. A wide range of organisations, which required the collaboration of European governments, operated in Western Europe[1]. Yet, as Haas (*ibid.*) noted: 'detailed data on how – if at all – cohesion is obtained through these processes is lacking'. The European Union continues to provide a fascinating example of the collaboration of an increasingly diverse range of actors, each enjoying different resource bases, political capacities and relative leverage – hence different degrees of structural power (Young, 1991) – which has culminated in the formation and maintenance of a complex international regime.

Historically, the collaborative European project has been beleaguered by the complexities of finding collective solutions to shared problems and yet the EU has proved to be a remarkably resilient regime. Scholars attempting to make sense of the European integration process have sought to address Haas' criticism and to identify the process through which cohesion is (or is not) achieved through the collaborative activities of member states. However, as the various contributions to this text and others (see Greenwood *et al.*, 1992; Mazey and Richardson, 1993a; Andersen and Eliassen, 1993) indicate, there has also been a proliferation of interest group activity and collective action at the day-to-day level of EU policy making, in addition to the collaboration between states which results in treaty based advances in the integration process. In the analysis of this more mundane, but equally vital, aspect of the European integration process, Haas' (1958: 4) observation continues to hold true. While there have been numerous attempts to identify and map the activities of interest groups and lobbyists at the EU level, little attention has been paid to the logic behind this collective action or to the impact of collective action on the actors involved: thus to the question of to 'how – if at all – cohesion is obtained' through these interactions.

Traditionally, the collective action literature focused on the selective (usually material) incentives which induced rational actors, on the basis of a cost–benefit analysis, to participate in a collaborative venture and thus allowed an organisation to minimise its free rider problem (Olson, 1965, 1971)[2]. From this rational choice perspective the preferences of the actors are viewed as exogenous[3] and 'theorists assume a sovereign individual whose preferences are not of theoretical concern' (Friedland and Alford, 1991: 251). In contrast, in this chapter it is argued that 'rationality as well as the appropriate contexts of its use are learned' (Friedland and Alford, 1991: 251). Thus, building upon the analysis elaborated by scholars of historical institutionalism, the preferences of the actors choosing to embark upon collective action at the EU level are considered to be endogenous, or developed within the institutional framework of the European Union. If preferences are viewed as endogenous, 'the meaning of rational action becomes unclear' (March and Olsen, 1989: 41) and a crucial question is raised: where are the preferences and values, on the basis of which actors weigh up the cost and benefits of particular incentives, derived from?[4]

The decision to embark on any form of collective action is, of course, made within the context of a set of opportunities facilitating collective action and of a set of constraints inhibiting the prospect of collaboration. Thus it is important to identify what these opportunities and constraints are, how they are generated, and how they might affect the preference formation of those actors faced with the prospect of participating in a collaborative venture. The hypothesis put forward in this chapter is that the institutional structure of the EU (the prevailing rules, norms and conventions), the activities of the EU institutions as purposive actors, and the symbolic or mythical dimension of EU governance all play an important role in explaining the propensity of other actors both to embark upon and to sustain their collaboration in collective action at the EU level. In short, that the 'political institutions organize these interactions in ways that shape interpretations and preferences' (March and Olsen, 1989: 41) and that 'not just the *strategies* but also the *goals* actors pursue are shaped by the institutional context' (Thelen and Steinmo, 1992: 8).

INTERESTS, INTERACTION AND LEARNING AT THE EU LEVEL

> And as with all learning processes, they need not merely use this new information for the guidance of their behaviour in the light of the preferences, memories and goals which they have had thus far, but they may also use them to *learn*, that is, to modify this very inner structure of their preferences, goals and patterns of behaviour.
>
> (Deutsch, 1953; 1966: 117; emphasis in original)

The process through which interest groups would come to mobilise at the EU level and the impact of increased interaction between interests and institutions at the EU level on the process of preference formation has long fascinated scholars of European integration. For both Haas (1958) and Deutsch (1968), the concept of a European political community or of a 'sense of Europeanness' were prerequisites for progress towards an integrated Europe. The 'mutual relevance' achieved as actors entered into iterated transactions with one another would, it was argued, help to shape the preferences of these actors and their propensity to work together in the future. Haas (1958, 1970), for example, emphasised the importance of interests, learning and authority– legitimacy transfers for the formation of a European-level political community. Haas' pluralist based neofunctionalism recognised the continuing importance of national political elites, and emphasised the key role played by interest based politics, in driving the process of political integration at the European level. National political elites might, for example, become more supportive of the process of European integration as they learned of the benefits which might ensue from its continuation, although they might equally, Haas recognised, become opposed to the integration process as they recognised its costs (Haas, 1958: 287–8). In either case, a re-evaluation of the preferences of the political elite (whether in favour of, or in opposition to, the European project) would result, ultimately, in the transformation of traditional nationally centred belief systems:

> As the process of integration proceeds, it is assumed that values will undergo change, that interests will be redefined in terms of regional

rather than a purely national orientation and that the erstwhile set of separate national group values will gradually be superseded by a new and geographically larger set of beliefs.

(Haas, 1958: 13)

In its focus upon the learning of integrative habits, as a result of prior cooperation, neofunctionalism displayed a clear link with both the functionalist (Mitrany, 1943)[5] and communication (Deutsch, 1966)[6] schools. Crucially, however, for Haas this was not a one way process. Although the attitudes of national political elites would influence the development of the integration process, supranational political elites also had a role to play in encouraging the process of integration. Thus, 'decision-makers in the new institutions may resist the effort to have their beliefs and policies dictated by the interested elites and advance their own prescription' (Haas, 1958: 19). It was through a complex interaction of belief systems that Haas envisioned the reorientation of the activities of national political elites, in response to European-centred interests and aspirations, would take place. Interestingly, Haas had found the ECSC legislature rather wanting in this respect – it had clearly not lived up to the expectations Monnet had of a federal executive – Haas felt, however, that the Assembly[7] might prove to be a more 'faithful prototype' of a federal parliament (Haas, 1958: 311).

Mitrany (1943) had specifically warned against the creation of territorially based supranational authority structures: 'for an authority which had the title to do so would in effect be hardly less than a world government; and such a strong central organism would inevitably tend to take unto itself rather more authority than that originally allotted to it' (Mitrany, 1943; 1966: 75). In contrast, in Haas' neofunctionalist approach, the very propensity of supranational organisations to maximise their powers was identified as an important element of the process through which a political community is formed. Indeed, the supranational institutions were allotted a key role as potential 'agents of integration' (Haas, 1958: 29). The supranational institutions were expected both to facilitate the transfer of elite authorities to the European level and to play the role of honest broker facilitating decision making betweeen recalcitrant national governments (Haas, 1958: 524).

Ultimately, Haas argued, as beliefs and aspirations were transformed through the interaction of supranational and national belief systems 'a proportional diminution of loyalty to and expectations from the former separate national governments' could be expected

(Haas, 1958: 14). A shift in the focus of national loyalties, and importantly of expectations, towards the new supranational authority structure would similarly be expected. The central importance of the transfer of loyalty in early neofunctionalist explanations of the process of political integration is undisputed. However, in his later work, Haas (1970: 633) recognised the difficulty of measuring this transfer and welcomed the contribution of Lindberg and Scheingold (1970), who stressed the importance of the extent to which authority for decision making had been transferred to the European level. The degree to which authority–legitimacy transfers had taken place would, they argued, provide a measurable indicator of progress towards a new political community.

The authority–legitimacy transfer was not, however, the sole defining criterion of political integration identified by Haas. Crucially, the process of political integration encompassed not only a change in the focus of the *'loyalties'* of the political elite but also in the focus of their *'expectations'* and *political activities'*[8] (Haas, 1958: 16). The reorientation of the preferences of the political elite, Haas argued, may result as much from their opposition to, as from their support for, the integration process. It is the reorientation of national expectations and political activities in response to supranational developments in Europe, or to the pull of the new centre, which are crucial for the process of political integration, not simply the extent to which the political actors are in support of the process of integration. Haas (1958: 288) considered that although elites with long term negative expectations of supranational activity might appear irreconcilable to the unification pattern, in fact, 'even the consistently negative-minded may be persuaded to adjust' (Haas, 1958: 296). Meanwhile, groups with short term negative expectations who mobilise in response to specific supranational policies which they oppose 'may, in self defence, become a permanent institution with a common – albeit negative – body of expectations' (Haas, 1958: 288). Any shift in loyalties, in response to the activities of the new centre, need not be absolute or permanent. Multiple loyalties may continue to exist. Hence, for Haas (1958: 15–16), it was more likely to be the convergence of a very disparate set of interests which would drive the process of integration and result in the establishment of a new political community, than any mass conversion to the doctrine of Europeanism. Ultimately, a self-interested shift in loyalty, or in the focus of political activities, by the political elite would increase the dynamic towards the development of the new political community whether it results from positive or from negative long term expectations of the integration process

(Haas, 1958: 297). It is this process which is usually referred to as political spillover[9].

Thus not only the sectoral expansion of competence at the EU level or major alterations in the constitutional structure of the EU would facilitate cohesion between the actors involved. The growing public perception of the EU as key actor was seen to be important, as was the role played by the supranational institutions in encouraging the reorientation of traditionally nationally based value structures and preferences. Crucially, the learning process, focused upon by Mitrany, Deutsch and Haas, was expected to play a key role in explaining the re-evaluation of the traditional preferences of key actors in the integration process. As will become clear below, many of these insights remain useful for our examination of the process through which actors take the decision to work collectively at the EU level today.

INSTITUTIONS AND THE EU POLICY PROCESS

> Preferences are neither clear nor stable. They develop over time. They are shaped not only by forces exogenous to politics and decision-making but also by the processes of politics themselves. Thus, the current interests of citizens are only a fraction of their interests as they unfold over their lifetimes, and that unfolding is affected by choices along the way.
>
> (March and Olsen, 1989: 146)

As structural explanations of the integration process came to dominate the field of integration studies in the 1970s and 1980s, academic preoccupation with the institutional aspect of EU governance, begun with Haas (1958), dwindled accordingly. Recently, however, this focus of study has been revived. In particular, scholars have increasingly come to ask the question 'what consequence does the process itself have for forming and reforming – perhaps for inventing or discovering interests and values?' (Lindblom, 1965: 15). The learning process undergone by actors involved in interactions at the EU level, and the impact of this learning process on the preferences of the actors involved, has increasingly come under scrutiny. As Sandholtz argues:

> Membership in the EC has become part of the interest calculation for governments and societal groups. In other words, the national interests of EC states do not have independent existence; they are not formed in a vacuum and then brought to Brussels. Those

interests are defined and redefined in an international and institutional context that includes the EC.

(Sandholtz, 1993a: 3)

National political and administrative elites, business elites and judicial elites have all had to learn to come to terms with the EU as an aspect of their daily lives: 'socializing new actors is therefore a central component of the Community–member state relationship' (Sbragia, 1994: 75). There is, likewise, increasing evidence of the mobilisation of transnational business elites at the EU level, which have, in turn, pushed for further integration in the EU (Sandholtz and Zysman, 1989, Sandholtz, 1992, Cowles, 1995a). Sandholtz (1996) has summed up this process rather neatly in the phrase 'membership matters'. A range of studies, which recognise the role of EU institutions in the integration process, has, meanwhile, begun to emerge both from authors favouring an intergovernmentalist perspective and from those who emphasise the central role of semi autonomous supranational institutions. Institutions have been characterised in a number of ways: as passive structures; as actively shaping expectations and norms; and as purposive actors seeking to influence the development of the EU.

The notion of institutions recognised as passive structures, that is as providing the norms, values and procedures, alterable only with unanimous consent, within which the day-to-day policy choices and major constitutional decisions are taken, is quite consistent with the intergovernmentalist perspective, which focuses predominantly on the structural leadership exerted by national governments in international negotiations (Moravcsik, 1993: 509). Following international regime theory, the critical role played by EU institutions in providing a passive structure which enhances the efficiency of intergovernmental decision making is recognised. EU institutions provide a framework within which to negotiate major history making decisions by ensuring a shared negotiating forum, joint decision procedures, a set of shared legal and political norms, institutions to monitor cooperation and defection and, not least, by disseminating ideas and information (Moravcsik, 1993: 508).

However, it is increasingly recognised that EU institutions also play an active role in the EU policy process. Thus, while emphasising the crucial role which national governments play in selecting between available alternatives when taking decisions in the EU, Garrett and Weingast (1993) have argued that EU institutions also play an important role in coordinating expectations and in shaping a 'shared belief system'. Analysing the role of institutions and ideas in EU policy making, they have argued that 'by embodying, selecting and publicising particular paths on which all actors are able to co-ordinate, institutions may provide a *constructed focal point*'. In this way, 'institutions not only provide individuals with critical information about defection but also help to construct a shared belief system that defines for the community what actions constitute cooperation and defection' (Garrett and Weingast, 1993: 176; emphasis in original).

Garrett and Weingast's (1993) emphasis on the development of a shared belief system is consistent with recent studies which, drawing on new institutionalist perspectives (March and Olsen, 1989; Di Maggio and Powell, 1991; Thelen and Steinmo, 1992), present institutions as more than simply arenas within which political action is played out (Bulmer, 1994a: 357) but as actively playing a role in shaping norms, values and conventions. March and Olsen (1989: 165) identified the role played by institutions 'as agents in the construction of political interests and beliefs' as an important aspect of integrative politics: of 'building community and a sense of common identity within which decisions are made'. Analysts applying the tools of new institutionalism in the EU context have also emphasised the dual role played by institutions (Bulmer, 1994b; Peterson, 1995). Thus, institutions are also presented as playing an independent role as actors in the policy process, able to 'develop their own agendas and act autonomously of allied interest groups' (Peterson, 1995: 81) and not simply as a structure in which other actors pursue their goals. Perhaps most importantly, from a historical institutionalist perspective, EU institutions have been recognised as able to 'generate endogenous institutional impetuses for policy change that go beyond the usual representation of institutional mediation' (Bulmer, 1994a: 372).[10]

The agency of the EU institutions is increasingly recognised and studies reveal how EU institutions have influenced the agenda setting, policy formulation and implementation processes. There is considerable evidence that institutions, as purposive actors, have an important role to play. Studies have highlighted the role of bureaucratic politics in the EU (Peters, 1992), the role of the Commission as agenda setter (Peters, 1994; Pollack, 1995), and the Commission's role in the promotion of the EU regulatory regime (Majone, 1989, 1991a, 1991b, 1992a, 1992b, 1993; Dehousse, 1993; Cram, 1993; Bulmer, 1994a). Likewise, the role of the European Parliament as conditional agenda setter has been examined (Tsebelis, 1994). Increasingly too, scholars have begun to assess the important political role played by the European Court of Justice (Weiler, 1991; Garrett, 1992; Shapiro, 1992; Garrett and Weingast, 1993; Burley and Mattli, 1993; Wincott, 1994) and, importantly, to examine the critical interactions between the Court and other institutions within the policy process (Alter and Meunier-Aitsahalia, 1994; Wincott, 1995).

Increasingly the leadership potential of EU institutions has come to be re-examined. In this context, for example, the role played by the CEU as an entrepreneurial leader during the negotiations over the Single European Act has been recognised (Sandholtz, 1993a; Sandholtz and Zysman, 1989). In the classic style of an entrepreneurial leader, the Commission officials displayed the characteristics of:

(i) agenda setters shaping the form in which issues are presented for consideration at the international level, (ii) popularizers drawing attention to the importance of the issues at stake, (iii) inventors devising innovative policy options to overcome bargaining impediments, and (iv) brokers making deals and lining up support for salient options.

(Young, 1991: 294)

The EU institutions have often played a critical role in bringing particular groups of interests together in the EU context and in creating policy networks. The Commission, in particular, may have an important role to play in providing the catalyst for collective action, whether amongst member states (Sandholtz and Zysman, 1989), big business (Sandholtz, 1992a, 1993b, Cowles 1995a) or amongst broader social interest groupings (Cram 1996b: 1997). The Commission has, for example, frequently offered 'selective incentives' (Olson, 1971) (ranging from funding opportunities to the opportunity to play a role in policy formulation) to encourage collective action. Likewise, the Commission plays an important part in initiating research and promoting particular sets of ideas which may encourage collective action amongst the various transnational and domestic interests. Critically, 'analysis and ideas are needed to discover opportunities of collective gains and to elicit support in favour of the most efficient way of exploiting such opportunities' (Majone, 1994: 5). Recently, the role of the European Court in encouraging the mobilisation of individuals at the EU level has also been highlighted (Alter and Meunier-Aitsahalia, 1994). Thus, an important aspect of the involvement of domestic and transnational interests in the EU policy process may be the critical role which supranational institutions or political leaders at the supranational level have played in encouraging and promoting the mobilisation of these interests (Sandholtz, 1992a & b; 1993b; Cowles, 1993).

COLLECTIVE ACTION AT THE EU LEVEL

There is increasing evidence of the involvement of a wide range of actors at the EU level and a significant expansion in the number of collective forums through which these actors may concert their activities. There has been a rapid increase in the number of Euro groups operating at the EU level, many seeking to gain information about, or to influence, the European policy process.[11] It is widely recognised that 'changes in the distribution of power between the Member states and the European Community have prompted a proliferation of interest group lobbying at the EC level' (Mazey and Richardson, 1993a: 3). The growth of EU competence and enhanced decision powers for EU institutions in certain policy areas (such as those concerning the single market) may help to explain the increase in the volume of lobbying at the EU level, in response to the pull of the new centre (Haas, 1958: 16). However, explaining the logic behind the collective action of traditionally nationally based interests at the EU level remains problematic:

> Alliances are the product of political processes not preexisting preferences . . . policy interests can be defined in different ways so that several distinct policies may be compatible with a group's interest. Potential group members do not always know their interests in a specific policy area, moreover, existing groups may be ambivalent or divided about their policy interests.
>
> (Weir, 1992: 194)

Many of the Euro groups operating at the EU level have emerged from earlier organisations founded at the national or international level (see other chapters in this volume). Clearly shifts in traditional behaviour patterns were in part a response to the changed institutional context in Europe. For example the establishment of European-level consumer organisations immediately after the signing of the Treaty of Rome (see Chapter 7) or of the newest European-level environmental organisations after the signing of the SEA (see Chapter 8). Even in policy areas where there has been a clear expansion of EU competences, however, actors continue to have choices concerning the course of action/level of activity most appropriate to achieving their desired ends.

As McLaughlin, Jordan and Maloney (1993) have argued, far from placing all of their eggs in one basket, large firms seeking to influence the EU policy process, or to gain more information about EU activities, continue to pursue multiple strategies. These may include collective action at the EU level but may equally include direct unilateral action at the EU level or, indeed, unilateral or collective action at the national or international levels.[12] Thus even where there is a clear shift in competence to the EU level, the decision to pursue collective action at the EU level is not inevitable. Similarly, the question of which collective forum to join and which partners to ally with can be influenced by a wide range of factors, from past experience of collaboration to political expediency or, indeed, the decision may be a reponse to institutional incentives at the EU level. These reflect, perhaps, a convergence of disparate interests rather than a shared set of pre-existing fixed preferences. Importantly, it has been argued that 'cooperation does not emerge self-created out of the soup of failed unilateral strategies. Some political actor (or actors) must propose cooperation and sell the idea to potential partners' (Sandholtz, 1992a: 3).

It is clear that EU institutions, viewed as rules, norms and conventions, provide constraints upon and opportunities for collective action; provide the parameters within which collective action might take place; and also have an important influence on the environment within which preferences are formed. As Pierson (1993: 598) has argued, 'incentive structures influence the probability of particular outcomes and the pay-offs attached to those outcomes. Individuals choose, but the constraints that frame their decisions provide strong inducements to make particular choices'. Crucially, however, the development of particular norms and standard operating procedures does not come about purely by chance but may actively have been encouraged by the semi autonomous EU institutions. Indeed, the promotion of particular policy developments at the EU level may have a significant impact upon the process of coalition formation at the EU level:

> Where groups have multiple, often conflicting interests, it is necessary to examine the political processes out of which political coalitions are formed...new ideas can cause groups to rethink their interests; consequently, the way in which various policies are 'packaged' can facilitate certain coalitions and hinder others.
>
> (Thelen and Steinmo, 1992: 8)

Most interesting, in this context, are those groups which have mobilised at the EU level, have altered their traditionally nationally based behaviour patterns, and are pursuing collective action at the EU level, in policy areas where there is little evidence of an increase in EU competence. For example, while the EU is becoming an increasingly important legislative force in the area of social policy, its regulatory power has been strictly circumscribed.[13] There is no binding EU legislation in the areas of homelessness, poverty, family policy, old age or disability – to name just a few of the areas in which a prolif- eration of Euro groups has emerged. Yet, in 1992 more than 100 networks of voluntary or community organisations were identified in Europe (Harvey, 1992: 277). Many of these operate in areas in which the EU could hardly be said to wield power. Indeeed, these have often been the very areas in which national governments have jealously guarded their national prerogatives. The challenge is clearly to explain why interests are mobilising around an institution with relatively little power in the policy area; and why are groups apparently shooting where the ducks are not?

Once again it appears that some actor (or actors) must perform the leadership role of 'educator, stimulating and accepting changing world views, redefining meanings and exciting commitments' (March and Olsen, 1989: 163). Analysis of the activities of Euro interests in the area of EU social policy, for example, reveals a close relationship between the activities and incentives offered by the European Com- mission and other EU institutions and the emergent pattern of collec- tive action. Advisory committees, networks, observatories and EU programmes all facilitate the participation of traditionally domestic interests at the European level. A range of powerful selective incen- tives (Olson, 1965) have been offered by the EU institutions, and by the CEU in particular, to encourage the participation of Euro inter- ests at the EU level and the development of transnational cooperation in the social field (Cram 1996b; 1997). Similarly, Greenwood observes that in the area of the professions, where consensus concerning the competence of the EU is lacking, 'the principal peak organisation in the domain arose not from the efforts of interests themselves but from the initiative of a Commission official' (see Chapter 6).

Even in those cases where the emergence of a Euro group or a new collective forum was a clear response to the increased institutional authority of the EU, the European institutions have often played a significant role in massaging the form in which these groups develop. In general, the Commission's preference for dialogue with representa- tive organisations at the European level provided a clear incentive for disparate groups to act collectively. More specifically, Commission support for the creation of organisations such as BEUC[14] or the

EEB[15] has had a clear impact upon the type of collective action pursued by consumer and environmental groups and the impact of this collective action in these fields. Crucially, 'institutional arrangements not only determine who decides, but also influence what is decided' (Majone, 1989: 102).

The impact of EU institutions on collective action is not, of course, limited to the areas of consumer, environmental and social policy but extends to key areas of industrial policy and the encouragement of collective action between major industrial actors. Today representatives from information and communication technology (ICT) firms (whether as individual actors, in committees or consultation groups, or as group members in industry federations and national and European standards bodies) are an omnipresent force in the EU ICT policy process.[16] DG XIII[17] now enjoys a rather symbiotic relationship with industry, which is involved at almost every stage of policy deliberation in the area. Yet, this did not come about without some effort on the part of the Commission. The involvement of major ICT firms in EU research programmes and ultimately in the administrative infrastructure for the development of EU ICT policy was, in part, a response to the selective incentives offered by the European Commission in the late 1970s (Sandholtz, 1992a; 1993b). Crucially, at this early stage power could not be said to lie in Brussels in the ICT sector. Although ICT firms proved willing to forge their own collaborative alliances and industrial cooperation had already begun to emerge in the early 1980s, prior to the main thrust of EU policy, the direction this cooperation took lacked a particular EU focus. Although a small number of EU firms had begun to cooperate with each other, cooperation with firms based outside the EU was, in fact, far more common (Mytelka and Delapierre, 1987: 241). This gives some indication of the global direction which the development of the ICT sector might have taken of its own accord if firms were left as entirely independent actors, untramelled by regulation or by incentives. Once again, a variety of choices were available to both firms and national governments: the question remains, why did ICT firms choose to work collectively at the EU level in the late 1970s and early 1980s? Did the decision to act collectively at the at the EU level really coincide with shift of 'ducks' (see Chapter 1) to Brussels or with the shift of *incentives* to the European level?

It is important to ask how the participation of Euro interests in the EU policy process, or in Euro groups, has affected the activities and preferences of those participants. Indeed, 'if interest groups shape policies, policies can shape interest groups. The organisational structure and political goals of groups may change in response to the nature of the programmes they confront or hope to sustain or modify' (Pierson, 1993: 598). Thus, collective action in an EU context may have important spillover effects or unintended consequences, not least of these being the fact that many of the collective forums in which Euro groups participate (for example: intergroups; advisory boards; standards bodies; networks) themselves become part of the EU institutional structure. Just as Haas (1958: 19) argued that 'once the institutions associated with the step of integration are established, a change is likely to take place' so too collective forums at the EU level can be viewed as emergent institutions contributing to the creation of new norms and standard operating procedures. Thus it is no longer only formal EU organisations such as the Commission, the Parliament or the Court or formal EU legislation which 'shape[s] how political actors define their interests and that structure their relations of power to other groups' (Thelen and Steinmo, 1992: 2). The impact of cooperation on the actors involved may become an important variable when examining the logic of collective action over time. Thus, it is vital to explore the *learning processes* undergone by the actors involved and the impact of collaboration on *communication patterns*, and to recognise the importance of the *institutionalisation* of collective action.

The role of EU institutions, both as structure and as agent, can be seen to have important implications for the development of the strategies and to some extent the goals of actors embarking on collective action at the EU level. Yet, the symbolic or mythical dimension of EU governance may play an equally important role in shaping the goals of the actors and altering their preferences: 'by most reasonable measures, the symbolic consequences of political decision-making are at least as important as the substantive consequences' (March and Olsen, 1989: 52). A crucial question remains to be answered: do groups act collectively to influence new powerful institutions at the EU level or does the EU become a central actor in any given policy area because actors have been persuaded to collaborate at the EU level or at least had been persuaded of the importance of the EU? The examination of the symbolic aspect of politics may be crucial in this respect, offering an insight into both the logic of collective action and the dynamics of political behaviour (Elder and Cobb, 1983: 1). Indeed, the ability to create at least a myth of the importance of the EU in a diverse range of policy areas may have a significant impact on the propensity of actors to collaborate at the EU level.

CONCLUSION: SYMBOLIC POLITICS AND COLLECTIVE ACTION AT THE EU LEVEL

> judgement and decision, though mental activities of individuals, are also part of a social process. They are taken within and depend on a net of communication, which is meaningful only through a vast, partly organised accumulation of largely shared assumptions and expectations, a structure constantly being developed and changed by the activities which it mediates.
>
> (Vickers, 1965: 15)

For the most part, 'people don't stop at every choice they make in their life and think to themselves, "Now what will maximise my self-interest?" Instead, most of us, most of the time, follow societally defined rules, even when so doing may not be directly in our self-interest' (Thelen and Steinmo, 1992:8). This of course is rather reminiscent of Mitrany's (1943), Haas' (1958) and Deutsch's (1966) focus on the learning of integrative habits. Indeed, Galtung (1973: 25), building on Haas' point, argued that even opposition to the EU in itself only reinforces its position as an important actor. The central importance of the EU in policy debates was, he argued, only likely to be strengthened further as opposing interests began to organise on a transnational basis.

Students of politics tend to 'underestimate the diffuse, interactive way in which meaning, intentions and action are woven together' (March and Olsen, 1989: 52). Clearly, the construction of even a symbolic appearance, or a myth, of EU centrality in key issue areas may have important implications for the formation of preferences on the basis of which interests/groups take decisions upon the utility of collective action from their perspective. It has become clear that leadership has played a crucial role in explaining the particular pattern of collective action which has emerged at the EU level. Once again, in providing the leadership required for cooperation, a key aspect of a leader's role is the relationship the leader:

> has, or can forge, with the ideological aspects of the state – its pattern of legitimacy, its cultural image and structure, its myths. A leader who can manipulate myths – who can deconstruct and construct the culture of the [nation state][18] itself – is in a very different position from one who is restricted to conforming to the text and playing out the script.
>
> (Cerny, 1988: 134)

However, as Mazey and Richardson (1994: 178) note, much of the pressure exerted by Euro interests is, in practice, pushing at an open door. The collaborative activities encouraged by the EU institutions are not, of course, solely concerned with creating a consultative partner, with establishing a constituency of support or with a piecemeal expansion of competences. Nor, as has become clear, is this their only effect. A less tangible outcome may be equally important. The general rules concerning the cofinancing of activities organised by NGOs in the framework of the HELIOS II Programme for people with disabilities state, for example, that: 'during the activity, the Commission contribution and the European Dimension should be highlighted in the opening and closing addresses. The EC flag should also be used as well as the European anthem when appropriate' (HELIOS II, Nov. 1993: 4).

This symbolic aspect of EU activities may be critically important in the sense of establishing some sense of a European identity. The close collaboration of Euro interests may contribute to a changing policy environment in the EU. Indeed, in the ICT field, the importance of participation in the various collective forums connected with the EU, in generating a technological community of individuals who know and trust one another, cannot be underestimated (Sharp, 1990). Similarly, many of those interviewed in the social field, have observed a growing sense of Europeanness amongst their members or, at least, a growing propensity to adopt a European approach to problem solving and a greater willingness to work together with their European counterparts:

> Certainly when I talk about this European Disablility movement, it was very evident, as you might imagine, at the European Day of Disabled People at the European Parliament. That's a very tangible example. Not necessarily in a militant way but in a way that is linked to a sense of identity and a sense of pride as well, a certain pride in being part of a specific culture or group.
>
> (Cram, private interview, 1995)

It appears that the effect of the catalytic role played by the EU institutions may have contributed to some extent towards the development of a set of 'shared assumptions and expectations' (Vickers, 1965:15) on the part of those actors drawn into participating at the EU level. This, in turn, appears to have had some impact upon the interests and activities of, not only the Euro groups, but also of their national member organisations and even of national policy makers (Cram, 1997: 132–9). As Vickers (1965: 29) has argued, 'policy-making assumes, expresses and helps to create a whole system of human values'. It is on the basis of these assumptions and preferences, developed in part at least within the institutional structure that is the European Union, that vital decisions on whether or not to pursue a collaborative venture are taken by groups working in the EU context.

NOTES

1 Haas noted in particular: the Organisation for European Economic Cooperation; the Council of Europe; the Western European Union; and the European Coal and Steel Community.

2 It is not my intention to rehearse these arguments in this chapter. For a critical review of the collective action literature see Jordan, Chapter 2 in this volume.

3 'The idea that preferences are produced and changed by a process that is exogenous to the processes of choice is fundamental to modern decision theory... Conventional theories of markets, for example, picture advertising and experience as providing information about alternatives and their properties, not as affecting tastes. Similarly, conventional theories of politics assume that a voter's exposure to and choice of a candidate do not change that voter's preferences for various attributes that a candidate might possess, although they may change a voter's belief about which candidates possess which attributes' (March and Olsen, 1989: 162–3).

4 The historical institutionalist approach views 'the question of how individuals and groups define their self-interest as problematical' (Thelen and Steinmo, 1992: 8). Conflict over the process of preference formation has been identified by Thelen and Steinmo (1992: 9) as perhaps the core distinction between rational choice institutionalism (exogenous preference formation) and historical institutionalism (endogenous preference formation).

5 For the construction of a 'working peace system' it was only, Mitrany argued, through cooperation in technical/functional organisations that it might prove possible to 'set going lasting instruments and habits of a common international life' (Mitrany 1943, 1966: 58). Without these habits, political/constitutional action could not be contemplated: while with these learned habits of integration such political/constitutional action may ultimately prove superfluous (*ibid.*: 97).

6 For Deutsch (1966: 96–7), mutually responsive transactions resulted from a complex learning process from which shared symbols, identities, habits of cooperation, memories, values and norms would emerge. Deutsch's vision of political integration did not insist on the presence of any specified institutional structure but rather depended on 'a historical process of social learning in which individuals, usually over several generations, learn to become a people' (Deutsch, 1966: 174).

7 Later to become the European Parliament.

8 Emphasis added.

9 For the purposes of this chapter the process identified by Haas as political spillover is most relevant. However, Haas, also recognised the importance of functional or technical spillover, which, he argued, was based on a quite

different logic from that which drove political spillover: 'sector integration... begets its own impetus toward extension to the entire economy even in the absence of specific group demands and their attendant ideologies' (Haas, 1958: 297). In neofunctionalist terms, the process of functional or sectoral spillover referred to the situation in which the attempt to achieve a goal agreed upon at the outset of cooperation, such as the harmonisation of coal and steel policy, becomes possible only if other (unanticipated) cooperative activities are also carried out, for example harmonisation of transport policy or economic policy. In this way cooperation in one sector would spill over into cooperation in another, previously unrelated, sector.

Similarly, Haas (1958: 317) identified a process of geographical spillover. Haas recognised that cooperation between one group of member states was likely to have some effect upon excluded states: not least by altering existing patterns of trade. In turn, the responses of non member states might, he argued, influence the process of integration; for greater detail see Cram, 1996a.

10 Paul Pierson (1996) adds to the growing scholarship on new institutionalist approaches with his recent article: 'The Path to European Integration: A Historical Institutionalist Analysis'.

11 see Aspinwall and Greenwood, Chapter 1 in this volume; see also Cowles Chapter 5, in this volume for the changing role of big business in this context.

12 See also Sidenius, Chapter 4 in this volume with respect to the range of options available to national-level interest organisations seeking to achieve their desired ends.

13 Binding EU regulations in the area of EU social policy are restricted to the areas of Health and Safety, Equal Treatment of Men and Women, Protection of Workers and Social Security for Migrant Workers (Cram, 1993; 1997: Chapter 4).

14 see Young, Chapter 7 in this volume.

15 see Mazey and Richardson, 1993b and Webster, Chapter 8 in this volume.

16 See Cram 1997, chapter 5 for the range of ways in which the ICT industry seeks to influence EU ICT policy.

17 The Directorate General responsible for information and communications technology.

18 Instead of 'nation state', in this case, read 'polity'.

4 A collective action problem?

Danish interest associations[1] and Euro groups

Niels Christian Sidenius

A variety of groups and associations carry out political activities. They take place at local, regional, national and international levels, they focus on politicians and administrators, and they are performed through a number of outlets and instruments. According to Olson (1965), political activity by collective units is a by-product of other services produced by the association, and by creating public goods political activity also creates a free rider problem. In order to attract and keep members associations have to supply selective goods, typically selective material goods. Olson's *Theory of Collective Action* has been much debated and contested, concerning the nature of incentives as well as the effect of group size (see, for example Salisbury, 1969; Moe, 1980; Sabatier, 1992); but this has not eliminated the crucial matter of collective action forms and incentives.

Most analyses of collective action have focused on attitudes and behaviour of individuals and firms, whereas little attention has been paid to the collective action problems confronting associations as member units. This chapter intends to investigate the nature of collective action and collective action problems for Danish interest associations in relation to Euro groups.

To deal with national interest associations and the way they coalesce in international arenas raises at least three points. First, whether associations are first or second order associations (Schmitter and Streeck, 1981; Sidenius, 1994), we cannot regard them as units acting similarly to individuals or to firms. We may expect that associations behave more, as well as less, rationally than individuals and firms do. On the one hand, they are probably in command of more information regarding the diversity of benefits and costs of participating in collective action, and at least the larger associations are able to make informed decisions on the basis of that information. On the other hand, as associations they are part of a group of political or semi political actors who have already opted for collective action, irrespective of whether or not they have been able to defeat their own problems of free riding successfully. The *raison d'être* of associations probably makes them more inclined towards joining associations at sectoral or geographically higher levels, because it reinforces the ideology and practice of associability.

Second, there will most likely be a difference between incentives, decisions and activity of associations at the national level compared with those at the international level. The concepts of internationalisation and multilevel governance (see, for example, Jachtenfuchs and Kohler- Koch, 1996) do not imply disappearance of policy implementation and production of services at the national level – which means that full scale incentives produced by associations are still at hand. As a consequence, one may hypothesise that international-level associational incentives and activity are more one-sidedly politically directed than they are at the national level.

The number of Euro groups has increased in recent years (for example, Andersen and Eliassen, 1993; see also Chapter 1 in this volume) and the major part of them is made up of national associations (Philip, 1991; see also Euroconfidentiel, 1996). However, this does not tell us much about the considerations of national associations whether or not to join and stay in a Euro group. The question is whether the decision to join a Euro group more or less automatically follows previous decisions in the national context on political and associational activity or it contains a genuine collective action problem.

Third, the population of national associations is very diverse as regards size, resources, scope, political influence, and the area of societal life that each of them organises. Associations are also different as to the extent to which they are impacted upon by the politics and policies of the EU (see Chapter 1). One may, therefore, suppose that different associational properties as well as dissimilarities in the way in which associations are impacted upon by the EU may lead to different approaches *vis-à-vis* membership of Euro groups.

This chapter analyses the political activity of Danish interest associations from the perspective of membership of Euro groups – to what extent do they join Euro groups and how can it be explained? The analysis sheds light on three separate assertions. First, the inclination of Danish interest associations to associate in Euro groups differs between groups in accordance with their associational properties and the way in which they are influenced by the policies of the EU.

Second, membership of Euro groups has to be seen as one among several options of political activity, implying that the collective action problem has been solved before the decision was taken to join a Euro group. And, third, membership of Euro groups is nevertheless perceived in terms of incentives; these incentives cannot, however, predominantly be characterised as selective material benefits.

THE INTERNATIONALISATION OF DANISH INTEREST ASSOCIATIONS

One may suppose that large, resourceful associations which focus on a broad spectre of policy, are more likely to deal with international aspects of policy than are small, single-focus associations without many resources. One may also suppose that associations within established policy areas such as labour market and trade policy are more inclined towards national as well as international political activity than are associations of newer policy areas, for example, consumer policy. Similarly, one may suppose that associations organising spheres of society which are strictly regulated by the EU, for strategic reasons will be more alert to policy opportunities in the EU context than other associations will be. Thus, associations of agriculture are more inclined to perceive policy matters in an EU context than are the associations of civil servants. We therefore assert that associations within the production of goods and services are more internationalised than associations within other areas of societal life. We also assert that associations within sectors facing international competition (for example, business) are more internationalised than associations within the public sector (for example, civil servants). In order to analyse these assumptions Danish interest associations are divided into four groups; workers, civil servants and academics, business and other associations.

Political activity: contexts and diversity

National interest associations become involved in political activity in varying contexts, with different interlocutors and on a number of policy matters. Here we distinguish between associations' political activity at the national level, their domestic political activity with regard to EU policy, their political activity *vis-à-vis* political and administrative institutions in Brussels, and, finally, their membership of Euro groups as a special outlet for political activity (Table 4.1).[2]

Table 4.1 Danish interest associations' political activity and Euro group membership (%)*

Associations	National political activity %	EU-related political activity %	Political activity in Brussels %	Euro group membership %
Workers (N=34)	79.4	58.8	61.8	55.9
Civil servants, academics (N=175)	76.6	37.7	33.1	41.7
Business (N=358)	69.3	49.4	39.1	50.0
Other associations (N=749)	58.7	21.2	20.3	27.0
All associations (N=1316)	64.5	32.1	28.2	35.9

Source: Author's survey (1993)

* The questions of the survey were:
● Has your association been in contact with political–administrative institutions at the national level or with the peak associations of the municipalities?   ● Has your association been in contact with political–administrative institutions at the national level or with the peak associations of the municipalities in EU matters?   ● Has your association been in contact with EU institutions or the Permanent Danish Representation in Brussels?   ● Is your association member of one or more Euro groups?
The associations were able to respond Yes or No. Table 4.1 displays the Yes responses, but it does not say anything about the frequency of contact or its policy impact.

Associations within the production of goods and services are more politically active than their counterparts in varying parts of civil society. And associations within private production, such as workers' and business associations, are more engaged in politics than the associations of civil servants and academics are. Generally, the associations of workers are more politically active than those of business, which, in declining order of activity, are followed by the associations of civil servants and academics and finally other associations. The only exception is that a larger share of associations of civil servants and academics are engaged in domestic political activity than is the case with the associations of business. This, no doubt, mirrors the size and institutionalisation of the Danish public sector and its regulations.

From the national foundation of interest associations one might have expected a horizontally declining order of activity – that national political activity was more frequent than international political activity – but this is not the case. What really distorts that expectation is, however, the frequency of Euro group membership, which – with workers' associations as an exception – comes second after national political activity. Obviously, it is more common to join a Euro group than to lobby for interests directly in Brussels. Euro group membership as a political activity is not similar to the other activities; it was an option taken before the expansion of EU policy, and membership may imply the existence of solidaristic motives of associability (Wilson, 1973; Moe, 1980).

European Union politics and Euro group membership

Relationships between EU politics and membership of Euro groups can be illuminated by focusing upon those interest associations that are influenced by EU policy. The assumption is that these associations more than other associations are inclined towards joining Euro groups (Table 4.2).

With very large variations between groups of associations, about 40 per cent of all associations state that they are increasingly influenced by EU policy. Of these associations, a little more than 60 per cent are also members of Euro groups. It does not make much sense to suggest that membership of Euro groups creates the impact of EU policies, so the relationship presented by the figures implies that membership of Euro groups is the dependent variable. The figures also show that

Table 4.2 EU impact* on Danish interest associations, and their membership of Euro groups

Associations	Impacted upon by EU policies		Impacted upon and Euro group member	
	(N)	%	(N)	%
Workers	34	76.5	26	69.2
Civil servants, academics	175	51.4	90	63.3
Business	358	64.8	232	67.7
Other associations	749	26.6	199	55.3
All associations	1316	41.6	547	62.5

Source: Author's survey (1993)

* Impact is the sum of the responses of great extent and some extent. The question of the survey was: In what way do decisions at EU level influence the work of your association? and the answer was that: EU decisions more and more influence the fields of activity of the association to a great extent, to some extent or to a negligible extent.

those groups most influenced more often join Euro groups than groups less impacted upon by EU policy.

The relation is monotonous, however, and it does not at all explain the variation in the behaviour of groups of associations. Table 4.2 makes it clear that some associations do not associate in Euro groups despite the fact that they are influenced by EU decisions. And from data of the survey we know that some associations have joined Euro groups although they claim not to be impacted upon by EU policy. The pattern of correlation is found in Fig. 4.1, including the cases of membership and non membership that are not explained by EU policy impact on associations.

Our assertions are partly confirmed. International political activity – in general as well as by membership of Euro groups – is more common among associations within the sectors of production of goods and services compared with other sectors of societal life. And international political activity is more disseminated among associations of sectors facing international competition than among associations related to the public sector. So, associational properties, state context and international environment do seem to make a difference as to international activity of associations. But Euro group membership as an example of international political activity is not convincingly explained by the impact of EU policy. What we do see is that some associations join Euro groups for other reasons than as a reaction to the growing influence from EU policy, just as other associations do not join Euro groups although they are impacted upon by EU policy. This latter group may represent the case of free riding – presupposing that an important task of Euro groups is to produce collective goods – but abstention from membership is not necessarily

		Euro groups	
		Membership	Non membership
	Associations influenced (N=547)	62.5	37.5
EU policy influence			
	Associations not influenced (N=408)	20.8	79.2

Figure 4.1 Influence from EU policies and Euro group membership (%)
Source: *Author's survey (1993)*

equivalent to free riding (Sabatier, 1992:125). The data available do not allow us to elaborate on this point.

POLITICAL ACTIVITY: EUROPEAN UNION AND EURO GROUPS

Political activity breeds political activity

No matter which theoretical underpinning is preferred – Olson's by-product theory or Truman's (1951) theory of a more spontaneous political action by groups – many interest associations actually behave as political units[3] and organise accordingly at the national as well as the international level (see Table 4.1, first and last column). To what extent does membership of Euro groups correlate with other kinds of political activity – domestic political activity in general, political activity regarding EU policy, and political activity *vis-à-vis* the political institutions of the EU. No doubt, membership of Euro groups can be seen as a producer of political and organisational activity; but generally we find it more likely that membership of Euro groups is an effect of other political and organisational activity (Table 4.3).

More than 60 per cent of those workers' and business associations which are politically active *vis-à-vis* domestic political and administrative institutions have also joined a Euro group (first column). In contrast to this, less than half of the associations of civil servants and academics and less than 40 per cent of other associations combine national political activity with membership of Euro groups.

The second column shows domestic political activity related to EU matters, for example, directives implementation. This political activity is less frequent than domestic political activity, but it is much more associated with membership of Euro groups. That holds for all groups of associations, although the frequency level of other associations lags behind a bit.

The third column combines political activity directed towards EU institutions with Euro group membership, and generally it shows the same level of correlation between political activity and Euro group membership as the second column. But this is only due to the increasing frequency of membership by business associations. Finally, the combination of the two internationally directed political activities by far predicts the frequency of Euro group membership in the best way; that is, four out of five associations which are either involved in domestic EU related politics or is having contact with EU institutions

Table 4.3 Types of political activity by interest associations (N) and Euro group membership (%)*

Associations	National political activity (1)		EU-related political activity (2)		Political activity in Brussels (3)		(2) & (3)	
	(N)	%	(N)	%	(N)	%	(N)	%
Workers (N=34)	27	63.0	20	80.0	21	76.2	18	83.3
Civil servants, academics (N=175)	134	46.3	66	75.8	58	74.1	42	88.1
Business (N=358)	248	62.1	177	72.3	140	77.1	112	82.1
Other associations (N=749)	440	37.0	159	64.8	152	61.8	103	71.8
All associations (N=1316)	849	46.6	422	70.4	371	70.4	275	79.3

Source: Author's survey (1993)
* The table counts interest associations which act politically in different settings (N), irrespective of the intensity of that political activity, and the percentage of the associations which have also joined a Euro group. For the questions, see Table 4.1.

are also paying fees to one or more Euro groups. This frequency level is only very marginally raised by adding national political activity to the other two variables.

The figures add up to the conclusion that membership of Euro groups to a very large extent correlates with other types of political activity, and Euro group membership is to be seen as the dependent variable. But, again, this does not mean that Euro group membership always correlates with the political activity just mentioned. A number of Euro group members are neither involved in domestic political activity (16.9 per cent of all relevant associations – N=366), with domestic political activity related to EU policy (20.4 per cent – N=765) nor with political activity *vis-à-vis* EU institutions (21 per cent – N=770). And business associations are more inclined towards this deviating behaviour than the other groups of associations.

To conclude, political activity – and in particular that which is internationally directed – fairly well predicts membership of Euro groups. But other causes of membership must be in force, too; and probably more for business associations than for other collective units.

Routes to Brussels

In order to fully evaluate Euro group membership we have to put it into the context of lobbying; that is, we have to portray Euro group membership in relation to other means of lobbying or routes to Brussels. Table 4.1 shows that almost three out of ten Danish interest associations perform politically *vis-à-vis* the policy making arena in Brussels – with very different levels of frequency, though. Table 4.1 only displays one route to Brussels, that is, through Euro groups,[4] but a number of other routes are at hand. For example, Table 4.4 deals with a spectrum of political channels to the EU institutions.

Membership of Euro groups is the most used route to Brussels, with direct initiatives from the association headquarters in Denmark and contact through national umbrella associations as the two next most used routes. In general, the table mirrors the fact that interest associations use a number of routes and not just one or two.[5] Besides the routes already mentioned we would like to point to the going together with other national associations and to the route made up of Danish political and administrative institutions.

At the other end of the spectrum is the very small use of consultancy firms, which probably reflects the tradition of associability in

Table 4.4 How to get in contact* with EU institutions (%)

Associations	A %	B %	C %	D %	E %	F %	G %	H %
Workers (N=21)	90.5	66.7	76.2	28.6	81.0	52.4	4.8	76.2
Civil servants, academics (N=58)	55.2	5.2	48.3	13.8	56.9	27.6	8.6	72.4
Business (N=140)	65.0	14.3	37.1	26.4	31.4	45.7	11.4	72.1
Other associations (N=152)	61.8	7.2	34.2	9.9	14.5	24.3	6.6	51.3
All associations (N=371)	63.6	9.4	39.9	17.8	31.3	34.5	8.6	63.9

Source: Author's survey (1993)
* The associations actually going to Brussels were asked to state whether they often, occasionally or rarely/seldom were in contact with EU institutions in various ways, A to H. The table adds the responses often and occasionally, in spite of that, in a number of cases (N) is rather little: (A) Direct from the association in Denmark; (B) From the association's office in Brussels; (C) Together with other Danish associations; (D) Through Danish trade associations; (E) Through Danish umbrella associations; (F) Through Danish authorities; (G) Through consultancy firm (lobbyist); (H) Through Euro groups.

Danish society (Olsen and Sidenius, 1991), as well as some reluctance to engage in direct lobbying in Brussels. At this end of the spectrum we also find offices in Brussels[6] and, partly, action through Danish trade associations.[7]

The variety of routes is a point in itself, because it indicates that, for many associations, being in contact with politics in Brussels is not a one shot business but the employment of a whole collection of instruments. This corresponds with the more general literature on lobbying (for example, van Schendelen, 1993; Mazey and Richardson, 1993a; Pedler and van Schendelen, 1994). The very frequent use of Euro groups suggests, however, that this outlet has a special position which makes it necessary to investigate more what Euro groups are doing for their members.

The importance and tasks of Euro groups

Danish interest associations evaluate beyond any doubt Euro groups as important; in the range from 83 per cent to 100 per cent, in total 87.9 per cent (N=473), they ascribe great or some importance to the tasks of Euro groups. And even more in unison, *in toto* 90.3 per cent (N=473), do the associations state that the importance of Euro groups has increased since 1985.[8]

Supposing that interest associations demand different services from Euro groups, we suggest that those associations more inclined towards

Table 4.5 The importance* of tasks performed by Euro groups (%)

Associations	General information %	Specific information %	Policy impact %	Liaison creation %
Workers (N=19)	84.2	84.2	78.9	100.0
Civil servants, academics (N=73)	49.3	68.5	64.4	75.3
Business (N=179)	65.9	82.1	75.4	80.4
Other associations (N=202)	54.5	56.4	42.1	73.8
All associations (N=473)	59.2	69.1	59.6	77.6

Source: *Author's survey (1993)*
* Importance is the sum of great importance and some importance. The question of the survey was: What tasks do these Euro groups primarily supply for your association? and the possible responses were: (a) Euro groups supply information about the general development of the EU;   (b) Euro groups supply information about specific policy issues or decisions of the EU;   (c) Euro groups impact upon the decisions of the EU;   (d) Euro groups provide contacts to associations in other EU member states.

joining a Euro group (workers' and business associations) focus more on policy related services than associations less inclined to join tend to do (associations of civil servants and academics and other associations). They, on the contrary, are supposed to focus more on general services and creation of liaisons (Table 4.5).

The creation of liaisons with associations of other member states and, secondly, the supply of information on specific issues are the most important tasks performed by Euro groups. In comparison, the supply of general information and the impact upon EU policies, though definitely not unimportant, are evaluated to be less important. Danish associations do not use membership of Euro groups as a mere tool of information gathering, which corresponds with the correlation between Euro group membership and other internationally oriented political activities (see Table 4.3). On the other hand, Danish interest associations in general do not yet regard themselves as important political players in Brussels – either through Euro groups, or through other means (see Table 4.4).

The striking feature of Table 4.5 is the variation between groups of associations. In a vertical comparison, the associations of workers and business emphasise the importance of policy impact by Euro groups much more than do the other groups of associations, a finding which holds for the supply of specific policy information as well. But the second vertical comparison does not match our suggestion that the associations of civil servants and academics and other associations take the lead with regard to supply of general information and liaison creation. On the contrary, in these respects, too, the associations of workers and business ascribe more importance to Euro groups than the other two groups of associations.

In conclusion, the associations of workers and business are closer to utilising Euro groups as tools of influencing EU politics than are the other groups of associations. Given the literature on lobbying, this finding was to be expected. We also see as a tendency that the more important one task is considered to be, the more importance is attached to other tasks as well. The extent and diversity of political activity – and the socialisation of members – creates a demand for various services supplied by Euro groups, and this demand feeds in itself on the importance of the services.

It is perhaps surprising that the associations do not focus more on the impact which Euro groups have on EU policies, but rather pay attention to the procurement of information. There has been quite a change, however, compared with the statements regarding the 1985 evaluation of the relative importance of Euro group services. Here the supply of general information was considered the second most impor-tant task, and the policy impact of Euro groups was by far the least important of the tasks, considered to be important by only 39.3 per cent of all associations (N=473). This change corresponds with the increased weight of the supply of specific information. Together the changes mirror a more policy-focused approach of Danish interest associations with regard to Euro groups and their impact on the EU. Euro group activity is part of this change, and their supply of services changes accordingly.

The predominant task of Euro groups is to act as forums for contact with similar groups from other member countries. This was seen as task number one in 1993 as well as in 1985, where its rank was even less challenged by other tasks. This kind of contact may provide information and form a basis of future policy impact by a group of national associations, but it substantiates that membership of Euro groups is a manifestation of an activity which is beyond the mere supply of information and policy impact.

COLLECTIVE ACTION OR ARMS RACE?

Euro group membership is not an isolated action but one that is very often connected with other kinds of EU directed political activity. Euro group membership is but one among several routes to policy making in Brussels, although the most important one, and Danish associations see a number of Euro group tasks as important to them. But does the national associations' option to join Euro groups actually represent a collective action problem, where a rational calculation fixes costs and benefits and where free riding is the logical reaction to a predominant production of collective goods? Or is Euro group membership excluded from the collective action rationality and founded on somewhat different political and social considerations?

The question is to what extent we can draw a parallel between Euro groups and those political action committees that are set up to lobby in Washington, DC, or to raise funds for the election campaigns of candidates preferred by firms, institutions or associations. In their analysis of political action committees (PACs) in the United States, Gray and Lowery (1995) – explicitly focusing on PACs connected to a sponsoring organisation – suggest that the formation of a PAC does not involve a collective action problem, because the decision to set up a PAC is not the fundamental one.

The argument is that when an organisation – a firm, an association, an institution et cetera – decides to promote its interests politically, it decides to lobby. This is the primary decision which is followed by considerations about how to get access to the relevant political and administrative institutions – agencies, committees at Capitol or Members of Congress – in competition or collaboration with other organisations. At this stage an organisation chooses between a number of instruments or routes of lobbying, and formation of a PAC is among these instruments. According to Gray and Lowery (1995), the collective action problem arises already with the decision to lobby; at this phase the organisation has the opportunity to consider the costs and benefits of lobbying and the option of free riding. Which advantages will it be able to appropriate even if it does not lobby, because other organisations may further the policies wished for (collective goods). Which advantages will it renounce by not lobbying, because it cannot get hold of them otherwise (selective goods). And which advantages will it not be able to utilise by not lobbying, because they are not lobbied for successfully by other organisations (collective goods).

On the surface, this argument can be applied to national interest associations' membership of Euro groups. Membership is in particular related to political activity with international orientations, and it is just one of several routes to EU politics. This implies that the collective action problem has already been solved.

There is at least one severe objection to this parallel. The setting up of a PAC by a sponsor only represents a collective action problem under one condition, and that is if some other political actor through a PAC or otherwise creates the good, which our sponsor demands, as a collective good. That collective good might be the election of a certain candidate for Congress who is in favour of a tough trade policy against Japan, which will benefit a number of US interests, including our sponsor. In this case our sponsor has the option of free riding, calculating that the hoped-for result of the election will turn out even without his effort. But the result of an election campaign is often very difficult to forecast – and due to the US election system one usually either wins or loses by making such a forecast – so reliance on a collective good made by other actors is not a safe gain. Further-more, seemingly alike societal interests – firms within the same trade – differ very often from each other with regard to markets, production profiles, capital structure, and so on. Hand in hand with more general lobbying, this disposes them to lobby their own special interests by turning the attention of the running candidates to their mixture of problems, which is also reinforced by the fact that general policies affect interests differently (Leone, 1986), implying that general policies are not pure collective goals (Hula, 1995: 242). The setting up of a PAC may therefore be conceptualised as an arms race rather than as collective action.

A national interest association's decision to join a Euro group is anticipated by its decision to become active politically, especially with regard to internationally related issues. This early decision raises in principle a collective action problem which is similar to the problem-atique of PAC formation. But from then on, the arms race approach to Euro group membership may be more relevant. This is because group membership involves uncertainty as to policy profile of the group, relevance of the policy impact and uncertainty concerning initiatives of group members, to which can be added the intangible benefit of the social contact within the group. From this a national interest association may conclude that it is more safe from a political insurance point of view to be an early member of the Euro group (see McLaughlin and Jordan, 1993; Sidenius, 1994; Hula, 1995: 244) than to stay outside and free ride more or less relevant collective goods. This argument holds in particular when membership does not exclude individual political action in Brussels, as the utilisation of several routes confirms is the case (see Table 4.4).

From Olson (1965) one may ask whether national interest associa-tions actually have the option of free riding membership of Euro groups. Although Olson's distinction between small and large groups is not quite clear, one may suppose that the number of potential members of many Euro groups is so small that none of them really has the option of free riding. The pressure for participation will overrule the rational calculation of costs and benefits and free riding as its possible outcome. To some degree this presupposes, though, some kind of common understanding of the political effects of participation among the interest associations in question, that is, the potential Euro group members, which ultimately is the product of the established Euro group.

The analysis and reasoning so far support the arms race approach more than the collective action theory. But this should not lead us to forget that not all politically active interest associations actually join a Euro group, or that membership does not necessarily last for ever. The asserted importance of social contact as a Euro group benefit seems to imply a mere bundle of membership incentives, the analysis of which may nuance our understanding of why national interest associations join Euro groups.[9]

DANISH BUSINESS ASSOCIATIONS IN EURO GROUPS[10]

Danish business has an almost century-long tradition of domestic associability and political activity (Olsen and Sidenius, 1991), and its dependency on international trade leads to the suggestion that business associations also tend to participate in international associations and political activity. This is confirmed by Table 4.1. We also suggest that the proclaimed efficiency standard of business, the tradition of associability and organisational self-interest add up to a mix of motives and cost–benefit considerations as to whether to join and sustain Euro group membership or not. We therefore expect a whole range of motives and incentives to contribute to explaining Euro group membership (Hula, 1995).

Many analyses focus on the organisation and activity of Euro groups, including their services to members and their interrelations with EU institutions. Attention is primarily paid to what Euro groups do, what services they produce for their members, what their goals are and how the organisation perceives its tasks and position (Greenwood *et al.*, 1992; Greenwood, 1995a). This is the supply side approach of Euro group activity (see also Chapter 1). Here, focus is on the demand side of Euro group activity, that is which services the members want the organisation to provide, how services are evaluated, and so on. Demand and supply are interrelated, here as elsewhere.

Incentives or benefits, not to mention their alleged importance, are conceptualised and categorised differently (for example, Olson, 1965;

Salisbury, 1969; Wilson, 1973; Moe, 1980; and Hula, 1995). Our point of departure is the typology put forward in Chapter 1 by Aspinwall and Greenwood, though with less weight on collective, social incentives than on the other types.

Services in 1996 and at time of entry

In order to test in particular the importance of selective material benefits for associations' decisions to join and stay as members of Euro groups, the majority of services in the survey fall in this category (Table 4.6).

Some selective material benefits are important, whereas others are not. The procurement of information (A, B in Table 4.6) and the access to advisory committees (D) are evaluated as important,

Table 4.6 The importance of services supplied by Euro groups: opinion balances* (%, N=137)

Services	At time of entry %	1996 %
A Procure general information about developments within the EC/EU	7.3	14.6
B Procure information about developments within your branch	38.0	39.4
C Influence EC/EU decisions	38.0	48.9
D Give access to EC/EU advisory committees, etc.	13.9	16.8
E Provide technical consultancy	−45.9	−48.9
F Provide legal advice	−53.3	−54.0
G Give access to services offered by other Euro groups	−45.2	−51.6
H Give access to consultancy firms	−61.3	−61.3
I Deliver services not obtainable elsewhere	−6.5	−13.9
J Provide a forum for social and professional contacts	37.9	43.8
K Establish contact with associations in other EC/EU countries	51.1	50.4
L Keep you up to date on the political development within your branch	39.4	46.7
M Provide greater strength through joint action in relation to the EC/EU	57.7	65.0

Source: *Author's survey (1996)*
* The term opinion balance is a little misleading as the figures in the table display the responses great importance minus minor importance, the possible response between them being some importance. There are disadvantages by using such aggregate figures, but for all practical purposes they are limited in this case.

whereas Danish business associations do not find various consultancy services important (E, F, G, H and to a lesser degree I). In other words, they do not demand as many and diverse services from Euro groups as are demanded from business associations at the national level. This is probably accounted for by the power of implementation of EU directives by the member states and by the difference of member units: firms, and small firms in particular, demand other services than associations do.

Collective material benefits (C, M in Table 4.6) are also important, that is influencing EU decisions through joint action is considered to be relevant Euro group services. By considering these services as collective benefits, it is presupposed that members in general are not able to promote their special interests through Euro groups. These usually have to aggregate interests before presenting policy proposals to the EU, and the promotion of national sector interests therefore takes place via other channels (see Table 4.4).

Selective social incentives are important, too. The existence of a forum for social and professional contact and the possibility of being able to make coalitions and to be attentive to sectoral development (J, K, L) seem to motivate membership of Euro groups. This mirrors the inclination of Danish associations to associate in wider contexts – sectoral associations into umbrella associations and national associations into Euro groups.

Responses are very similar from the time of entry to the summer of 1996. The general change is that services evaluated positively at the time of entry – confirming their importance to members – are evaluated even more positively in 1996; and that services evaluated negatively at the time of entry, are evaluated even more negatively in 1996.

In sum, selective material benefits are less important to Euro group members than selective social and collective material benefits are. This contrasts with the Olsonian suggestion of the importance of selective material incentives for potential and current members, and it is more in line with other theories' emphasis on the importance of an array of benefits (Wilson, 1973; Moe, 1980; Hula, 1995).

Time of entry and demand of services

The time of entry into a Euro group is supposed to make a difference as to the evaluation of the Euro group, its position and its services. The stages of European integration and different member state affiliation to the EU is expected to colour membership experience. Here we operate with three periods of entry.

The first period covers the time until Danish membership of the EEC, that is, the time up to 1973. Business became more and more in favour of Danish membership of the EEC, and European integration had some momentum, although several times blocked by France. The second period, from 1973 until 1985, is one of integrationist stability and fierce domestic debate of the membership question. The last period since 1986 involves an expansion of European integration and a change in the Danish opinion from very sceptical (membership itself was at stake) to reluctant integrationist – in spite of the no referendum in 1992 and the four exceptions to the Maastricht Treaty at the Edinburgh Summit. Through the periods, the importance of the EU to Danish business increases, and one may therefore expect a more and more positive evaluation of Euro groups and their services, especially with regard to getting access and influencing EU decisions (Table 4.7).

The differentiation of time of entry lends some support to the suggestion. Some selective material benefits are evaluated in a more positive way in the two latest periods than in the first period. This holds for A, B and D (Table 4.7) but not for the other selective material benefits (E, F, G, H and I), which would have to be evaluated in a less negative way. It also holds for collective material benefits (C and M) but not for the three selective social benefits (J, K and L), of which two change in an unexpected direction.

Only one service, that is access to advisory committees, and so on (D), matches completely the expected change, and it is very little. In the aggregate (the sum of the values of each service), the activity of Euro groups is appreciated most in the period 1973–1985. To sum up, time of entry is not an independent variable explaining the importance of Euro groups' services to their members.[11] This differentiation of data does not give rise to a more positive evaluation of the effect of selective material incentives in making potential members sign up for membership.

Offices in Brussels and demand for Euro group services

National interest associations have for years set up offices in Brussels, but recently it has become more common to set up some permanent presence in Brussels (van Schendelen, 1993). This also holds for Danish interest associations (Bregnsbo and Sidenius, 1993). Does this have an implication for the evaluation of Euro group services?

Danish interest associations use a variety of routes to the EU institutions, most prominently Euro groups, but also their own offices

Table 4.7 The importance of services supplied by Euro groups by time of entry, opinion balances[a] (%, N=133)[b]

Services	pre-1973 (N=35) %	1973–1985 (N=53) %	1985–present (N=45) %
A Procure general information about developments within the EC/EU	2.8	9.4	6.7
B Procure information about developments within your branch	34.3	43.4	37.8
C Influence EC/EU decisions	20.0	54.7	33.3
D Give access to EC/EU advisory committees, etc.	−2.8	2.1	4.5
E Provide technical consultancy	−45.7	−51.0	−37.7
F Provide legal advice	−58.6	−45.3	−64.4
G Give access to services offered by other Euro groups	−48.5	−51.0	−35.6
H Give access to consultancy firms	−54.2	−64.1	−64.5
I Deliver services not obtainable elsewhere	−5.7	−1.9	−22.2
J Provide a forum for social and professional contacts	48.6	34.0	35.6
K Establish contact with associations in other EC/EU countries	60.0	43.4	53.3
L Keep you up to date on the political development within your branch	40.0	35.9	44.4
M Provide greater strength through joint action in relation to the EC/EU	42.8	67.9	60.0

Source: *Author's survey (1996)*
[a] See Table 4.6   [b] The cases only add up to 133 because four associations did not respond to the question of time of entry.

in Brussels (see Table 4.4). It has also been shown that there is a sequence of decisions as to lobby and using various routes of lobbying. The first decision is about whether or not to engage in lobbying, the second about the choice of most feasible instruments, or routes, of lobbying. The setting up of an office in Brussels only adds to the instruments of lobbying, from which we would not expect a different demand and evaluation of Euro group services compared with the evaluation by members without their own offices. And in particular, we would not expect varying uses due to the importance ascribed to Euro groups by Danish associations.

But maybe this is too formal an argument. The introduction of a new instrument of lobbying might have an impact upon the division of labour between all instruments, and the setting up of offices in Brussels seems to be similar to some Euro group advantages. Presence in Brussels brings the association close to the EU policy making institutions, to other national interest associations in Brussels and to the whole supply of information at hand in Brussels (A, B, K and L, Table 4.7). The most stable advantage of Euro groups to this alternative is probably a more direct access to the policy making institutions and the uniting of associational force *vis-à-vis* these institutions (C, D, J and M). Table 4.8 displays figures on effects of offices in Brussels.

Business associations with an office in Brussels do not substitute their own activity for Euro group services. Rather, associations otherwise in Brussels tend to evaluate the potentially substitutable services more positively than associations staying at home do. The expectation

Table 4.8 The importance of services supplied by Euro groups by associations' presence in Brussels: opinion balances[a] (%, N=136)[b]

Services	With office (N=70) %	Without office (N=66) %
A Procure general information about developments within the EC/EU	14.3	13.6
B Procure information about developments within your branch	40.0	39.4
C Influence EC/EU decisions	52.9	44.0
D Give access to EC/EU advisory committees, etc.	20.0	12.1
E Provide technical consultancy	−62.9	−33.4
F Provide legal advice	−58.5	−48.4
G Give access to services offered by other Euro groups	−47.2	−34.9
H Give access to consultancy firms	−62.8	−59.1
I Deliver services not obtainable elsewhere	−21.4	−4.5
J Provide a forum for social and professional contacts	45.7	42.4
K Establish contact with associations in other EC/EU countries	54.3	47.0
L Keep you up to date on the political development within your branch	51.4	40.9
M Provide greater strength through joint action in relation to the EC/EU	68.6	60.6

Source: Author's survey (1996)
[a] See Table 4.6.
[b] The cases only add up to 136 as one association did not respond to this question.

about the most stable advantages of Euro groups may be correct but cannot be proved on these data, which, on the other hand, do not contradict it.

The selective material services (A, B and D in Table 4.8) are evaluated a bit more positively by associations having their own office in Brussels. The implication of this is that presence in Brussels matters, because being there increases the possibility of using more intensely some Euro group services, and further decreases the need for other services (E, F, G, H and I). Collective material benefits (C and M) are also evaluated more positively by business associations, when they are themselves present in Brussels. The closer associations get to the policy making institutions in Brussels, the more they experience institutional complexity, and the more they appreciate the role of Euro groups as political units. Also with regard to selective social benefits (J, K and L) does presence in Brussels on a permanent basis enhance the appreciation of Euro group services. The creation of contact and mutual understanding is strengthened by closeness. Business associations may set up offices in Brussels in order to increase their room for manoeuvre as individual actors, that is to increase lobbying, but that very same device also adds to the fruitfulness of business associations' membership of Euro groups.

Exit, voice and loyalty

Joining an association neither implies eternal membership nor that one accepts or acquiesces in all policies and ideas of those in charge of the association. According to Hirschman (1970), members of organisations can either choose to leave them (the exit option) or work to change their policy and practice (the voice option). The choice of option depends on the degree of loyalty to the organisation, its goals, members, and so on, because 'loyalty holds exit at bay and activates voice' (Hirschman, 1970: 78).[12]

Danish business associations – whether they are first or second order associations – experience exit as well as voice, membership turnover and efforts at reformulating goals and practices. An example of this is the early 1990s change of organisational forms and scope of business umbrellas.

When they decide to go international, to join a Euro group, they tend to be very loyal. This does not mean, though, that no associations have ever considered the exit option, that is, reconsidered the value of membership, but for all practical reasons the exit option has not been executed.[13] About 20 per cent of the associations (28 of 137), have deliberated whether to exit their Euro group for a variety of non exclusive reasons. The major reasons are too little efficiency (17 per cent of all associations); and too little Euro group activity (14 per cent), which parallels a more general critique of Euro groups (for example, Grant, 1993). Some associations also state that membership costs outweigh the advantages or that the Euro group has too little influence (10 per cent, each) – mirroring that an Olsonian collective action issue has been at stake. But exit considerations have nothing to do with the influence of the association in the Euro group, nor with increased importance of other channels to the EU institutions.

The importance of Euro groups to Danish interest associations (see Tables 4.4 and 4.5) is thus paralleled by their opting out of the exit option. We would suggest that the discontent mentioned therefore results in voice, that is, efforts at improving or reforming the Euro group from within (Hirschman, 1970: 79). But not all intra-organisational activity results from voice as it is mingled with a supposedly much bigger pool of activity based on more fundamental loyalty.

Joining a Euro group implies paying the membership fee and introduces, on a partly voluntary basis, certain political and administrative tasks within the group. The large majority of Danish business associations, 93 per cent (127 of 137), state various non exclusive intra-organisational activity in Euro groups, which mirrors loyalty as well as voice. Participation in the general meetings of the Euro group is the most common activity (88 per cent of all associations), closely followed by participation in working parties (80 per cent). A fairly large proportion (64 per cent) have also served as members of the executive committees of Euro groups, whereas fewer (20 per cent) have performed administrative tasks. This diverse and encompassing activity indicates a high level of integration and responsibility as to the function and cohesion of Euro groups. Collective good incentives and selective social incentives attract members with political goals who are also keen on intra-organisational participation (Knoke, 1988). The indirect assessment of membership is supplemented by a more direct one (Table 4.9).

The picture is far from unambiguous. A clear majority of associations state that membership of Euro groups is a must (A), underlining the importance of a general standard of associability. But two-thirds of the associations also claim that Euro groups should provide selective benefits to their members (C in Table 4.9). An interpretation is further complicated by the large number of 'agree and disagree' responses, indicating some complexity in the evaluation of membership benefits (B). But apart from that, question B indicates that more

Table 4.9 General attitudes to membership of Euro groups (%, N=137)

Statements	%					
	1	2	3	4	5	6
A It is a natural thing for national associations to be members of a Euro group	70.1	24.8	3.6	0.0	0.0	1.4
B Our association would benefit by the work of the Euro group even without being a member	1.5	24.1	32.8	29.9	7.3	4.3
C Euro groups ought to grant their members special advantages	27.7	40.9	17.5	4.4	0.7	8.7
D It is more important to have contact with foreign associations than with Danish associations	5.8	10.2	52.6	27.7	2.2	1.4

Source: *Author's survey (1996)*
1 Agree completely;   2 Agree;   3 Agree and disagree;
4 Disagree;   5 Disagree completely; and   6 Don't know/no response.

associations think they are better off due to their membership than they would be outside the Euro group. In Olsonian terms: Euro groups produce selective as well as collective goods, and the value of the former exceeds the membership fee. We may hypothesise that quite a number of members would prefer more selective goods than are actually supplied (B and C), but that the exit option is rather unlikely (refer to the figures above) due to the high degree of loyalty (A).

As a tendency, associations find their national networks the more important ones, but actually the majority find it difficult to determine the relative importance of national compared with international networking (D). This is supposed to indicate an increasing weight of international interrelations and a difficult time coming up for those national business associations which are not able to adjust to the challenges of changing policy making structures.

One may suppose that time of entry matters, when national business associations establish their attitudes to Euro group membership. The suggestion would be that newer members demand more services than older members do, because the latter have become more integrated into the spirit of international associability and may have developed other outlets of supply of services (see Table 4.10).

Time of entry is important in explaining membership attitudes. The responses to question A (Table 4.10) are almost unanimous, but the change corresponds with the suggestion that membership duration increases the spirit of associability. On the other hand, the responses

Table 4.10 General attitudes to membership of Euro groups by time of entry: opinion balances[a] (%, N=133)[b]

Statements	pre-1973 (N=35) (%)	1973–85 (N=53) (%)	1986– present (N=45) (%)	All (N=133) (%)
A It is a natural thing for national associations to be members of a Euro group	100	98.1	88.9	94.9
B Our association would benefit by the work of the Euro group even without being a member	5.7	−9.4	−28.9	−11.6
C Euro groups ought to grant their members special advantages	65.7	71.7	51.1	63.5
D It is more important to have contact with foreign associations than with Danish associations	−5.7	−15.1	−22.2	−13.9

Source: *Author's survey (1996)*
[a] (Agree completely + Agree) minus (Disagree completely + Disagree).
[b] The cases only add up to 133 because four associations did not respond to the question of time of entry.

to question C do not confirm our expectation, because old members actually expect more special advantages from membership than newer members do. But do the responses to question B fit in with this? A small majority of first period members would benefit without being members, whereas a larger proportion of third period members would not. With regard to a focus on collective benefits versus focus on selective benefits, as question B is factual and question C normative, this difference does not reveal a serious inconsistency of attitude.

Probably the best explanation is that first and third period members perceive benefits differently. The former demand more selective benefits, because they see Euro groups' services as mainly collective benefits; and the latter demand growth of selective benefits in a more modest way, because they already see selective benefits as outstripping collective benefits. To some extent data can explain the divergent perceptions of Euro group services by differences in demand for services. Early members tend to emphasise social selective benefits (J, K and L of Tables 4.6 to 4.8) more than latecomers do, whereas the latter tend to emphasise selective material benefits (A and B of Tables 4.6 to 4.8) more than early members do.

Summing up, the exit option does not stand prominently in business associations' perceptions of Euro groups, whereas loyalty and voice are very pronounced. Although membership is an obligation, members do appreciate Euro group production of selective benefits, in varying ways, though, according to time of entry.

CONCLUSION

Differences between national interest associations lead to variations in internationally oriented political activity. Euro group membership varies, too, and it is in general correlated with international political activity of associations, whereas it correlates with EU policy impact less than might have been expected. To Danish interest associations, Euro group membership is the most prominent route to the policy making arena in Brussels. But national associations' Euro group membership cannot without serious qualifications be looked upon as a collective action problem, and this adds momentum to the arms race approach.

Exit is an option for Euro group members, so a rational calculation of costs and benefits is worthwhile, and exit has been considered by some interest associations, though without being executed. This abstention cannot be explained by members' lack of focus on selective benefits, which are recognised as well as wanted. The composition of the demanded services from Euro groups proves that some selective material benefits are important to members, but even more so are selective social and collective material benefits.

This adds up to the conclusion that Euro group membership is determined by an array of motives which are partly mirrored in the demand for services. The importance of collective benefits, the high degree of loyalty and the ensuing participation in intra Euro group affairs qualifies the conclusion in the way that membership could be 'interpreted in the light of normative political and cultural commitments' (Plotke, 1992: 175; see also Sabatier, 1992).

The interpretation of Euro group membership as dependent on an array of motives and benefits is partly competing, partly compatible with the arms race approach. It is competing, because membership by benefits involves some kind of calculation, that is, economic rationality, whereas the arms race approach has passed this rationality in favour of multiple lobby instruments. And it is compatible with the arms race approach, because both reject the Olsonian focus on selective material incentives. Euro group membership is to be understood on the basis of a combination of the arms race approach, normative political and cultural commitments and inducements of an array of selective and collective benefits.

NOTES

1 The unit of analysis is national associations, typically first and second order associations, some of which have joined European second and third order associations, i.e. associations of associations. Direct membership groups (first order associations) at the European level are thus omitted from the analysis, but a number of Euro groups, including some with Danish membership, have become first and second order associations, e.g. CEFIC, ACEA and UNICE (Greenwood and Ronit, 1992; McLaughlin and Jordan, 1993; Collie, 1993).

2 The data in Tables 4.1 to 4.5 are from a survey on Danish Interest Associations: Resources, Structure, Tasks and Contact with Public Authorities' (Author's survey 1996) which was carried out from late autumn 1992 through to spring 1993 by Niels Christian Sidenius, Peter Munk Christiansen and Jørgen Grønnegård Christensen, Department of Political Science, University of Aarhus. The unit of the survey is nationwide interest associations, which were registered by the means of a variety of sources as no authoritative source exists. The size of the group is about 1,900 (this is our best estimate), and 1,316 associations responded to the questionnaire, i.e. about 69 per cent of the group. Industrial associations are under-represented in the survey in comparison with the associations of workers and civil servants and academics, but we do not think that it creates a systematic distortion of data.

3 Within the population of interest associations, i.e. collectively organised groups, we only distinguish between politically active and non active associations, that is the latter are only potentially political bodies. This differs from Jordan (1994), who distinguishes between potentially political bodies, pressure groups and policy participants. Our politically active associations seem to resemble Jordan's pressure groups pretty much.

4 The fact that Euro group membership is more frequent than political activity in Brussels may at first sight look paradoxical. It rather indicates that Euro group membership is motivated by other incentives than lobbying is.

5 The only major change, by adding together the 'occasionally' to 'often' categories of contact concerns workers' associations; Euro groups shift from being number 1 to being number 3–4, and Danish umbrellas shift from being number 3 to being number 2.

6 As is indicated in the section of business associations, Danish business associations in Euro groups, the number of offices in Brussels has increased from 1992/93 to 1996. This no doubt amounts to a more intensive use of association offices as a route to EU institutions.

7 The less frequent cooperation through trade associations may be explained by the fact that most associations of the survey can be conceptualised as trade associations which either cooperate with 'other Danish associations' or 'through umbrella associations'.

8 Where focus is on change from 1985 to 1993, the results of the analysis have to be taken with some caution (this includes the even larger span of time in the next section). The respondents may not have been able to remember exactly what things were like, or they may not have performed the same tasks in the association; as a matter of fact they may not even

have been on the payroll of the association. In this context, with a possible tendency of overestimating the previous importance of Euro groups, the increased importance of Euro groups seems to be a substantiated conclusion.

9 Ideally, in order to conclude on the issue of membership incentives we also have to look at the associations which have decided not to join a Euro group. In principle, this is possible, but not feasible as non members probably do not have an informed basis for an evaluation of tasks and services of Euro groups. The validity of such data would be questionable.

10 Data for this section are created through a special survey carried out by the author from late May through mid August 1996 (Author's survey 1996). The population of the survey were those business associations which in the 1993 survey stated that they were members of one or more Euro groups, i.e. the potential number of cases was 179. The associations which did not respond to the questionnaire were reminded once or twice, and by mid August 137 associations had responded, i.e. 77 per cent of the population. For various reasons, 13 associations were not able or did not want to participate in the survey, which reduced the number of cases to 166. A modified rate of response is thus 83 per cent.

11 It can be shown, however, that the old members of Euro groups – i.e. associations which joined Euro groups in the first and, particularly, the second period – evaluate their services much more positively than the new members do (time of entry in the last period). This may be accounted for in various ways. One explanation is that the new members have not yet become socialised; a second explanation is that Euro groups have run into difficulties in making the supply of services match the demand; and a third explanation is that the new members are more inclined to approach the EU through various channels than the old members are.

12 Obviously, this does not hold for cases with formally or informally compulsory membership, e.g. the regional chambers of German artisans or previously the Danish Chamber of Commerce.

13 Four of the thirteen associations refered to in Note 10 stated that they were no longer affiliated to a Euro group or did not have any contact with one. Unfortunately, they did not want to elaborate on their reasons for leaving; anyway, the exit ratio is very small.

5 The changing architecture of big business

Maria Green Cowles

One of the most important developments in the European Union (EU) has been the mobilisation of large multinational firms.[1] The collective action of European big business signalled the arrival of new politically powerful actors in the Brussels policy making process. Today, the European Roundtable of Industrialists (ERT) – an organisation of chief executive officers from forty-five leading European companies – is arguably the most influential interest group in Brussels. Unlike most Brussels based organisations, the ERT directs its agenda setting strategies at the European Council as well as the European Commission. The EU Committee of AmCham – the group of American multinational corporations – is recognised as one of the most efficient interest groups. Every month, the EU Committee sends out more than 10,000 documents – position papers, reports, letters, and so on – to specifically targeted Commission, Council, European Parliament and media officials. European big business has even emerged as an important international actor in the EU. In the Transatlantic Business Dialogue (TABD), large companies, with support from national industry associations, have organised themselves to shape the US–EU trade and investment agenda.

Perhaps due to the important role of firms today, some scholars of European integration have mistakenly assumed that European big business organised early on in the Community's development and actively participated in the policy making process. In fact, the collective action of European big business has been a slow process, characterised by a number of different phases throughout EU history. In each phase, European companies have mobilised for different selective and collective incentives (for an overview of these incentives, see Chapter 1.) They have created different forms of organisation, and have focused on different industrial concerns. For example, members of the earliest big business group were company leaders who organised for selective social incentives and gathered over sumptuous dinners and cocktails. Learning about the Community's institutional arrangements and industrial programmes that might impact their firms were of secondary concern. By contrast, today's large firm organisations generally mobilise for collective political incentives (see Plotke, 1992; Coen, 1997). Many of these groups are small, direct-firm organisations dedicated to shaping the agenda on specific Community issues through the use of organised, well-financed lobbying schemes.

This changing architecture of European big business is significant in that it challenges traditional forms of industrial collective action in Europe. The creation of European-level big business organisations has allowed large companies to bypass long established European as well as national industry associations in influencing EU legislation and programmes. Thus, European and national industry associations – long recognised as the voice of industry – must now coordinate or compete with large companies not only for influence in EU industrial and regulatory policy, but also for membership and dues.

The purpose of this chapter is to examine large firms' collective action in the EU. Why did these large companies organise themselves at the European level? How did the collective action of big business differ from that of traditional industry associations? What influence has the mobilisation of European multinationals had on these associations? Why and how are big business association strategies changing in the post single market era? In addressing these questions, the chapter will explore the changing architecture of European big business organisations in the history of the European Union.

THE MISSING PLAYER

The creation of the peak organisation of European industry coincided with the establishment of the European Economic Community (EEC) in 1958. The Union of Industrial and Employers' Confederations (UNICE) was a typical Eurofederation – a federation of national industry associations. Interestingly, the motivating factor behind UNICE's creation was not to promote the European customs union, but to create a defence mechanism against Commission activity (Sidjanski, 1967). To use the language of collective action, UNICE's initial organising impulse was not to pursue a collective good, but to avoid a collective bad (see Chapter 2). UNICE was formed to gather information on and to monitor the development of the EEC. Thus, it also provided national industry associations with selective material incentives – namely, information on Community activities (Cowles,

1996a: 340–43) (today, UNICE tends to be a proponent of European integration).

As indicated in Chapter 2, the collective action problem of a European peak association such as UNICE is not apparent as the national associations were already mobilised in the member states. In the case of industry, the national associations had also organised collectively in other international forums. Between 1948 and 1957, for example, approximately sixty European interest groups were created in response to the Marshall Plan (Hammerich, 1969, as cited in Cowles, 1994). In 1948, the French industry association brought fifteen other national associations together as the Council of Industrial Federations of Europe (CIFE) to provide input to the Organisation for European Economic Cooperation (OEEC) on Marshall Plan activities. When the European Coal and Steel Community was ratified in 1953, a special CIFE subgroup was set up to monitor the nascent Community and 'to prevent the spreading of further "authoritarian" integration projects' (Ehrmann, 1957: 418). In 1958, the subgroup broke away from CIFE to become UNICE.

While a number of industry Eurofederations were created in the early years of the Community, European big business groups were not. There were several reasons for the firms' absence. National patterns of industry association, i.e. the manner in which associations are organised, were one key reason why large firms did not mobilise in Brussels in the early years of the Community. In most countries in continental Europe, firms were not allowed to be direct members of the national industry associations – which were also federations of federations. The situation was different in the UK, where the Confederation of British Industry (CBI) allowed companies to join the association directly. This national pattern of association was further reinforced by cultural considerations. In Germany, for example, direct lobbying by firms or groups of firms 'can raise suspicions of inappropriate political manipulation by capitalist interests' (Kohler-Koch, 1993). Thus it is preferable for industry associations to carry out such activity officially. Therefore companies continued to rely on their national industry associations (which were members of UNICE) for information on the EU.

National business–government relations were another factor that influenced the firms' inactivity in Brussels. For the most part, large companies were national champions, either nationalised or receiving preferential treatment, and thus did not share a strong European orientation. Many firms were also preoccupied with rebuilding their own national markets after the war. As one pundit noted: 'There is no such thing as European industry – there is German industry, British industry, French industry, etc. Vive la différence!' (Rowley, 1974). At the same time, EC officials did little to encourage industry activity in Brussels whether by European associations or large firms. The Commission's socialisation of European industry groups was weak and ineffectual, and disinterested at best. Early studies on interest group activity, for example, reveal that Commission officials were often aloof in meetings with industry group officials (Feld, 1966). While the general distrust of Community industry groups such as UNICE did not bode well for Commission–industry relations, it was also clear that high level European officials did not seek close relations with industry groups. The Action Committee for the United States of Europe, for example, was comprised entirely of leaders from Christian and social democratic parties as well as trade unions (Yonsdorf, 1965). Noticeably missing from the Action Committee's ranks were the leaders of business associations. Moreover, the committee's chairman, Jean Monnet, was not interested in recruiting the companies, because he believed they were 'too nationalistic' to support the European integration project (Cowles, 1994). That many of these companies were involved or were perceived to be involved in World War II activities also did not sit well with political authorities. For their part, European big businesses were more intrigued by the General Agreement on Tariffs and Trade than in the Community project.

THE CONTEXT OF CHANGE

While European big business may have been a missing player in the EU's formative years, large European companies began to organise themselves by the late 1960s and early 1970s. Using the model outlined by Aspinwall and Greenwood in Chapter 1, a number of intervening variables can be identified that helped shape the incentives for firms' collective action. These overlapping variables include the state context, the external environment and the EU context, as well as the changing nature of the firms themselves.

In certain respects, the state context – notably the traditional business–government relations – was an important 'negative' factor in shaping large firms' decisions to organise at the EU level. As mentioned above, for cultural and historical reasons, national industry associations were the traditional representatives of industry *vis-à-vis* government elites. Their authority in EU matters was reinforced by virtue of their membership in European industry groups such as UNICE. The EU's institutional voting rules also benefited the national associations. For example, the Luxembourg Compromise of 1965, which returned the EU to a unanimous voting system, meant that EU policy making followed the 'national route' (Averyt, 1975). If an industry association disagreed with a proposed directive, for example, it merely had to convince its own government to veto the legislation (Cowles, 1996b).

The changing international environment in the 1970s and 1980s brought new competitive pressures to large companies – and with these pressures, new strains on their relationship with national industry and government officials. Multinational corporations faced new challenges posed by international organisations that sought to control or constrain their international activity. For example, the United Nations (UN) and later, the Organisation for Economic Cooperation and Development (OECD), proposed a Code of Conduct for multinational firms in their world-wide operations. Later, following the economic malaise of the 1970s, European firms found themselves facing growing competition from Japanese manufacturers (Sandholtz and Zysman, 1989). Seeking to shore up and improve their balance sheets, European big business began to pressure for greater access to European markets and an improved regulatory environment to enhance their competitiveness. Large European companies became frustrated with the perceived inability or unwillingness of national industry representatives and government officials to address their concerns (Cowles, 1994). A dissatisfaction with the national route of European policy making provided incentives for European big business to organise politically at the European level.

The international environment influenced large companies' actions in another way. By the late 1970s and early 1980s, a number of companies had begun to develop more global competitive strategies. French firms in particular began to invest more overseas (Savary, 1984). In certain respects, these large companies went global first and European second. The lessons they learned overseas in other markets and in interactions with other firms prompted them to redefine their home market as the European as opposed to national market.

The European context also was critical in shaping the incentives for large firms' collective action. As noted above, UNICE was created to monitor the creation of the EU. The EU's institutional environment, however, should not be overemphasised in the case of the 1985 programme and the Single European Act. While a number of interest groups mobilised as a result of the 1992 programme, the major European big business groups organised prior to the 1992 programme.

In the case of the European Round Table of Industrialists (ERT), business leaders were key players in promoting the single market programme in the first place. In many respects, large firms themselves were the agents for the EU's institutional change during the 1980s.

Laura Cram's discussion in Chapter 3 and elsewhere (Cram, 1997) of the Commission and institutional learning is also helpful in understanding the firms' decision to organise collectively. After EU leaders initially shunned large companies in the EU's early years, certain Commission officials began in the late 1960s to play an important policy entrepreneur role in creating incentives for big business participation in EU activities. This Commission role was carried out in many ways: providing information to firms; bringing leaders of key industry leaders together to discuss European solutions; offering monetary contracts for participation in EU projects; and allowing companies to provide data and actively to solicit proposals that would shape EU regulatory policy. In fact, the relationship between the Commission and large firms became mutually reinforcing by the mid 1980s: Commission officials encouraged the firms' participation in the EU policy making process and, in turn, European big business served as a constituency for the Commission *vis-à-vis* the member states. While this relationship has become more nuanced with the mobilisation of countervailing interests in the post 1992 period, the Commission–big business linkage remains important in EU policy making today.

Finally, the nature of European big business itself is important in understanding the firms' decision to organise collectively in Brussels. As mentioned above, the inability of national industry federations to address large firms' concerns adequately prompted European big business to consider organising itself in the European capital. The fact that these large companies had clearly defined concerns as well as sufficient resources to open up Brussels offices facilitated the decision to mobilise. The relatively small numbers of large firms as opposed to small and medium sized companies also facilitated collective action. Olson, of course, first made the size of group argument in his seminal work (Olson, 1965). That is not to say that European companies did not face cultural and historical traditions that hindered firms' mobility. German big business, for example, became involved in European business groups rather belatedly given the strong national industry associations (Cowles, 1996b). Nonetheless, European companies faced far fewer cultural obstacles than did consumer groups, as outlined in Chapter 7 and by Young elsewhere (in Wallace and Young, 1997).

PHASES OF EUROPEAN COLLECTIVE ACTION

The mobilisation of European big business did not come all at once. Nor did all firms organise for the same purposes (Camerra-Rowe, 1994). While it is difficult to create all-inclusive categories, one can conceive of large firms' collective action in at least four broad but often overlapping phases. In the first phase, leaders of major European firms mobilised for selective social incentives. In the second phase, individual firms organised for collective economic incentives within European sectoral associations or informal sectoral groups. In the third phase, multinationals associated themselves again for collective political reasons, but across industrial sectors. Lastly, European big business organised for collective political reasons around specific policy issues. In certain respects, the phases built upon one another. For example, it is difficult to imagine the creation of cross sectoral big business groups in phase III if several of these companies had not organised themselves along sectoral lines in phase II. The various phases of large firms' collective action are highlighted in Table 5.1.[2]

Phase I: social cohesion

In 1967, the Groupe des Présidents des Grandes Entreprises Européennes (the Group of Presidents of Large European Companies) laid the groundwork for associating big business in Europe. Indeed, the group emerged as the first major example of big business collective action at the European level (Cowles, 1996c). The creation of the Groupe des Présidents is also notable in that it was created shortly after the EU's infamous 'empty chair crisis' and the resulting Luxem-

Table 5.1 Phases of large European firm collective action

Phase and decade of origin	Dominant incentive	Dominant format	Commission role	Examples of organisations
1 – 1960s	Selective social	Informal group of individuals	Yes	Groupe des Présidents
2 – 1960s, 1970s	Collective political	Transformed Eurofederations	Mixed	Pharmaceutical, information technology
3 – 1980s	Collective political	Direct large firm associations	Mixed	ERT, EU Committee
4 – 1990s	Collective political	Direct large firm Associations	Minimal	ENER-G8, ICRT

bourg Compromise. Thus, while some political observers were predicting the dark days of the Community, large European companies were expressing interest in the EU for the first time.

Thus, in 1967, a dozen presidents and CEOs of major European companies met to discuss EU issues. A senior director of Euratom, Monsieur Von Geldern, served as the Groupe des Président's key organiser or policy entrepreneur. Von Geldern, a former top level director at Philips, the Dutch electronics firm, was appalled at the European Commission's poor knowledge of European industrial concerns. He also was aware of industry's own indifference toward the EU. Von Geldern believed it was important to organise European business leaders so they could meet and exchange information and ideas with Community officials. Von Geldern also thought that such meetings would help promote the larger goal of European integration. Most of the company members did not share Von Geldern's vision of a unified Europe at the time.

The Groupe des Présidents members came together due, in part, to Von Geldern's tenacity as well as the selective material incentives to be gained by membership – namely, information on the European Union. For the first time, company leaders could receive information unfiltered by the national associations. The selective social incentives offered by the organisation were the most important incentives for membership, however. The Groupe des Présidents gave company leaders from various EU member states the opportunity to socialise with one another. The organisation became a dining club, a fraternal group for CEOs and not an important interest group in Brussels. In 1988, the Groupe des Présidents was disbanded, with several of the members choosing to join the politically active European Round Table of Industrialists (ERT).

While the Groupe des Présidents never became a lobbying organisation in Brussels (it never intended to be) the organisation did begin a dialogue between industry and the Commission that had been largely absent. In many respects, the Groupe des Présidents opened the door for other companies to organise themselves in Brussels in the 1970s and 1980s. The Ravenstein Group, an organisation of company representatives in Brussels, is one such example (Cowles, 1994).

Phase II: the initial transformation

The next phase of big business mobilisation can also be traced to the mid 1960s. It was at this time that individual companies began to organise themselves within their European-level sectoral associations due to collective political incentives. These companies desired not merely to gather information on Commission activities, but actively to influence the outcomes of EU legislation. This phase coincided with the development of EU regulatory policy issues that impacted firm activity. As Giandomenico Majone points out, 'the real costs of most regulatory programmes are borne directly by the firms and individuals who have to comply with them' (Majone, 1991a). Thus, while many business groups continued to follow the 'national route' of EU policy making, it was no coincidence that several companies whose operations were affected by EU regulatory policy began to follow the Community's legislative agenda carefully.

In 1965, for example, a group of firms from the European pharmaceutical industry encouraged the Community to pass its 'very first piece of transnational regulation' – Directive 65, which involved greater European regulation of the industry (Greenwood *et al.*, 1992). The European pharmaceutical industry wanted the Commission to regulate medicine safety throughout the world in the aftermath of the thalidomide tragedy. Of course, the legislation was also a means to protect the industry from potential future regulatory action. Two years later, several firms in the chemical and pharmaceutical industries began to pay close attention to the Commission's activities, notably Directive 67/548 on the classification, packaging and labelling of dangerous substances. One American company estimated that the passage of one of the environmental programmes alone would cost it about $10 million (Cowles, 1994).

The activities of the chemical and pharmaceutical firms revealed the willingness of large companies not to rely on their national associations to represent their interests. The firms also demonstrated their intention to carve out a greater role within existing European associations. The companies began to push for a greater say in the European industry associations. As a result, today, for example, European chemical companies now play a role equal if not dominant to that of the national chemical associations within CEFIC, the European chemical association. The fact that a handful of large companies dominate both the chemical and pharmaceutical industries has facilitated this transition.

The transformation of industry associations by European companies even reached UNICE, the peak industry association, in the aftermath of the 1979 Vredeling proposal. Influenced by debates within the UN and OECD, the purpose of the Vredeling proposal – also known as the multinationals directive – was to institutionalise employee participation in national firms to ensure employees received adequate information about company operations. Some observers, however, viewed the Vredeling proposal as a vehicle for promoting collective bargaining in Brussels (Cowles, 1994; 1996a).

The Vredeling proposal immediately raised concerns among multinational firms. Many companies viewed the legislation as a means to reduce their management prerogative and to control operations. Several large firms soon discovered that they could not rely on their national governments to veto the proposed legislation. European big business also discovered that the national associations in UNICE had failed to take action against the proposal. In fact, no UNICE official had taken responsibility for reviewing this key legislation of interest to the multinationals.

As a result, in 1980, a group of large firms met in Brussels to discuss how they could better defend and represent their interests. Initially, the group met to agree upon strategies that it would later press upon UNICE members and officials prior to their meetings. In time, the European Enterprise Group (EEG) was born as members realised that there was a need to develop a coherent multinationals' voice on EU policy matters. One of the EEG's key objectives was to transform UNICE by creating a multinationals' group within the peak association that would represent their interests. Over the years, the EEG, along with key UNICE officials, succeeded in transforming UNICE policy groups and committees to include large firms in addition to national industry associations. As discussed below, the culmination of this effort was the creation of the UNICE Advisory and Support Group (UASG) in 1990, which included two dozen companies which contributed money, and often personnel, directly to UNICE. The EEG continues to exist today as a coordinating body between the UASG, the ERT and the EU Committee (Cowles, forthcoming).

The second phase of big business mobilisation also coincided with the economic crisis in Europe and the growing awareness of the global economy. Many companies that began to associate in Europe in the Ravenstein Group and Groupe des Présidents had become increasingly global in their corporate operations. American companies like Ford, IBM, Exxon and 3M as well as European firms like Shell, Unilever, ICI and Philips already had developed a strong international profile. However, other large companies, many of which were 'national champions' supported directly or indirectly by national governments, remained primarily focused on their national markets. By the late 1970s, prompted by the failure of national programmes to address global competitiveness, several of these firms began to look for solutions outside their nation state and outside their national industry associations.

With the encouragement of Industry Commissioner Etienne Davignon, a number of firms began to seek European solutions to the economic crises of the time. Unlike his predecessors, Davignon worked directly with large European companies to develop industry-wide restructuring plans such as the Davignon Plan for the steel industry. In 1979, he also met with the leaders of major European information technology companies to develop a Europe-wide research and development agenda in what became known as the European Strategic Programme for Research and Development in Information Technology (ESPRIT).

Thus, beginning in the late 1960s and continuing through the 1970s, a number of companies began to organise themselves informally at the European level. In the case of some industries such as the information technology industry, the Commission played an important role in facilitating the collective action of these firms (Cawson, 1992). In the case of others such as the chemical and pharmaceutical industries, companies mobilised on their own. The collective action of these firms resulted in the initial transformation of European industry associations.

Phase III: direct firm membership

The third phase of big business mobilisation in the early 1980s witnessed the creation of some of the most powerful organisations in Brussels – the EU Committee of AmCham and the European Round Table of Industrialists (ERT). Like the second phase of mobilisation, the large firms' incentive for association was political in nature. Again, both groups of firms were further motivated by the recognition that the member states and national industry associations were either unable or unwilling to address these key regulatory issues adequately. This third phase of mobilisation was different, however, in that firms did not attempt to transform existing organisations. Rather, they sought to create politically powerful big business organisations of their own that would compete with traditional industry associations. This third phase witnessed the creation of direct large firm membership groups.

In 1978, a small committee of American multinationals inside the American Chamber of Commerce in Belgium was created to follow and, if possible, influence important legislation directed at multinational firms (Cowles, 1996a). By the next year, the companies had become increasingly concerned with the Vredeling initiative and its extra-territorial dimension. As proposed, the Vredeling required multinational firms in Europe whose headquarters were located outside the EU (namely American companies) to establish consultation procedures between the parent companies and subsidiaries.

While several American companies became members of the EEG, they recognised that they were still at a disadvantage in that they had no member state to champion their concerns in the Council of Ministers. Moreover, although they had significant operations throughout Europe, the companies could not be assured of adequate representation within the national industry associations, especially in those associations which discouraged American participation outright. Thus, American companies had little choice but to create a strong direct firm organisation in Brussels. On 1 January 1995, the companies established the EU Committee as an organisation separate from the American Chamber.[3] Today, the EU Committee is recognised as one of the largest, most influential groups in Brussels.

Another important group to emerge in the 1980s was the ERT. With the strong support of Commissioner Davignon, Pehr Gyllenhammar, CEO of the Swedish firm Volvo, the Swedish car manufacturer, brought together a group of leading European CEOs and board chairmen to form the ERT. Many ERT members were concerned with European competitiveness *vis-à-vis* their American and Japanese competitors. They were also dissatisfied with the slow progress in creating a common European market. The ERT's initial purpose was to relaunch the European economy with a major industrial initiative – a programme that created a pan European political–legal framework in which European companies could conduct their business (Cowles, 1995a); in other words, a single European market.

While ERT members enjoyed privileged relations with national government officials, they were not convinced that national government leaders would find the political will to create a single European market. After all, governments had failed to take decisive actions toward creating a unified European market throughout the 1970s. ERT members were also convinced that the various national associations, individually or within UNICE, did not have the political clout to launch a major industrial initiative. The business leaders reasoned that only they could provide the initiative for the creation of such collective goods as a single European regulatory market and trans-European networks (road, rail, telecommunications, etc.) that would facilitate the free movement of goods, services, people and capital within the single market.

This last point brings to the fore Mancur Olson's all-important problem of free ridership. Why would a group of European business people agree to organise themselves at the European level and then invest the time and resources to receive a good from which everyone will presumably benefit? Olson's answer, of course, was that these firms or business leaders would not join the group unless they received selective benefits of their own. Clearly, ERT members received selective social incentives such as fraternising with other CEOs and belonging to an elite organisation with high level contacts in national and EU administrations. They also received selective material incentives such as potential contracts for the building of the trans-European networks. At the same time, however, one cannot dismiss the importance of collective political incentives in driving the organisation of this group. Why? There appear to be two primary reasons. First, as David Marsh noted, large firms in general are often driven by collective political incentives, for they recognise that even if others benefit from these political activities, the will also benefit. After all, the relative improvement of all participants in the market place is part of the law of comparative advantage to which most business people adhere. Andrew McLaughlin and Grant Jordan, however, have provided an equal if not more compelling reason for joining groups based on collective political incentives (McLaughlin and Jordan, 1993). They point out that many groups in Brussels believe that if they do not take the political initiative, no one else will. Clearly this was the case of the ERT, which found that neither the member states nor the national industry associations were capable of undertaking actions deemed vital to the business community. Today, the ERT continues to find new issues and policies that reinforce and maintain the collective political incentives undergirding the organisation (Cowles 1995b).[4]

Phase IV: specific issue groups

In recent years, the collective action of large European companies has developed a new format. While the underlying incentive for organisation is a collective political one, the groups have moved from organising around sectoral or trans-sectoral issues, to mobilising around specific policy issues.

One reason for this development is the changing institutional setting and maturation of the single market itself. At the time when the ERT first proposed relaunching the EU with the single market initiative, the unanimous voting system dominated EU policy making. In the aftermath of the Single European Act, of course, the qualified majority vote returned for single market issues. As Aspinwall and Greenwood noted in Chapter 1, EU institutional changes such as the qualified majority voting system have largely ended the national route traditionally followed by various interest groups. Companies and other interest groups now recognise that in EU regulatory policy, the most important work is done in the initial proposal writing. European companies must be in Brussels to influence the process early on. Moreover, companies and associations are forced to work with others in order to present a transnational position to Commission officials and/or to secure votes to pass or defeat a legislative measure. This coalition building has further promoted the mobilisation of companies at the European level. At the same time, the maturation of the single market has led to new legislative agendas. Now that the vast majority of single market directives have been agreed to (although not all have been implemented), EU policy makers are turning their attention to those issues that initially were too sensitive to tackle; and those areas where general directives now require more specific legislation. As a consequence, large firms are beginning to form *ad hoc* alliances around these new issues.

One of these new groups is ENER-G8, a coalition of eight energy intensive manufacturing companies. This group was created in 1995–6 specifically to address the internal energy market initiative. In recent years, debates on the internal energy market have largely been dominated by the key producers of energy – nationalised firms or dominant private companies that are predisposed to protecting their national monopoly. Indeed, the voice of the energy consumer was largely missing from the debate. Therefore, eight powerful companies – AKZO Nobel, BASF, Mercedes-Benz, Dow Europe, ICI, KNP BT, Pilkington, and Thyssen – decided to pool their resources and create the industrial consumers' voice. According to one official in President Jacques Santer's cabinet, ENER-G8 has emerged as one of the most important new voices in Brussels.[5] Moreover, ENER-G8 has placed pressures on the energy producers, who have traditionally relied on their ties with national government to influence EU legislation, to become more organised at the European level.

Another new group is the International Communications Round Table (ICRT), comprised of a diverse group of companies including Bertelsmann, Dow Jones, Dun & Bradstreet, IBM, ICL, Macmillan, Matra Hachette, Microsoft, Philips Media, Reuters, Sony, and others. The collective political incentive underlying the ICRT is the development of an information society in Europe. Thus, these companies are seeking to influence the debate over intellectual property protection, electronic commerce and encryption.

Recently, European big business has organised itself in another policy arena for the first time – foreign policy. While European firms have mobilised around EU regulatory issues since the mid 1960s, they had not used their big business organisations for foreign policy purposes. For example, no European big business organisation existed to influence the Uruguay round of GATT negotiations. One reason for this is that the member states must approve the Commission's negotiating mandate in these negotiations. A second reason is quite simply that European companies in general have not played an important role at the national level in shaping international economic negotiations. Any discussions with the government on trade talks were usually conducted by the national trade associations.

The creation of the Transatlantic Business Dialogue (TABD) marked the first time that European companies organised themselves in a meaningful way at the European level to influence the EU's international economic agenda. Interestingly, it was the US Commerce Department that promoted the TABD as a means to mobilise European companies on transatlantic trade issues. The US government thought trade negotiations would advance further if European industry was incorporated in the debate at the European level (Cowles, 1997). For their part, many European companies joined the TABD for political reasons – namely, to ensure that the American government and companies continue to promote strong transatlantic ties at a time when Americans have increasingly become interested in the Far East.

While the European Commission helped recruit the first TABD chairmen, European companies now drive the organisation and process. Once again, a handful of key companies, notably Philips, ICI, Daimler and BASF, spearheaded the initiative.

CHALLENGES TO THE NATIONAL ASSOCIATIONS

The collective action of European big business has not come without some cost to the historically dominant national industry associations. While groups of multinational firms have not supplanted the national associations, they have presented these organisations with considerable challenges.

First, the mobilisation of large firms has challenged the traditional leadership of the national associations. Today, for example, UNICE claims to be the 'voice of European industry'. While Commission officials recognise UNICE's claim as the peak industrial association, they will often call upon the ERT to give programme advice, to co-sponsor a conference, or to lend its name to a European initiative. Indeed, Commission officials are often more interested in speaking with the captains of European industry, who have considerable ties to national politicians, as opposed to an association official who, depending on her or his position, has little corporate experience and less political clout.

Equally important, the creation of large company organisations has produced competition for membership. Participation in the various interest groups can be costly. Often, firms must choose from amongst several organisations. In the early 1980s, a number of large firms threatened to leave UNICE and their national organisations in order to fund a new European-level industry group which they believed would be more responsive to the interests of large companies. Among other issues, the companies were concerned that national industry associations were not funding UNICE adequately enough to be an effective organisation. They also were displeased that the companies which paid for the associations had little say in the matter. In order to assuage the companies, national industry associations agreed to create the UNICE Advisory and Support Group (UASG) mentioned above (Cowles, forthcoming). Today, a number of European associations – such as CEFIC – are being transformed from within. Many of these associations are changing their purpose from information gathering to political action as a result of pressures by large companies. A primary reason for this change is the growing strength of the EU itself over the past four decades. As noted above, when the Commission proposed legislation that impacted the bottom line of major companies or offered contracts to companies for trans-European projects, European big business took note. Similarly, as powers of the European Parliament develop today, large companies no longer approach EP members for informational purposes, but to influence their votes on key legislation.

Of course, there are times when large companies do not want to take the lead on particular issues. For example, companies generally prefer that the industry associations speak out on European social policy matters. Sensitive matters, therefore, can often be deflected to the association as opposed to the firms themselves.

Perhaps the area most challenged by the collective action of big business is the traditional business association relationship itself. In continental Europe, for example, the relationship between individual firms and associations has been a hierarchical one. The confederation of federations model reinforced this relationship. The presence of multinational firms and their European organisations in Brussels has, at times, reversed this relationship. For example, instead of giving advice to its member firms, the German industry federation now finds itself speaking to German companies (whose officials in Brussels far outnumber that of the BDI) in order to find out information on the Brussels policy making scene (Cowles, 1996b). Similar situations have arisen in French industry, where a separate group of large French firms competes with the French industry association both in Brussels and in Paris (Schmidt 1996). Some of the small industry associations, for example those in the Netherlands, have seen their large European companies bypass them completely on numerous policy matters.

The influence of big business and their organisations in Brussels is beginning to have an impact at the national level as well (Cowles, 1996d). BDI officials, for example, have seen to it that German companies have an organisation similar to the UASG in the BDI Cologne headquarters. Of course, as more and more industrial matters are decided in Brussels, some association officials worry that the links forged between European big business and national government officials on EU matters will naturally spill over to national matters as well. Time will tell the extent to which the politics of Brussels will impact that traditional relationship between the national associations and governments.

CONCLUSION: THE CHANGING ARCHITECTURE OF EUROPEAN BIG BUSINESS

As indicated in Table 5.1, the collective action of European big business has changed in many ways over the EU's history. For example, the incentives, format and focus of the large firms have varied. Whereas company presidents once organised in the 1960s largely for selective incentives, today's direct firm organisations are created due to collective political incentives – namely, to influence the shaping of specific EU legislation. Although the EU initially shunned European big business during the Monnet years, it is clear that the European Commission has played an important role since the 1960s in encouraging the mobilisation of large firm associations.

As mentioned above, the collective action of major European companies has also changed the traditional roles and memberships of national and European associations. Moreover, there is evidence to suggest that the mobilisation of these large firms has prompted other interest groups to organise to defend their interests in the EU better. More likely than not, we will continue to see a transformation of interest group activity as the EU matures. One likely development, already detected, is the development of *ad hoc* coalitions between industry, consumer and environmental organisations.

Clearly, the changing architecture of European big business has shaped the mobilisation of EU interest groups in general. More likely than not, these large firms will continue to affect interest group activity in both Brussels and the national capitals. The manner and extent to which these companies influence the EU will be an important subject for future study.

NOTES

1 This chapter is largely drawn from Maria Green Cowles, *The Politics of Big Business in the European Union*, forthcoming.
2 I thank Grant Jordan for suggesting the original categories and idea for this chart.
3 The EU Committee went through several name changes (EEC Committee, EC Committee, etc.). The most current name is used in this chapter.
4 Recently, the EU Committee of AmCham launched a separate group, the European–American Industrial Council (EAIC), modelled after the ERT. The EAIC thus allows top level officers from American firms to meet with EU and national officials directly on EU matters.
5 Interview with Commission official, Brussels, 28 June 1996.

6 The professions

Justin Greenwood

Survey results (in Chapter 1) indicate a number of significant differences between Euro groups representing the professions, and those of other interests. The lowest response rate to the survey was experienced from groups representing the professions (45 per cent – thirty-one groups). Whilst the low number of replies received makes it difficult to draw valid conclusions, analysis of results indicates that groups representing the professions have a higher proportion of organisations with a turnover of less than 50,000 ECU (43 per cent – nine organisations), and less than two staff members (27 per cent – eight), than any other type of interest. This context partly helps explain the lower response rate. Groups representing the professions formed later, and came to Brussels later, than did business groups; and they are less likely to have a Brussels base than are any other category of interest. Unlike the rest of the constituency of Euro groups, the UK, after Brussels, is the most important base for European-level professional associations, accounting for 25 per cent (seventeen) of all of those listed in the 1995 European Public Affairs Directory (Landmarks Publications, 1994), and the 1992 Commission Directory (European Commission, 1991a). Taken together, these factors indicate a lack of strength of European-level organisation for interests representing the professions. There are a number of explanations for this weakness: the limited demand for use of the single market by the service based professions, including professional mobility across member states; the difficulties of finding common issues which impact across the variety of professional interests; the lower level of EU competencies over professional life in comparison with other fields; the relative lack of institutional incentives upon professional interests to organise and develop at the European level, particularly in comparison with other domains such as social and citizen interests; and extreme differences in the relationship between the state and the professions between member states; and, relatedly, differences of national traditions of organisation and development of the professions. These factors deeply influence the pattern and logic of collective action issues at the European level, and in comparison with other interests analysed in this book, make the professions something of an exception. Collective action amongst professional interests displays greater difficulties than for any other interest domain we analyse in this collection. Indeed, perhaps an alternative starting point to observing the weakness of interest representation for the professions at the European level is to register surprise that European-level groups in this domain number more than a handful.

There are no less than three European-level pan sectoral groups which claim representation of general professional interests. Despite each of these containing quite separate membership constituencies, their interest domains overlap considerably. This architecture in turn reflects the problematic definition of what constitutes a 'profession', which is a highly contested concept. Early attempts at definition focused on the traits of professional groups versus non professionals (Greenwood, 1965), including attributes such as the use of systematic theory, authority, community sanction, an ethical code and a professional culture. More recent definitions, however, have focused more on the processes of professionalisation, and the ways in which such processes allocate social and economic power to these groups (Wilding, 1982; Friedson, 1986), and enable groups to define their own boundaries and exercise closure (Murphy, 1988). The criteria for definition used by such authors centres on the capacity to define and control their work, and thus on the political ability of these actors to exercise their knowledge in exclusive ways. Such a definition, however, only partially resolves questions such as whether occupations like social work should be viewed as professions, which their own representative organisations would claim, or more as semi professions; or precisely which groups of engineers have professional status. Some groups which claim professional status might more accurately be covered within this text under the trade union heading. Even here, the lines are unclear because some groups claiming to represent professional interests are organised under the auspices of the European Trade Union Confederation, ETUC. Indeed, the theoretical and empirical boundary problem of precisely which groups are to be considered a profession is largely unresolvable. Because of these uncertainties, some of the associations representing professions have considerable difficulty in defining the parameters of their own membership constituency. In such circumstances, collective and solidaristic identity is somewhat difficult to achieve.

Further complications centre upon culturally bound issues and questions of competence (Harris and Lavan, 1992). One interest might achieve general acquiescence of professional status within a particular country, while in another country such status is open to question. Related to these differences of acquiescence are the degrees of competence required to enter and operate within a profession, and the modus of regulation operational in different countries.

These complications are most visible by examining the markedly different relationships between the state and social groups in the member states, arising from distinctive historical influences. For instance, in France a strong, centralised state, in part a feature of national defence requirements due to a fragmented border, and of competition with the Church for political space, meant that the control of professional training has historically rested in the hands of the central state. In the UK, on the other hand, the absence of such circumstances for a strong state meant that the state has always had to compromise and negotiate with social groups, with relationships characterised by mutual understanding and informal mechanisms to resolve conflicts. In turn, this meant the investiture of private associations with capacities to perform public functions, such as self-regulation, and the development of powerful self-governing associations of the professions able to exercise social closure and to attract high social status (Dankelman, 1996). This partly explains the depth and strength of the professions in Britain compared with elsewhere (EURO-CADRES, 1995), with twice as many professionals included within the UK interprofessional associations than in any other member state. In Germany, however, corporatised arrangements between the state, employer and trade union interests meant that, whilst incorporated access to the state for other groups was more difficult to obtain, so too was the delegation of powers for self-determination (Dankelman, 1996). Consequently:

> German architects, with almost no public regulation to protect their domain, try to use Europe to gain restrictions on access to their profession. The French architects, for their part, see European rules as a danger, since they are more vulnerable to foreign competition.

> (Dankelman, 1996: 13)

In these circumstances, meaningful European-level collective action will always be extremely difficult. Partly because of such differences, there are also different national traditions of coalescence with other types of interest, with certain professional interests affiliated to wider units, or operating independently. In turn, these differences can be reproduced at the European level, with one branch of the profession from one country ultimately represented by a different European association to the same branch in another country. Thus, Italian civil engineers educate and licence architects, who are organised separately elsewhere in Europe. But there is also a basic problem of mutual recognition. For instance, British midwives provide family planning services, whereas those in Ireland do not, and Dutch midwives often operate as sole specialists at births. Dentistry in Italy is subsumed within general medicine; and there are no counterparts to British solicitors and barristers (Orzack, 1991). For some of the professions embedded within member states, simply understanding the differences in arrangements in other countries was a basic problem to be solved before any type of collective action was possible. Unsurprisingly, there has therefore been a proliferation of national associations operating alongside European federations in Brussels for many of the professions.

THE LANDSCAPE OF EU-LEVEL ASSOCIATIONS OF THE PROFESSIONS

Peak associations claiming representation of professionals

At the peak level, three associations organise professional interests:

1 SEPLIS, representing the liberal professions, formed in 1974.
2 EUROCADRES, the Council of European Professional and Managerial Staff, which operates under the auspices of ETUC, and represents salaried, unionised professional and managerial staff. EUROCADRES was formed in 1993.
3 CEC, the Confederation Européenne des Cadres, representing independent organisations of managerial staff primarily in industry and commerce. CEC is not affiliated to ETUC. It was created in 1989.

SEPLIS and its member interests

SEPLIS was formed in 1974 from the idea of a Commission official whose own department of liberal professions within the Commission had been disbanded, and who therefore identified the need for liberal professions to have a voice in European public affairs. Entrepreneurship for group formation therefore arose from outside of professional interests themselves. Until 1989, it was the only European organisation representing cross sectoral professional interests in Europe. Although it is a small organisation, with two part time executives, a part time secretary, and a non-salaried president, it is somewhat larger than it was for most of the 1970s, when it struggled to mature beyond embryonic status.

SEPLIS is best conceptualised as an umbrella organisation of professional associations. The first category of these are inter professional associations from individual member states, of which there are twelve; Greece and Italy have no organisation, while Luxembourg is not a member, and Switzerland has observer status. The second type are European-level sectoral associations, of which twelve are SEPLIS members. Through these organisations, SEPLIS claims to represent the interests of some 2.7 million liberal professionals in Europe, who are responsible for the employment of 9 million individuals. Groups such as doctors and engineers, who are salaried state employees in some countries, are not members, because they do not quite fit SEPLIS's own definition of what constitutes a liberal profession (those engaged in independent practice and the backing of statute law relating to their profession, with a high level of specific and intellectual training, personalised service, involving a relationship of trust, independence, and care with the client – SEPLIS, 1996a).

Partly reflecting the difficulties of meaningful collective action across professional groups, sectoral members of SEPLIS have sought to limit its role to that of a listening post and information provider for its members, because they prefer to take the lead role on issues directly affecting them. Thus, in the passage of the recent Directive on Comparative Advertising, the role of SEPLIS was purely to provide information to its members, who then sought to exert influence over the content of this measure. The coordinating role performed by SEPLIS is strictly limited to where it is absolutely necessary to take cross sectoral positions, and the provision of discussion seminars and events with speakers. This is in direct contrast to the approach taken by the Commission: in the 1960s and 1970s it sought to enable the free movement of professionals through sectoral directives, but because of the immense difficulties encountered, changed strategy in the 1980s to pursue integration by means of general directives. One measure of the lack of influence of SEPLIS over European public affairs is that it was not at all consulted by the Commission during draft and passage stages of these general directives, dating from 1988 (First General Systems Directive) and 1992 (Second General Systems Directive), when it was the only European-level cross-sectoral professional interest organisation in existence in Brussels. Given that the directives were aimed right across the spectrum of professions, and taking into account the cross sectoral remit of SEPLIS, this appears somewhat strange. However, as is evident later, part of the problem was that earlier sectoral initiatives had involved excessive consultation, resulting in considerable delays.

Another measure of the lack of influence of SEPLIS is that its best institutional contacts have historically been with the somewhat marginalised Economic and Social Committee (ESC), where it has been a full member, and opposite to which the offices of SEPLIS are situated. There has recently been an attempt by SEPLIS to strengthen contact with division E2 of DG XV (Internal Market and Financial Services), containing twenty-two policy officials responsible for matters concerning the professions. There remains, however, little consultation of SEPLIS by DG XV, and limited contacts with DG V (Employment, Industrial Relations and Social Affairs) and DG XXIV (Consumer Policy) have been initiated by SEPLIS. Indeed, the organisation has never been contacted by any of the Commission services seeking expertise or information, one of the classic roles in public affairs performed by Euro groups. In common with a number of other groups, however, SEPLIS will have a role in the Commission's Citizens First campaign to explain to European citizens how the EU can benefit them, in that the Commission will use SEPLIS to disseminate information through its member organisation on issues such as how to take advantage of worker mobility in the single market. However, the limitations placed on SEPLIS by its members make it far more of an information processor than an organisation influencing, or seeking to influence, European public affairs. It has a largely reactive role, and indeed only intervenes in public affairs when specifically asked to do so by its members. Historically, its impact has been over-dependent upon the strength of the elected president. It is not recognised by the Commission as a social partner, because, as the Commission records in its communication to the Council and Parliament on social policy, 'its representativeness remains to be established' (Commission, 1993: 41).

Partly because it has failed to be recognised by the Commission as a social partner, SEPLIS is completely isolated from both EURO-CADRES and CEC, and has never once been in contact with these organisations. Its fraternal contacts concerning the social dialogue have been restricted to UEAPME (European Association of Craft, Small and Medium-Sized Enterprises), where, given the concentration of professionals in small practices, its most natural soulmate might be found, although even here contact has been highly infrequent and not at the decision making level. Rather unsurprisingly, given these circumstances, it feels itself to be a loser on key decisions which have emerged from the social dialogue, such as the parental leave accord, permitting leave of up to three months during the first eight years of the life of a child. Although there has been dialogue with the European consumers' organisation, BEUC, the relationship between the two organisations is best characterised as one of conflict, arising from attempts to liberalise the services offered by independent professions, where each has broadly opposing interests. Indeed, in common with most interests, the single market represents both a threat and an opportunity for the professions. On balance, SEPLIS sees the single market as too consumer oriented, particularly where the construction of a free market attacks the monopolies which professions have enjoyed on the supply of services, and threatens favourable self-regulatory arrangements which have prevailed at the national level. This negative perception of the EU partly explains why the main period of growth of professional interest representation in Europe has occurred relatively late, in a period spanning the past ten years. Those interests which have, on balance, seen the single market as more of an opportunity tend to have established themselves somewhat earlier, in an attempt to shape the opportunities their way. Those professions for whom national comforts were sufficient to make them insular later found to their cost that such a reactive stance could ultimately lose them privileges at home.

The issues on which SEPLIS has been working in recent years include: those arising from the social dialogue, such as the parental leave accord; mutual recognition of professional qualifications; comparative advertising; the provision of services by the professions to the general public, including the current passage of the legal services directive; the abandoned general directive on liability of service providers; the Citizens First initiative; and the Defective Services Directive, on which its opposition departed from that of many of the sectoral professional groups, who took a more favourable view. As will be evident from the discussion below, the other peak professional associations have also been active on a number of these issues, yet, significantly, there is virtually no contact between these organisations.

EUROCADRES

EUROCADRES is a quite different type of organisation from SEPLIS. Formed in 1993 following a decision of the ETUC executive in December 1992, EUROCADRES seeks to group together professional and managerial salaried staff in both Western and Eastern

Europe who are organised in trade unions. This focus upon salaried, unionised staff is quite different from the focus of SEPLIS membership, where the emphasis is upon independent, liberal professionals. Although there is a small degree of overlap of individual member constituency with SEPLIS, in practice the overlap is negligible because of the type of organisations both associations represent. EURO-CADRES estimates that its membership constituency includes 4 million staff in the International Standard Classification of Occupations (ISCO) groups 1 and 2 (fully professional and managerial occupations), of whom 3 million are from the member states of the European Union. EUROCADRES' direct members are private and public sector unions from the national level (whether wholly, or partly, representing professional/managerial staff), and EU-level sectoral organisations of unionised professional and managerial staff in public and private sector organisations. These members provide the funding for EUROCADRES, together with ETUC and EUROFIET. Although EUROCADRES receives no core funding from the European institutions, it does draw upon the resources of ETUC, itself significantly financed by the Commission.

EUROCADRES has a secretariat of two executives and a part time secretary, with offices located in the Brussels premises of EUROFIET, the European branch of the international trade union organisation of professional and managerial workers. It operates with an annual assembly and an active steering committee of eighteen, and it draws upon the resources of the organisations appointing members to the steering committee in its work. As part of the ETUC structure, its concerns are those of the trade union movement, and it takes the view that Europe should not be a deregulated market. Although it has virtually no links at all with SEPLIS (with which it has never met), and only informal contacts with CEC, it has worked closely with the Engineers Association FEANI (Federation Européenne D'Associations Nationales D'Ingénieurs), where there is some degree of membership overlap in the field of electrical and telecommunication engineers. Apart from this, it has not worked with most of the other sectoral professional associations. Like SEPLIS, it is therefore rather isolated in its work, at least outside of the trade union movement. However, as is evident from the discussion below, the issues on which it focuses are not dissimilar from those of SEPLIS.

The main strength of EUROCADRES is its trade union constituency, which has afforded it recognition as one of the second level social partners and gives it excellent access to DG V and DG XXII (Education, Training and Youth). It is therefore an institutionalised actor for labour market-related issues, and its status as a social partner provides it with the ability to influence key issues in European public affairs. It has been particularly active on core trade union-type issues concerning unemployment amongst professional and managerial staff. Its contact with the other services which routinely affect its interests, such as DG XV, tends to be more issue specific, over concerns such as: the Citizens First initiative; the mutual recognition of qualifications; obstacles to free circulation, including those presented by supplementary pension schemes; parental leave; and equal opportunities. Many of these issues also concern SEPLIS, CEC and sectoral professional groups, which makes the lack of contact between them all the more remarkable. On the whole, despite its relatively short existence, EUROCADRES appears to have a much greater degree of involvement in European public affairs than does SEPLIS. Thus, the majority of issues on which EUROCADRES has been active have involved the Commission initiating contact with it.

Confederation Européene Des Cadres (CEC)

Formed in 1989 from the International Confederation of Professions, CEC represents an estimated constituency of 1.5 million salaried managers in industry, the public sector, trade and commerce, through national cross sectoral associations of managers, and European-level (or international) sectoral associations. It has offices in Paris (inside the corresponding international association), and a dedicated office in Brussels. It is not affiliated to ETUC because it is dedicated to representing independent organisations of workers. It comprises fourteen national cross sectoral associations of managers (all member states with the exception of Finland, Greece and Ireland, and two for the United Kingdom, plus Norway), and eleven sectoral associations, ranging from bank to mining managers.

There is no membership overlap between SEPLIS and CEC. Although on paper there is a clear division between the three peak associations, with SEPLIS representing the liberal professions, CEC representing salaried managers, and EUROCADRES representing unionised managers, in practice there is domain overlap, as all represent a constituency of professional interests as classified by the ISCO. As CEC (CEC, 1995: 1) records in its literature, its constituency includes inter professional associations, and its national members include the names of managers, professionals, and executives within their titles. This broad constituency is also reflected in its objectives, which include the desire:

— to ensure adequate representation of European managers and professionals within the European Union

— to coordinate and provide guidance in the work of affiliated organisations in order to define harmonised solutions to problems affecting the whole sector.

(CEC, 1995: 1)

All three organisations represent similar employment concerns at the European level, and all address DG XV. Thus, the list of issues CEC has been active on recently includes the parental leave accord, the Citizens First campaign, supplementary pensions, home working, and, to a slightly lesser extent, the mutual recognition of qualifications. Like EUROCADRES, CEC has only experienced limited contact with other European-level sectoral organisations of professional interests outside of its own membership. Similarly, CEC is officially recognised as a (second level) social partner, and both are therefore active on the same range of issues, including the social aspects of the 1996 IGC. Although both represent the interests of salaried employees, the limited contact between these two organisations can be explained partly because of the difference in perspectives which unionisation and non unionisation brings. Whilst the relationship between the two is not problematic, EUROCADRES does make a point of claiming in publicly available documentation that it is a far more representative organisation than CEC (EUROCADRES, 1994). For its part, CEC has rather better contacts with business associations such as UNICE, UEAPME, and EuroCommerce, with which it has been active on high politics issues such as monetary union.

The three peak organisations representing professional interests to some extent defy expectations about coalition formation. Although they do have distinct membership constituencies with clear demarcation lines between them, all of these three associations work on a very similar range of issues. This might otherwise predict either a good degree of contact between them, or at least a considered position among the actors on coordination. Yet only two of them, EURO-CADRES and CEC, have ever met deliberately. Indeed, one of the respondents from the three peak professional organisations interviewed had not heard of one of the other organisations. There is considerable difficulty in finding substantive issues across the professions where there is a popular and common demand for European action, making meaningful cross sectoral collective action somewhat difficult. The Commission, rather than the professions themselves, has sought to find common cross sectoral issues, and has settled on the single market adjunct of promoting professional mobility. Perhaps most telling of all, however, is that when the Commission was drafting the general system directives of 1989 and 1992 concerning issues of free movement of professional workers, inter sectoral European-level organisations representing the professions were either not in existence or not consulted. Similarly, none of the European-level sectoral interests were consulted on a series of measures which represent, to date, the most significant action taken by the European institutions to affect the professions.

European-level sectoral professional interests

Significantly, the majority of sectoral professional associations at the European level are not full members of SEPLIS, CEC or EURO-CADRES. Some of these associations are located in far flung corners of Europe (not necessarily even in the EU), and are in certain cases little more than letterhead associations, with care-of addresses via a particular individual person, firm, or international association, sometimes during a rotating secretariat. In some cases, there are no staff attached exclusively to European-level associations, but rather the secretariat is provided by a national member association. Some professions with considerable power at the national level, such as doctors, have rather lightweight professional representation at the European level. Thus, despite the presence of a Euro association since 1959, the Comité Permanent des Médicins de la Communauté had no permanent Brussels presence until very recently (Lovecy, 1996).

There appears to be a higher proportion of associations with these types of characteristics in professional domains than in other domains. Similarly, there are more international associations representing particular types of professional interests which have not yet spawned a dedicated European bureau than is evident elsewhere. In other cases, there are multiple representatives of domain interests. Some of these are specialist, sub sectoral functional divisions; in some cases, these are family associations of specialities operating from the same premises, such as associations of notaries, while in other sectors, associations are quite separate (such as accountants, and accountants serving SMEs – small and medium sized enterprises). Although these divisions are based on clear functional lines, sometimes such specialisms do compete. For instance, the relationship between associations representing opticians, and ophthalmic opticians, has at least historically been highly conflictual, based on the desire of the latter to exclude the former from the ability to provide certain types of services to the general public (Orzack, 1992).

Other domains simply have multiple representative outlets without clear functional lines, where division arises more from tradition and preference. Thus, there is the European Lawyers Union (Luxembourg), and the Council of Bars and Law Societies of the European Community (CCBE) (Brussels); while in Germany we find the European Union of Dentists, and in Brussels the Liaison Committee for Dentistry in the EC (Brussels) (another sub sector, dental hygienists, is based in Glasgow). Other European-level professional associations are joined in Brussels by national offices of their members, usually because of the inability of the European association to reach meaningful agreement amongst its members. Thus, the CCBE, dating from 1960, is now accompanied by a variety of national law associations in Brussels. While the presence of multi-representative formats does not in itself imply competition, the extent of associational fragmentation, locations outside of Brussels, undivided (into European) international associations, sectoral associations not affiliated to peak associations, parallel national associations with Brussels offices, and empty shell groups, in professional interest fields, are indicative of weak and problematic patterns of collective action.

Unlike in the business domains, it is not possible to find examples of European associations in the professions which are extremely well resourced and unequivocally influential in European public affairs. At the national level, such groups do exist, because the resources they bear have greater significance in national contexts. Thus, associations of lawyers, for instance, are extremely powerful actors in some member states. In part, this is because at the national level professional interests and processes of professional recognition are linked to wider issues of social and economic power, and partly because of the greater degree of competence hitherto existing over professional affairs at the national level. At the European level, the degree of these competencies is partial, in that only a very limited transfer of competencies to the European level for the professions has occurred (Lovecy, 1993). Partly in consequence, and partly because of national differences, it is possible to find only a handful of even moderately developed and partially effective Euro groups; those which do exist tend to suffer from classic lowest common denominator problems (Arnison, in Neale, 1994), and sometimes act more in a listening post capacity than in representative functions. In a survey of British professional groups, Neale found a marked preference for developing their own channels of interest representation to Europe, rather than using Euro groups

(Neale, 1994). However, some caution should be exercised in the sense that, as Neale has pointed out, some European-level business associations afford an avenue of representation for interests (Neale, 1994). Both CEFIC and EFPIA, for instance, have taken positions on core issues of interest to learned associations, such as wider European policy for science and technology funding, including the funding of higher education, while UEAPME has articulated concerns shared by professional interests in small enterprises.

The most organised professional interests at the European level are those of engineers, lawyers, certain interests allied to medicine, architects, surveyors, and accountants. The European (general) engineers association, FEANI, is an exception amongst these in that its foundation in 1951 predates the Treaty of Rome. Despite such an early presence, this association was unable to secure a directive for its members to be able to practice in other member states, an important issue for engineers, who have a long tradition of occupational mobility. Other associations were formed later, often with the specific purpose of achieving a sectoral directive aimed at the mutual recognition of qualifications within their field (Laslett, 1991). This has been the area where the EU has affected professional interests most, and has been the most important catalyst to the development of European-level professional associations. Nevertheless, it has been more an issue of single market completion taken forward by the Commission than one arising from systematic and across the board demand from interests representing different professions.

From the 1960s onwards, directives aimed at particular sectors of professional groups were sought to eliminate national legislation and procedures which discriminate against other qualified and licensed professionals in other member states. Thus, sectoral measures were passed to enable doctors, nurses, dental practitioners, veterinary surgeons, midwives, architects and pharmacists to practice in another member state, to offer temporary services in another country if requested to by a client, and to receive recognition of qualifications if migrating. A less encompassing directive aimed at enabling lawyers to practice in other member states was also passed, in 1977.

The process of establishing sectoral directives proved extremely tortuous and difficult to reach agreement. The first directive, aimed at doctors, was not agreed until 1977, while a directive aimed at pharmacists took sixteen years to achieve, and one for architects, dating from 1967 until final passage in 1985, took over seventeen years. Another aimed at engineers dating from 1969 was completely abandoned, not least because of the inability of FEANI members to reach agreement on standards amongst themselves, and, despite later creation of a register aimed at producing a system of recognition, the influence of FEANI received a setback (Neale, 1994). Similarly, an ambitious set of directives aimed at opticians, concerning rights of establishment, to provide services, and mutual recognition of qualifications, was also abandoned largely because of the failure of the professional bodies concerned to reach agreement. This latter failure is somewhat symptomatic of the wider issues concerned: examining and dispensing opticians were involved in a turf fight over who should be allowed to provide certain services, which was complicated by national differences in patterns of service delivery (Orzack, 1992). Inter sectoral competition between professions has also hampered the passage of integrative measures, such as disputes between lawyers and accountants over the provision of legal and financial advice services (Lovecy, 1993).

Where directives were successful, issues surrounding the unevenness of professional practice across the member states were considerable factors in their delay. Thus, for architects, disentanglement of qualifications allied to engineering in Italy were necessary, and special arrangements were needed for those who had taken three-year qualifications in architecture in a particular sector of German higher education (Laslett, 1991). As will be evident later, national interest associations, partly on these grounds of differences, were also significant factors in delays of passage of sectoral directives.

Other individual proposals aimed at physiotherapists, accountants, psychologists, librarians, tax consultants, journalists, and surveyors, have also been abandoned (Laslett, 1991; Orzack, 1992). This lack of progress on sectoral initiatives provided the basis for a sea-change in approach. Considerable Commission resources had been tied up by sectoral initiatives, and a number of reorganisations within the Commission had failed to speed the process up. Following agreement at the 1984 Fontainebleu summit, as part of the drive towards a single market, the sectoral approach was abandoned in favour of outline generalised directives on the mutual recognition of qualifications aimed at the entire constituency of professions, and reliant upon the development of detailed arrangements at member state level (Orzack, 1991; Button and Fleming, 1992; Harris and Lavan, 1992). The first of these, the First General Systems Directive (FGSD) aimed at all professions not otherwise covered by sectoral directives, was agreed in 1988, and came into force in January 1991. The second, the Second General Systems Directive (SGSD), covering occupations requiring less than three years qualification (and therefore beyond the scope of this chapter) was passed in 1992.

The passage of the sectoral directives attracted considerable interest representation. However, this arose mainly from the national capitals. Orzack records that:

> The Community's Commission, and Council of Ministers, as well as its Parliament and Economic and Social Committee, labored long and hard to prepare drafts of directives in a number of fields. Each draft was extensively scrutinized within these Community bodies but even more intensive reviews occurred in the separate countries. Governments for each member state examined and passed drafts and then negotiated bilaterally with other govern-ments and at Community meetings... in some countries and for certain professions, governments sought out practitioner groups and educational bodies and solicited their views on these texts. Official personnel of the Community sometimes passed along drafts, often informally. Draft texts came under legal and profes-sional microscopes. A great deal of lobbying occurred, both at national government levels and at the Community itself, as extens-ive delays characterized Community consideration of draft directives.
>
> (Orzack, 1991: 143)

During the passage of these directives, then, interest representation occurred, on balance, mainly at the national level. At the European level, interest representation mainly arose in the implementation phase, through Committees established by Council decisions for each of the eight sectoral professions covered, to coordinate and review progress. Although these included places for representatives of the professions, Orzack has characterised what he terms these sub bureaucracies as cumbersome and costly (*ibid.*), and of limited effec-tiveness. Some interaction arose between European-level professional associations and the Commission, although the impact of this is inconclusive (such as the failure of the law association, the CCBE, to achieve anything more encompassing than the rather limited 1977 directive), and of less importance than interest representation through the national route. Throughout, the Commission had been careful to engage professional opinion, usually at a high level of detail, some-times incorporating chunks of text written by professional associa-tions. Yet the high degree of consultation was in turn largely responsible for the delayed passage of these directives. In conse-quence, the Commission decided upon its own course of action for the FGSD, and the passage of this involved almost no consultation whatsoever.

As for the FGSD itself, it is minimalist in scope, based not upon harmonisation of qualifications, but upon mutual recognition of them – the lowest common denominator form of European integration. Neither does it place a duty to encourage or facilitate freedom of movement; rather, it is concerned with ensuring that barriers to recognition are removed (Harris and Lavan, 1992). The FGSD is highly dependent for operation upon the work of national governments to coordinate and oversee the work of licensing authorities for each profession, the source of a great deal of unevenness in implementation. In many cases, the competent authorities appointed by national administrations to oversee implementation are the national professional associations. This has in turn strengthened their role at the domestic level and with regard to their European association counterparts. Unsurprisingly, the lack of impact of European-level associations throughout the process of the GPSD (General Product and Safety Directive), from initiation through to implementation, left them embittered. For the lawyers, the past president of CCBE described it as a 'sudden and unwelcome... shortcut... greeted with considerable scepticism and opposition from most of the Bars of the Community. The proposal has all the hallmarks of a typical bureaucratic solution to a difficult problem' (Orzack, 1991: 148), and 'an element of danger... harmonization at any price... bogus equivalence based on the great fallacy of confusing unity with conformity' (*ibid.*).

Orzack has parodied opposition to integrationist measures amongst professional interests, which illustrates the degree to which these are still entrenched within their national capitals:

1 *National insularity* – 'we have the highest standards in Europe'.
2 *Pure nationalism* – 'foreigners cannot understand local standards of practice and cannot tell us how to prepare specialists'.
3 *Moral protectionism* – 'outsiders should not be able to compete against local professionals, threatening economic rewards merited by lengthy education and extensive experience'.
4 *Educational imperialism* – 'different knowledge traditions can disrupt a country's profession, particularly where it doesn't match our own high standards'.
5 *Turf protection* – 'people with similar titles but different ranges and levels of skills should not be allowed to practise here'.
6 *Services will be ruined*: 'migrants will flood in, increasing competition, reducing quality of services, and lowering income'.
7 *Ethical considerations* – 'outsiders do not practise in accordance with local standards'.

8 *Control of profession* – 'outsiders used to government controlled regulation of their profession will not be able to accept a culture of self-regulation by professional bodies'.

9 *Modes of compensation* – 'outsiders will experience difficulties in adapting from schemes with different modes of recompense for service provision'.

(Orzack, 1991: 148–9)

As with all characterisations, these generalisations mask considerable variations, and not all professional interests can be regardedas protectionist dinosaurs, hostile to liberalisation and integration measures. The European accountancy association, FEE, for instance, claims to have taken positions on a number of occasions broadly in favour of liberalisation (Orzack, 1992). Nevertheless, many of the professions have responded negatively to many of the implications of the single market, and Commissioners have complained of resistance from them (Orzack, 1991). Often, they are quite happy with arrangements which they have negotiated and developed with domestic authorities over a number of years from a position of strength, with powerful intermediary associations which have acquired high degrees of competence in controlling entry to the profession, and in regulating service standards. Intrusion from the European level is therefore unwelcome. Although some associations have purposefully sought directives at the European level on helpful issues for their members, such as the mutual recognition of qualifications, on other issues such as deregulation of service provision they have been less than enthusiastic. In turn, this raises the interesting general question as to the ways in which perceptions of transnational authority conditions collective action questions. One hypothesis worth exploring further, for instance, concerns whether interests which respond negatively, and reactively, to the European agenda might tend to take the national route of interest representation to Brussels and keep political resources invested largely at home, while those which see Europe more positively and in a more opportunistic sense might instead tend to work more at the European level.

Another perspective concerns the differences between national- and European-level, groups within the same domain. It is difficult to imagine why, for instance, legal professions in countries where considerable authority has been parcelled out to national associations would want to seek developed Euro competencies. These national associations may accordingly have sought to prevent or limit the autonomy, size and scope of their European association. The corresponding European association, on the other hand, partly acting from the basis of self-interest in growth and expansion, or simply to find a distinct role to justify its existence, or because of its day-to-day contacts with the Commission, may seek further integrationist activities. The outcome may depend on whether the European association is able to carry enough of its national members with it, or whether internal decision making allows for sufficient dissent without paralysis.

For the professions, to whom on balance the EU has been more of a threat than an opportunity, domestic associations remain strong while their transnational associations remain relatively weak. Even in the relatively better organised European-level professional associations, such as the CCBE, contacts with the European Commission are insufficiently strong, and consequently the Commission still needs to turn to the national associations. National and sectoral differences remain so strong that groups have often found it very difficult to build agreement amongst members, and consequently interest representation is often dealt with on an issue-by-issue basis using different alliances of national associations. Indeed, the UK and the German bar associations have gone their own way in making representations on the December 1994 draft directive on the right of establishment for the legal profession. Historically, for many professional interests in the member states, the question has been why they should abandon their lucrative, comfortable and often protected territories at the national level, domains in which they have played no small part in creating, for a far less certain future in Europe. As was evident from comments obtained in interviews with sectoral associations, there is a lasting problem of national protectionism. Although a variety of changes are now disrupting professional power at the national level, in terms of integration theory, professions have hardly consistently sought the transfer of competencies from the national level to the European level. As is evident from some of the other chapters in this collection, the policy entrepreneur, more often than not, has been the European Commission. Thus, teacher and student mobility schemes have grown exponentially over the past decade in a context of almost a complete absence of voice from the interests concerned. Further initiatives aimed at free movement of these target groups are now developing under the integrationist banner of the Commission-designed Citizens First initiatives rather than in consultation with the relevant interest organisations. Functional spillover there may be, but political spillover is, in many cases, hardly in sight.

THE FUTURE OF PROFESSIONAL INTEREST REPRESENTATION IN EUROPE

The European project involves the chance to be involved in designing a new set of rules. Although actors use the European level to pursue their national goals, particularly in the case of the professions, such interests can no longer afford to remain largely at the national level. However, the recent creation of some European-level professional associations suggests some degree of recognition of this reality within the domain. Indeed, the relatively recent entry of peak associations such as the CEC and EUROCADRES, and the social partner status accorded to them, may signal the beginning of a new era of professional interest representation in the EU. There are now strong signs that the macroeconomic social partners are taking forward the agenda of promoting occupational mobility, and the increasing momentum of the social dialogue, and the ways in which the interests within it are being increasingly caught up by such a momentum may drive the integration agenda for the professions in the future more than those associations more directly concerned with the professions have hitherto done.

Others, however, see things differently. Thus, from a case study article of the engineering profession in 1995, Evetts argues that 'international professional associations, such as FEANI, are becoming increasingly influential in the reregulation process for service providers in the single European Market' (Evetts, 1995: 770). FEANI for instance, has created a register of higher and lower qualifications, and the award of an international professional title to those who meet standards of seven years university engineering education plus professional experience. These systems are rapidly acquiring currency, in that some 8,500 British civil engineers have been awarded the title. As has occurred at the national level with self-regulatory schemes, systems such as these are bound to develop significance for the associations which develop them. Indeed, FEANI has already progressed further, and since 1992 has been working to develop a pan European system of accreditation and certification for engineers, and a new postgraduate qualification based on a credit transfer scheme (Evetts, 1995). Similarly, Lovecy draws attention to a common code of conduct prepared in 1989 by the CCBE for lawyer–client relations in the provision of cross border services, which has now been adopted by its members (Lovecy, 1996). Further evidence of some growth in influence of professional interest groups at the European level is indicated by Preston, who considers that the accountancy profession has come to dominate the development of company law and taxation (Preston, 1995).

Professional interests operating at the European level have now become engaged in a much broader set of issues than simply those concerned with the mutual recognition of qualifications. Evetts provides two examples, concerning the proposed directives on liability of providers of service, and joint cross border practice, where professional interests intervened in European public affairs. The first of these was withdrawn, and the second has been blocked. However, although she cites these two cases as evidence of the growing influence of transnational professional associations, some caution should be exercised, not least because the first of these involved considerable representation by business interests, and the second involved intervention primarily (but not solely) by the more powerful national professional associations. In the case of liability of service providers, some sector-specific directives are now under consideration, including one for lawyers which progressed from the Commission in December 1994, and which the European bar association, the CCBE, has grave reservations about; indeed, its own draft text, submitted to the Commission, was largely excluded in the final draft. Since the withdrawal of the general draft directive on the liability of service providers, a number of replacement measures have been introduced, such as directives on distance selling, and measures on after-sales service and those which have provided much clearer rights for consumers of professional services. Together, these measures have, on the whole, been opposed by professionals selling services to the public. It is also worth pointing out that Evett's conclusions on the effectiveness of FEANI are not shared by most other analysts. As Millman (1994) points out, the international professional title for engineers developed by FEANI has taken off in Britain, but not elsewhere, and FEANI has been slow to establish itself. Neale (1994), meanwhile, argues that the influence of FEANI has been in steady decline since its failure to achieve a sectoral directive at the European level.

Recent scholarship indicating increasing influence is nonetheless an issue well worthy of debate, in that it at least questions an otherwise rather uniform characterisation of European professional associations as essentially weak. There are signs of change, both at the peak and sectoral levels of European-level interest organisation among the professions. Some of the sectoral associations are now beginning to develop, with the most organised having secretariats of half a dozen or so staff. Some previously conflicting interests, such as dispensing and examining opticians, now collaborate in single European associations. The present arenas in which professional associations are playing concern fundamental cross sectoral issues, such as the social dialogue, a proposal for a third general systems directive on the mutual recognition of professional qualifications, the Citizens First campaign and draft legislation on comparative advertising, as well as a number of important sector-specific initiatives. Most recently, the Commission has published proposals to simplify EU rules for business and craft professionals wishing to work in other member states, which involved extensive consultations with European-, as well as national-level, professional associations. If professional interests are to develop further, they will however have to address the issue of cross sectoral coordination. At present, there are no signs of inter sectoral coordination arising. The peak associations which do exist lack the encompassing breadth of membership or the ability to initiate it, and, unlike business domains, there are no informal collectives of interests lurking behind the scenes. European-level interest representation for the professions has some way to go before it matches these types of sophisticated patterns.

CONCLUSIONS

European-level collective action amongst professional interests displays abiding problems. European-level associations tend to be either non existent, symbolic, weak, or functionally divided. The principal peak organisation in the domain arose not from the efforts of interests themselves but from the initiative of a Commission official. Affiliation to such organisations among potential interests is at best patchy, and, where it exists, members sometimes work to limit the role of European-level associations rather than develop it, based on a preference to take action themselves. The landscape of representation lacks maturity through the absence of informal collectives, the display of fragmentation through multiple organisations, and the presence of national-level organisations in Brussels alongside European associations. Coalition formation between European-level professional associations, similarly, is either weak or non existent, even where associations are working on similar issues. Such weaknesses have meant that the Commission has almost abandoned attempts to engage European-level professional interests in consultation. Because consultation which does exist tends to be addressed to national-level associations, there is a lack of institutionalised incentives for interests to invest significant resources in organising at the European level.

The heart of the problem appears to be national differences in the composition of professional interests, and their relationship with the state. In some cases, the European level has represented a threat to domestic professions by challenging control over regulation and service provision; which has been granted through historical relationships with state authority, whereas in other countries the European level has provided an opportunity for enhanced autonomy of professional interests. Because actors use the EU for their own national goals, such differences mean that the process of Europeanisation has, if anything, strengthened national diversity among the professions. Professional interests have not been alone in such a problem. Union organisations, in particular, faced similar problems of diversity in perspective arising from different relationships with the state, creating differences between labour interests in different countries as to whether EU-level action represented an opportunity or a threat; thus, German labour interests turned to Europe simply as a means to export conditions of higher labour market costs, whereas those from southern Europe worried about the impact of such a demand upon inward investment. Prevailing working conditions in Germany, arising from the incorporation of labour interests into the state machinery, meant that the EU level could offer workers little advancement in the quality of working conditions for those workers actually in employment, whereas for British labour interests the EU level represented the only realistic prospects for improvement. German labour interests therefore had little incentive, other than defensive reasons of employment protection from mobile capital seeking lower cost production conditions elsewhere, to shift resources away from the national level, where their interests were well catered for. Similarly, businesses from Germany, the Netherlands and Scandinavia sought to export higher environmental standards imposed upon them in these countries to elsewhere across Europe as a means of creating a level playing field in production costs. And yet EU-level collective action among labour interests, and coalition formation amongst business interests in environmental arenas, has developed strongly in recent years. The key difference between the professions and such other types of interests appears to lie in the degree of difference between professional interests at the national level, and the extent to which some of the professions have power and autonomy at the national level arising from their relationships with state authority. In some of the member states, for instance, the medical profession enjoys considerable state-licensed autonomy to exercise virtually monopolistic control over entry to the profession, and for self-regulation of professional conduct. These devices provide the source of power and status of such professions. In other countries, the role of medical practitioners as state employees results in the exclusion of such groups from the title of liberal professions. Under such circumstances, it is not difficult to see why actors have paid scant attention to European-level associability. Thus, the Comité Permanent des Médicins de la Communauté, although established in 1959, remains a lightweight association which has only recently located itself in Brussels. Similarly, such differences between arrangements in states and in definitions of professions precludes even associability to peak level European associations; thus, doctors are excluded from full membership of SEPLIS. At the peak-level, where associability is possible, meaningful collective action is difficult because for some professions Europeanisation has assisted the national strength of professional interests by enhancing their ability to exert powers of social closure, whereas for others it has made it more difficult. In another sectoral example, such national differences as to what constitutes a profession, and of norms and cultures in national professional practice, also disables European-level organisation of architects, who are organised into entirely different sectoral associations across member states. For some national architects' groups, the European level represents a threat to professional autonomy at the national level, whereas for others it provides an opportunity to claim independence from the state. These extremes of difference are difficult to reconcile, and explain why, at the sectoral level, a number of European-level professional associations exist alongside national organisations of the professions based in Brussels. Not only is meaningful platform building almost impossible in European-level associations, but the very formation of these groups and the definition of members is problematic. Policies, it seems, only make politics where actors have the ability to respond to them.

7 European consumer groups

Multiple levels of governance and multiple logics of collective action[1]

Alasdair R. Young

Although organising consumers at the national level is difficult, consumer groups are among the better resourced organisations in Brussels. At the national level consumer organisations in Europe have pursued a number of different strategies to attract members. These different traditions mean that national and European consumer movements are fragmented. Although each of these traditions is represented at the European level, the European consumer organisations pursue similar approaches to their members and none relies on selective incentives to attract or keep members. This chapter describes how consumers are organised at the European level and sets out to explain the apparent paradox of their relatively high level of resources.

I will argue that three main factors combine to enable consumers to organise relatively effectively at the European and, to a lesser extent, the international levels. First, the Olsonian logic of collective action (discussed in detail by Grant Jordan in Chapter 2) does not bite as deeply at the European level as at the national. Second, following from Grant Jordan's discussion of Gray and Lowery (1997), a different rationale applies when groups which are already politically active consider cooperating. Third, as Laura Cram argues in Chapter 3, the European institutions have played an important role in creating incentives for and promoting consumer cooperation at the European level.

The Olsonian logic of collective action does not pose the same problems for consumer groups at the European level as for consumers at the national. For one thing, the number of national consumer organisations is very small compared with the millions of individual consumers in each member state. In addition, the groups' preferences tend to be fairly congruent: unlike the members of European trade associations, their members are not competitors.[2] Thus a regulation that benefits one consumer group will not necessarily harm another.

This is not to say that the groups' interests are identical; in fact their different priorities provide an added incentive to participate in order to try to steer the Euro group in the direction they want to go (see Chapter 2). Further, the leaders of the national associations are likely to be more ideologically committed to their objectives than the members of their organisations, let alone the non members (Sabatier and McLaughlin, 1990). Thus they would have little incentive to free ride and strong inclinations to contribute.

Second, and probably most important, as consumers have already decided to pursue political objectives collectively at the national level, the decision to cooperate at the European and international levels is less a question of whether to cooperate than of how to achieve objectives. Significantly, consumer organisation at the European and international levels is most developed in the areas of food stuffs and standards: two issue areas important to consumers in which the respective levels of governance have significant impacts. Agricultural prices and food quality standards are set at the European level and standards for food hygiene are developed at the international level. The vast preponderance of product standards is agreed at either the European or international levels.

Cooperation between national consumer organisations is facilitated by several factors. As alluded to above, national consumer organisations, at least within a particular tradition, tend to have congruent interests. The EU's style of consumer policy, which tends to raise the level of protection in the countries with the lowest standards without threatening the level of protection afforded by the highest standard countries, means that even divergent interests can be readily reconciled in a common position. Further, the fragmentation of the consumer movement tends to mean that ideological divisions that might impede cooperation if they were contained within one group are externalised, making it easier for each group to reach common positions.

An additional incentive for consumer organisations to cooperate at the European and international levels is that, by and large, they do not have the resources to pursue unilateral strategies. This limited capacity to act unilaterally is reinforced by their credibility in the eyes of policy makers being largely dependent on their being perceived as representative. Thus unlike large firms (discussed by Grant Jordan, Chapter 2; and Maria Green Cowles, Chapter 5), consumer organisations are compelled, for the most part, to put essentially all of their eggs in the collective basket.

These limitations may contribute to the strong sense of solidarity that exists among the national consumer organisations. It is reinforced by the perception that business interests wield a lot of influence in Brussels and that only the combined efforts of the national consumer organisations can hope to provide a counterweight. This solidarity is evident in the fact that free riding (at least cheap riding) is explicitly tolerated; smaller and poorer consumer organisations tend to pay smaller membership fees.

Third, while there are strong incentives for consumer organisations to cooperate at the European level, the role of the European institutions in actively encouraging and supporting European-level cooperation among consumer organisations cannot be discounted. The European Commission has promoted, funded and consulted European consumer organisations. The European Parliament has provided a willing ear for consumer concerns and has acted as a loyal patron.

I shall begin by outlining briefly the traditions that have helped consumers overcome collective action problems at the national level, before describing the institutional incentives for national consumer groups to cooperate at the European level. After examining the features and priorities of the European organisations, I will explore the interactions between them, their cooperation with other European interest associations, and their collaboration with consumer groups beyond the EU's boundaries.

THE ORGANISATION OF CONSUMER INTERESTS AT THE NATIONAL LEVEL

Despite antecedents in the nineteenth century, the consumer movement in the developed countries did not really come into its own until the late 1950s and early 1960s. Its emergence was due to the convergence of two interrelated socioeconomic changes. First, during the 1950s economic relations rapidly became more complicated: the number and complexity of consumer goods available increased dramatically; marketing techniques became more sophisticated; and complicated purchasing transactions, such as hire purchase and consumer credit, began to emerge (OECD, 1983). Second, prolonged economic growth contributed to both prosperity and greater expectations about the quality of life defined in more than simply economic terms (Vogel, 1989; Weale, 1992). Higher levels of education and a more active media also contributed to greater understanding of the shortcomings of the *status quo* and louder demands for change (Weale, 1992). Such demands, combined with growing concern about the apparent political influence of big business, contributed to the mobilisation of organisations defending consumers' interests (Vogel, 1989).

The first seed of the consumer movement had been sown much earlier, in Rochdale, England, in 1844, when the first consumer co-operative was established in order to improve the social and domestic conditions of its members. Using capital generated from membership subscriptions, cooperatives were able to establish stores, build housing and commence manufacturing some products. Thus they were able to provide alternative sources of products, shelter and employment to the dominant local company. As their members were consumers, the cooperatives had a wider interest than just providing competition in company towns and began to champion consumer interests more generally. Thus the very first consumer organisations used selective benefits in order to overcome the logic of collective action. The individual cooperatives formed national associations to share information and promote their collective interests. Shared values and, at least initially, small numbers made such cooperation relatively straightforward. The cooperative movement was sufficiently success-ful that in 1895 the International Cooperative Alliance (ICA) was founded in London.

Family associations and women's groups also were early champions of consumers' interests. Their members also tended to organise at the local level and then form national federations. They tended to be mobilised more by social selective and collective incentives, such as the desire to promote social change, than by more material induce-ments. The involvement of family associations in consumer issues stems from their concern for the ability of families to afford their basic needs. The women's groups have been active on consumer issues because of the traditional role of women as managers of the house-hold budget and the purchasers of most household goods (Meynaud, 1964). In June 1947 the International Union of Family Organisations (IUFO) was established in Paris.

During the 1950s independent consumer unions began to emerge in Europe. They tended to be direct membership organisations, that is their members were individuals, not groups, although some were federations of local or regional organisations. Many generated rev-enue and members through subscriptions to their publications – such as *Consumer Reports, Which?* and *Que Choisir?* – which contain comparative test results. These publications have been sufficiently successful that the consumer unions tend to be the best resourced of the national consumer organisations. In addition, it is possible that some people subscribe to a group's magazine without subscribing to its ideology. This tends to give the secretariats of the independent consumer unions greater autonomy than those of the other national consumer organisations. The consumer unions organised themselves internationally in April 1960 when the Consumer Union (US), the Consumers' Association (UK), Nederlandse Consumentenbond, Union Belge des Consommateurs and the Australian Consumers Association founded the International Organisation of Consumers Unions (IOCU) in the Hague.[3]

During the late 1950s and early 1960s the trade unions also became more actively involved in promoting consumer interests (EURO-C, 1994). They did so at least in part because wage gains could be eroded by high prices (Meynaud, 1964). Thus unions sought price controls and market regulation, denounced misleading advertising and promoted comparative tests. By this point trade unions had been organised at the international level for several decades: the International Federation of Free Trade Unions (ICFTU) split off from the World Federation of Trade Unions in 1949; and the World Confederation of Labour (WCL), previously the International Federation of Christian Trade Unions (IFCTU), had been established in 1920.

The fifth tradition of consumer organisation is organisation at the subnational level. This is not an entirely separate tradition since, as noted above, other consumer traditions involve at least a degree of local organisation. There are two inducements for organisation at the local level: first, most purchases are made locally; second, selective social incentives – such as personal satisfaction from contributing to the realisation of a desirable objective or appearing to be a good citizen (see discussion in Chapter 1) – are much stronger. In some countries, such as Germany, subnational governments also play an important role in setting consumer policy, providing an additional incentive for organisation at the local level. Local governments elsewhere are often responsible for policing and enforcing consumer protection regulations. Because of their local focus, subnational groups have been relatively slow to organise transnationally, except indirectly through national federations.

In addition to these five traditions of consumer cooperation, in many countries there is also strong tradition of government support for consumer organisation. During the 1960s and 1970s, many western governments responded to the growing political and economic importance of the consumer movement (both in terms of organisation and the forces that contributed to it) by creating government departments responsible for consumer affairs and establishing mechanisms for consumer representation in the policy process (OECD, 1983). Further, many governments provide financial assistance to consumer organisations. According to Jordan and Maloney (1996), such patronage usually serves primarily to reduce the level of subscription from individuals, thereby increasing the propensity to join. I do not treat state sponsorship as a separate tradition, because, with a few exceptions, it largely supports the other traditions.

The distinct traditions of consumer organisation at the national level have relied on different mixes of selective and collective, social and material incentives to attract members. At one end of the continuum are the independent consumer unions, which depend heavily on their comparative test magazines to attract members. At the other end are the family and women's organisations, where the desire to bring about change is a much more important motivating factor. Selective social benefits may also be important factors in prompting participation in such groups and local consumer organisations.

A EUROPEAN CONSUMER MOVEMENT?

At least one of the traditions described above is evident in each member state, and often several coexist, although one is usually more vigorous than the others. In the UK, for example, the independent consumer union, the Consumers' Association (CA), is the dominant actor, but most of the other forms of consumer organisation are also present. The Cooperative Union represents the consumer cooperatives and the National Federation of Consumer Groups (NFCG) brings together local consumer organisations. The National Consumer Council (NCC), although politically independent, is financed and appointed by the government. The trade unions, represented by the umbrella Trades Union Congress (TUC), however, play little role in consumer matters. The UK is unusual in that there is a peak association to coordinate the national consumer groups' activities in Europe, the Consumers in Europe Group (CEG). CEG grew out of the need to respond to government requests for a consumer view on how accession to the then European Economic Community (EEC) would affect them. Although CEG's larger members also belong directly to one of the European organisations, many others[4] rely on CEG for information about developments in Europe and to represent their interests in the European consumer organisations[5] and before the Commission and European Parliament. An indication of the network of national and European consumer organisations is provided for the UK in Figure 7.1.

In other member states the pattern of traditions is very different. In Sweden the state, cooperatives and trade unions have been the primary promoters of consumer interests (OECD, 1983) and the independent consumer movement is very weak. In Germany, not surprisingly,

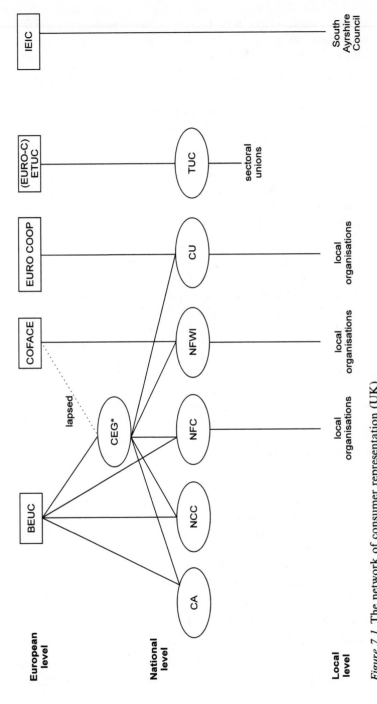

Figure 7.1 The network of consumer representation (UK)

Source: *Author's survey (1996)*

* CEG has 31 member organisations – those depicted here are those that also belong directly to European organisations.

regional consumer organisations are more important than in the UK. Family associations are particularly active in France. Each of these traditions is present at the European level:

- independent consumer unions: the European Consumers' Organisation (BEUC);
- family and women's organisations: the Confederation of Family Organisations in the European Community (COFACE);
- cooperatives: European Community of Consumer Cooperatives (EURO COOP);
- trade unions: the consumer unit of the European Trade Union Confederation (EURO-C); and
- regional organisations: the European Inter-regional Institute for Consumer Affairs (IEIC).

A sixth European-level organisation active on consumer issues is the European Consumer Safety Association (ECOSA), which supports regional, national and European activities relating to safety education and the prevention of home and leisure accidents and promotes research concerning the safety of products and services. As it is an association of consumer protection professionals, including government officials, industry representatives and academics, it is not a consumer organisation *per se*. I will consequently leave it out of my discussions.

These different traditions have significant implications for the organisation of consumer groups at the European level. First, consumer movements did not develop evenly throughout Europe. On the whole, consumers tend to be better organised in the northern member states than in the southern ones. The consumer movements in Greece, Ireland, Portugal and Spain are considered particularly weak. Second, these different traditions have lent the associated European organisations different priorities and perspectives. In addition to consumer interests, the cooperatives also have the concerns of retailers. The unions, and to a lesser extent the family associations, are concerned with the welfare of workers as well as of consumers. The consumer unions do not have to grapple with potentially contending interests, but their reliance on the subscriptions of generally upper middle class consumers may mean that they are less concerned with the interests of poorer consumers.

INSTITUTIONAL INCENTIVES FOR EUROPEAN COLLECTIVE ACTION

With the exception of IEIC, to which I will return later, the European consumer organisations (at least their precursors) were among the earlier groups to organise at the European level. In each case institutional developments, or at least perceptions of them, played a crucial role in inducing that organisation. Another striking characteristic is that the earlier consumer organisations were formed after related international associations had been established. Indeed, initially European-level cooperation among family associations and among trade unions was organised by the respective international organisations. A significant difference between the European organisations and their international counterparts is that from the start they were to be more than just information clearing houses. They were created to monitor and seek to influence European legislation on behalf of their members.

The cooperatives were the first to organise at the European level. Eleven cooperatives from five of the then six member states (Luxembourg was the exception) established EURO COOP in June 1957, just three months after the signing of the Treaty of Rome. The secretariat, based in the Belgian member organisation, was to inform members of problems posed by the creation of the EEC for consumers and cooperatives, and the Political Committee was to examine the consequences of the EEC for consumers and to propose means of safeguarding their interests. The signing of the Treaty was also the impetus for the organisation of family associations and trade unions at the European level (Meynaud, 1964). In 1958 the International Union of Family Organisations (IUFO) established a European Action Committee to be responsible for problems posed by the creation of the EEC. Also in 1958 the ICFTU established the European Organisation of the International Confederation of Free Trade Unions (EO/ICFTU) and in 1959 the IFCTU created the European Organisation of the International Federation of Christian Trade Unions (EO/IFCTU). In 1969, in response to the creation of the customs union and the establishment of the free movement of labour, these two organisations were converted into independent European organisations; the European Confederation of Free Trade Unions (ECFTU) and the European Organisation of the World Confederation of Labour (EO/WCL), respectively (Kirchner, 1977).

The creation of BEUC and the further development of COFACE and EURO COOP were directly promoted by the Commission. In June 1961 the Commission organised a session of study days in Brussels for consumer organisations. At this session, then Commission Vice President and Commissioner for Agriculture Sicco Mansholt advised Europe's consumers to unite, noting that 'the general interest of consumers in the common market are not represented to the same extent as are those of producers' (quoted in European Commission, 1991b: 13). One of the key areas in which he noted that consumers needed to be involved was the Common Agricultural Policy (CAP), which was at that time in the final stages of development (Meynaud, 1964).

There were two direct results from this meeting: the founding of BEUC and the creation of the Commission's Contact Committee for Consumer Questions, which in turn influenced the development of the European consumer movement. In September 1961, the independent consumer unions that had participated in the Brussels meeting signed a protocol on cooperation. In March 1962 they established BEUC with a rotating secretariat (Meynaud, 1964).

The Commission established the Contact Committee in April 1962 in order to provide a forum for consumer input into the policy process. The five members were BEUC, COFACE, EURO COOP, EO/ICFTU and EO/IFCTU, each of which had two seats. In early 1962 both COFACE and EURO COOP reorganised, at least in part in preparation for participation in the Contact Committee. COFACE created a working group on consumer policy and EURO COOP established an independent secretariat in Brussels.

Subsequent institutional developments further influenced the organisation of the European consumer groups. BEUC established a permanent secretariat in Brussels in 1973, the year after the leaders of the member states agreed at their Paris summit to adopt, *inter alia*, an EU consumer policy. The accessions of Denmark and the UK, with their developed independent consumer unions, also provided an impetus for establishing a permanent secretariat. In 1994 the European Trade Union Confederation (ETUC), the successor to ECFTU and the EO/WCL, established EURO-C in response to the Commission's decision regarding trade union participation in the Consumers Consultative Council (CCC),[6] the successor to the Contact Committee and the principal forum for consumer representation in the Commission. EURO-C is composed of representatives of 'the consumer departments of organisations affiliated to the ETUC or trade union based consumer protection organisations' (EURO-C *Newsletter*, March 1994: 1).

As the basic institutions of the consumer organisations were essentially in place by the mid 1970s, the launch of the Single European Market (SEM) programme in 1985 did not profoundly affect how the organisations are structured, but it did lead to significant increases in their levels of activity and, consequently, to their staffs and resources. BEUC's policy staff, for example, doubled from three to six between

1980 and 1992. There were two related reasons for this upsurge in activity. The first was simply in response to the increased importance of European decisions for consumers. The second, which reinforced the first, was the perception that the SEM was the creature of producers and that consumers had to mobilise in order to defend their interests.

The push towards the SEM did, however, provide the impetus for the establishment of the newest European consumer organisation, IEIC. It was founded in 1989 as a means of developing cooperation between border regions in order to address better the problems associated with increased cross border shopping encouraged by the SEM programme (personal correspondence, 31 May 1996).

THE EUROPEAN CONSUMER ORGANISATIONS[7]

Despite the different traditions they represent, the European consumer groups have several important common characteristics. First, they share some organisational objectives: to inform their members of developments in European policies, to represent their members in trying to influence those policies, and to provide a forum for coordinating activity and sharing information among the member organisations. Second, the selective benefits which are provided are nominal. BEUC, for example, does not even restrict its newsletter to member organisations. The European consumer organisations do provide access for their members to Commission working groups, but not in the sense of a selective benefit. Because of the large imbalance between their resources and responsibilities, the European consumer organisations depend on their members to represent them in advisory committees. Only in the old CCC were the European consumer groups able to give their member organisations access to a Commission advisory body in a form more closely resembling a selective benefit. Even then only a few member organisations could be nominated for fixed terms. The June 1995 reform of the CCC (the fourth major reform since it was established as the Contact Committee in 1962),[8] however, eliminated this potential selective benefit by restricting each European consumer organisation to only one seat.

These fundamental similarities aside, the European consumer groups operate with varying degrees of membership control, concentrate on different issues and command different types of expertise. A more detailed discussion of each of the European consumer associations follows.

The European Consumers' Organisation (BEUC)

Because of the relative affluence of its members, BEUC is the best resourced of the European consumer organisations (see Table 7.1). The Secretariat enjoys a fairly high degree of autonomy within the guidelines set at the biannual meetings of the General Assembly and bimonthly meetings of the Executive. It drafts most position papers and circulates the drafts to the members for comment. Only some-times and on some issues are these drafts based on prior consultations with member organisations. Food is one of the few policy areas in which a working group composed of representatives from member organisations drafts proposals. Once a draft has been circulated, it is up to the director to decide if there is sufficient agreement among the members to advance an official position. Nonetheless, efforts are made to find a consensus. Usually particularly contentious points are dropped in order to maintain broad support.

A central problem for all of the consumer organisations, but one that is particularly acute for BEUC because it tends to advocate more liberal policies, is bridging the gap between the policy preferences of groups from countries with high levels of domestic consumer protec-tion and those from countries where consumer policy is still in its infancy. On occasion, some national associations, such as the UK's CEG, may resist EU action for fear that their domestic protection will be eroded, while others may see EU action as the most viable route to improving the lot of domestic consumers. Finding a consensus is often facilitated by the EU's reliance on setting only minimum levels of consumer protection, which permits the more advanced countries to maintain their measures while pulling up the laggards. When such relatively simple solutions are not possible, the Secretariat is at pains not to be dominated by the largest and most vigorous member asso-ciations, such as the Consumers' Association (CA).

BEUC advocates the most purely consumerist view of all of the European consumer organisations. As such, its support for increasing consumer choice through liberalising trade and increasing competition meshes well with the objectives of the SEM programme, and it receives a receptive ear in parts of the Commission. The Directorate-General for Competition Policy (DG IV), for example, supplied BEUC with inside information regarding the block exemption on automobile distribution in an attempt to generate external support for its position (Holmes and McGowan, 1997). BEUC's vocal support for CAP reform does not, however, coincide as neatly with EU policy, and relations with the Directorate-General for Agriculture (DG VI)

Table 7.1 European consumer organisations

Name	Founded	Number of members	Number of countries	Type of member	Size of secretariat*	Core budget
BEUC	1962 (permanent secretariat 1973)	26[a]	16[a]	National independent consumer organisations	16 plus stagiers	~1 mecu
COFACE	1958 as part of IUFO, became independent in 1979	76[b]	15[b]	Family organisations, women's groups, consumer groups, and disabled persons groups. (mostly national)	3.67 plus stagiers	~0.7[d] mecu
ETUC (EURO-C) (1994)	1973	46[b]	22[b]	Trade unions (consumer departments of ETUC affiliated organisations and trade union based consumer protection organisations).	3	n/a
EURO COOP	1957 (independent secretariat 1962)	16[c]	16[c]	National consumer cooperative organisations	6[e]	~0.57 mecu[d]
IEIC	1989	22[b]	6[b]	Regional and local governments and consumer groups	n/a	n/a

Sources: BEUC (1995); COFACE (1995); CEG (1995); EURO COOP (1993); personal interviews by the Author.
Notes: * Only those dealing with consumer affairs, in full time equivalents.   a 1994.   b 1995.   c 1993.
budget, not just core funding.   e total resources, not just those engaged with consumer issues.   d entire consumer

are rather adversarial. BEUC's advocacy of liberalisation is tempered by its concern for higher standards, better rules on product safety and food quality and hygiene, and more consumer-friendly financial services. As a consequence, BEUC operates across a wider range of policy issues than any of the other European consumer organisations.

As is the case with many Euro groups, BEUC relies heavily on its member organisations, several of which have large staffs, to help it cope with the breadth of its responsibilities. Staff from its member organisations often represent BEUC's interests in the Commission's advisory and consultative bodies and sometimes help to track European legislation. The member organisations also have a substantial capacity to conduct research, which provides the Secretariat with the information it needs to participate effectively in the EU's policy process. Much of this information and expertise is generated as a by-product of its members' product (and service) testing activities, but BEUC also has the capacity to conduct explicitly policy oriented research. For example, in conjunction with one of its French members, Union Fédéral des Consommateurs (UFC), it conducted a study for the Commission on consumer complaints concerning guarantees and after-sales services.

The Confederation of Family Organisations in the European Community (COFACE)

COFACE is a very different sort of organisation from BEUC. Its more numerous members tend to be less affluent and have a wider range of social concerns. Consequently, consumer affairs are not its sole focus and it has fewer resources to allocate to promoting consumer interests (see Table 7.1). Nonetheless, a relatively large number of COFACE's member organisations are active with regard to consumer protection at the national level and participate in its Consumers Committee.

COFACE's policy making structures are also more formally democratic than BEUC's. As with BEUC, the annual General Assembly defines general policy guidelines, however, working groups, composed of representatives from interested member organisations, play a more prominent role, formulating all specific policy proposals. All positions must be approved by the Administrative Council, COFACE's most important deliberative body. The member organisations are supposed to vote in national blocks, although they do not always do so, and each country has a COFACE committee which meets regularly to agree positions prior to meetings of the Administrative Council.

Each country gets four votes and a two-thirds majority is required, although votes are rarely not unanimous.

Reflecting the concerns of its member organisations, COFACE is less concerned than BEUC with the economic aspects of consumer policy, focusing rather on health and safety protection, informing and educating consumers, and ensuring their access to justice. It also takes a more holistic approach to consumer policy than BEUC, considering the side-effects of consumer regulation on families. For example, because some of its members have rural bases, its attitude towards CAP reform is more ambivalent than are those of the other European consumer organisations.

COFACE's members do not command the same degree of technical expertise as BEUC's, but they do have the capacity to gather extensive information about consumer concerns and attitudes. In 1994, for example, COFACE conducted a cross national study on how well consumers understand safety symbols on labels.

The European Trade Union Confederation's consumer unit (EURO-C)

As noted earlier, EURO-C was only created in 1994 as the ETUC's 'voice on behalf of consumers'. Although other interested organisations can be associate members, all full EURO-C members are ETUC members, and even the trade unions that have a strong interest in consumer policy are members of the ETUC first and EURO-C second.

Because it is not an independent organisation, EURO-C's decision making structure is very different from those of the other consumer organisations. One of the ETUC's confederal secretaries (appointees below the deputy secretary general) provides general policy direction and approves specific EURO-C proposals, which are drafted by the EURO-C secretariat after a fairly informal process of consultation with interested members.

Despite its consumer focus, the concerns of the ETUC's members mean that EURO-C's approach to consumer policy can differ significantly from those of the other consumer groups, particularly BEUC. EURO-C sees its niche in the pluralistic European consumer movement to be 'social and solidarity-based consumer protection' (EURO-C, 1994: 2). This means that it is rather sceptical about the benefits of increased competition through liberalisation, although it favours reform of the CAP. In other policy areas, however – such as ensuring the quality and safety of foodstuffs, asserting the liability of service providers, improving the consumer orientation of financial services, and enforcing high standards in after-sales service – it takes positions more closely aligned to those of the other European consumer groups.

The European Community of Consumer Cooperatives (EURO COOP)

EURO COOP is the founding father of the European consumer movement, and it was particularly important in pressing consumer issues on the Commission in the early days of the EEC. It also organised and financed the Consumers Contact Committee from 1962 until its demise in 1972. It has since lost its primacy to BEUC. As it is composed of consumer cooperatives, promoting consumer interests is not its sole function; it must also represent their interests as retailers.

The Members' Assembly, which meets at least once a year, sets general policy and reviews the performance and finances of the organisation. It also elects the Management Committee, which establishes policy guidelines and ensures the implementation of decisions taken by the Members' Assembly. The Management Committee appoints the Secretary General, who is responsible for pursuing EURO COOP's policy objectives.

As its member organisations are particularly active in food retailing, EURO COOP specialises in EU food issues and is an active proponent of CAP reform. Pending wholesale reform of the CAP, EURO COOP has focused its efforts on improving the quality of produce. EURO COOP has also been active on product labelling and packaging and packaging waste.

The European Interregional Institute for Consumer Affairs (IEIC)

IEIC's members differ from those of the other European consumer organisations in two important ways: they include public authorities and are organised only at the subnational level. The IEIC is the youngest of the European consumer organisations, having been founded by seven regional organisations in 1989. It is also the only one of the European consumer organisations not to be based in Brussels; its secretariat is located in Lille.

IEIC's organisational structure is quite complex. The annual General Assembly provides direction to and elects the Board of Governors, which implements its resolutions and manages the association's working groups. There are currently four working groups dealing with access to justice and cross border disputes, education and consumer training, consumer information and new technologies, and consumer affairs. The Secretariat is responsible for the day-to-day management of the association and prepares policy proposals for consideration by the Board. If there is insufficient time to consult the Board, all member organisations are contacted by fax. The secretariat then incorporates the responses and faxes the final document to the members.

The association is particularly active in the areas of consumer information, training, and education. In 1994, for example, IEIC, under a Commission contract, produced a series of booklets and posters informing citizens of European consumer protection legislation. In order to advance consumer knowledge, the association also regularly conducts and coordinates studies and surveys on prices and commercial practices in different European countries. As part of its consumer education efforts, IEIC has since 1993 organised the European Young Consumer Competition, which is cofinanced by the Commission. Although active on a wide range of consumer policy issues, IEIC focuses on issues associated with cross border shopping, particularly the settlement of cross border disputes and access to justice. Its member organisations are also actively involved in supporting cross border information centres, providing 40 per cent of their funding.

Institutional sponsorship

As noted earlier, the Commission has long promoted consumer organisation at the European level. In addition to the political support discussed earlier, the Commission also subsidises the groups' activities. In 1994, for example, it contributed 300,000 ECU towards BEUC's core operations and 200,000 ECU to each of the other organisations. This represented roughly one-third of their operating budgets. The Commission also provides funding for specific projects, such as consumer education or studies of consumer concerns and attitudes. Each year there is a fierce struggle over the consumer budget with the Commission generally aiming to maintain funding levels, the Council of Ministers seeking to slash them and the European Parliament advocating their augmentation. In 1994 the Parliament not only resisted the Council's attempts to cut the budget, but even succeeded in securing more funding than the Commission had proposed.

Institutional pull in policy terms has, however, tended to be relatively weak. The three institutional focal points for consumers are the Commission's Directorate-General for Consumer Policy (DG XXIV), the European Parliament's Committee on the Environment, Public Health and Consumer Protection and the Parliamentary Intergroup on Consumer Affairs. In large part policy pull has been lacking because until quite recently European consumer protection tended to be pursued indirectly through other policies (Young, 1997b). In addition, the European institutions concerned with consumer policy were rather weak until the early 1990s. In the Commission consumer affairs was the poor relation in the Environment and Consumer Protection Service, later DG XI, before being made an independent service in 1989 and finally becoming a full directorate-general in March 1995. Even still it is one of the smallest directorates-general and has only recently gained the capacity to monitor adequately developments in other directorates-general that are relevant to consumers. Consequently, the European consumer groups have developed links with other directorates-general.

The Parliament's role in promoting European consumer policy has developed as its general powers have been enhanced by successive treaty revisions. Particularly since 1989, it has been an active player on consumer affairs, amending several important directives in the consumer's favour. Parliamentary Committee and Intergroup meetings also provide opportunities for consumer and other groups to exchange information and identify potential fellow travellers.

COOPERATION BETWEEN EUROPEAN CONSUMER GROUPS

Due to the different ideologies and priorities that stem from their different memberships, the European consumer organisations frequently find it difficult to cooperate. The most extreme example of this occurred in 1993, when BEUC sought, largely unsuccessfully, to have the ETUC expelled from the CCC and have EURO COOP's status reviewed on the grounds that, although they promote consumers' interests, neither organisation is a consumer group.[9]

On occasion, however, some of the groups will form alliances to advance particular objectives. BEUC appears to be the least inclined to participate in such alliances, although it has a good working relationship with COFACE. The two groups jointly provide the secretariat for the Parliament's Intergroup on Consumer Affairs. COFACE is the organisation most willing and able to cooperate with the others, having also worked with EURO-C and EURO COOP. The three groups, for example, recently joined forces to campaign for limits on the use of hormones in food products pending the implementation of a ban.

In addition to such *ad hoc* cooperation, agriculture and foodstuffs is one of two issue areas – technical standardisation being the other – in which cooperation between the European consumer groups is highly developed and institutionalised. Issues related to food prices, quality and safety are arguably among the most important to consumers. The average British consumer spends 18 per cent of his or her income on food. That proportion rises to 25 per cent for the poorest 10 percent of the population (NCC, 1995). In addition, the OECD estimates that the CAP increases prices by the equivalent of £134 per person per year (NCC, 1995). Cooperation between the European associations on this important issue is relatively simple because their policy preferences are largely compatible. They essentially agree that the CAP causes high consumer prices and poor quality produce (NCC, 1988). In slightly different ways they argue for a policy that will reduce prices, reflect actual demand and reduce surpluses, while protecting those who work in agriculture. Thus they support a shift from price supports to income support. Differences in emphasis and detail can, however, lead to disagreements.

Consumer representation on twenty-five of DG VI's Agricultural Advisory Committees is coordinated by the CCC's foodstuffs section. Logistical problems with how these committees are run, however, hamper the effectiveness of this coordination (NCC, 1988). Further, the composition of the committees is heavily weighted in favour of producers. Consumer representation on the Directorate-General for Industry's (DG III) Advisory Committee on Foodstuffs is simpler as the two consumer representatives are nominated by the CCC. Consumer participation is also arguably more effective than in DG VI's committees as the membership is less skewed towards producers.

The European Association for the Coordination of Consumer Representation in Standardisation (ANEC)

By far the highest degree of cooperation between the European consumer groups is in the area of technical standardisation. The independent European Association for the Coordination of Consumer Representation in Standardisation (ANEC) was established in February 1995. It is composed of eighteen national members, one selected by the consumer organisations of each member state of the EU and European Free Trade Area (EFTA), and four representatives from the CCC and two from the Consumer Consultative Council of the EFTA Secretariat (EFTA CCC). In 1995 it coordinated the activities of more than 100 national consumer representatives and forty-four ANEC observers active in 175 technical committees and working groups of the European Standards Committee (CEN) and the European Electro-technical Standards Committee (CENELEC). It also participates in both organisations' General Assemblies. ANEC is less involved in the European Telecommunications Standards Institute (ETSI), but it has a representative on the Users' Group and one national consumer representative participates in the Human Factors Working Group (see Figure 7.2).

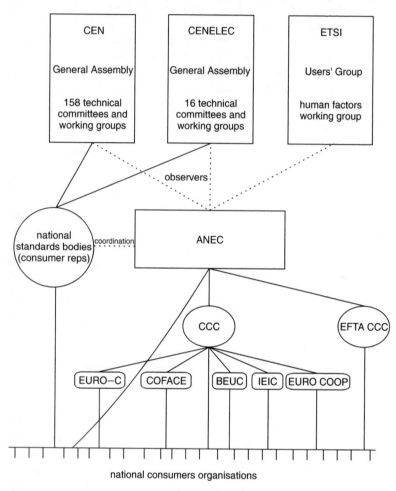

Figure 7.2 Consumer representation in European standardisation
Notes: CEN, CENELEC and ETSI: technical committees and working groups in which ANEC observers or consumer representatives from national standards bodies participate. Some national consumer organisations are represented directly in the European consumer organisations (EURO-C, COFACE, BEUC, IEIC and EURO COOP) and in some countries' national standards institutes. The consumer organisations in each member state select one representative to the CCC and one to ANEC (they may be the same person).

The importance of standardisation in the EU increased dramatically after the Council's May 1985 adoption of the New Approach to Technical Harmonisation, which delegated the development of detailed technical standards to CEN, CENELEC and ETSI. The first consumer observers had, with the Commission's assistance, gained access to CEN working groups in December 1982 and to CENELEC's in April 1983. These observers were appointed by the CCC and both their and the national consumer representatives' activities were coordinated and supported by SECO (the European Secretariat for Coordination in Standardisation), which was run on behalf of the CCC by BEUC under contract from the Commission.

The new approach, however, greatly increased the quantity and significance of the work of the standards bodies. In response the Commission published a green paper (European Commission, 1990) on the future development of European standardisation. Among its proposals was improving the participation of the social partners, including consumers, at every level of the standard setting process. ANEC is the product of the EU and EFTA CCCs' response to that Green Paper (ANEC, 1995a).

ANEC's General Assembly approves the annual work programme, accepts general policy objectives and nominates observers to the standards bodies, all of which are proposed by the Steering Committee. It takes decisions by simple majority with each national representative and each of the delegates from the EU and EFTA CCCs having one vote. The steering committee, composed of the President and nine members, is appointed by the General Assembly to administer the association. Six members must come from national organisations, two from the CCC and one from the EFTA CCC. Each member has one vote and decisions are taken by simple majority. The detailed organisation of consumer representation is handled by the Co-ordination Group, which is composed of representatives from each member country, the chairs of ANEC's working groups and invited experts. The six working groups – child safety, electrical appliances, environment, gas appliances, machinery and traffic safety – are made up of interested national representatives, the ANEC observers on the relevant committees and external experts. The level at which positions on particular standards are agreed depends on how technical the issue is, with more political and wide ranging decisions being taken higher up in the organisation. As ANEC is still a young organisation, at the time of writing these boundaries are still being worked out.

Participation in CEN's and CENELEC's General Assemblies permits ANEC to propose new work items, including the revision of standards that it considers too lax. Being an observer on technical committees and working groups enables it to comment on proposals, but not to vote. Roughly half of the member states' national standards bodies have some form of institutionalised consumer representation.[10] If the national consumer organisations can sway their respective national delegations, they can effectively vote by proxy. The consumer representatives included in national delegations are supposed to vote according to the national position, but when, as is the case on some committees for some countries, consumers are the only national representatives, they have more leeway.

ETSI is the youngest of the European standards bodies, and the least amenable to consumer interests. Unlike CEN and CENELEC it is not composed of national standards bodies, but of large producers and users. ANEC, however, is becoming more active in ETSI's User Group, which establishes user requirements before the industry representatives start to develop standards.

COOPERATION WITH OTHER EUROPEAN INTEREST GROUPS

Due to the complexity of regulatory politics, there is rarely a straightforward consumer–producer antagonism in policy making. Consequently, consumer groups' preferences are often compatible, if not identical, with those of particular firms or industries. In such instances, they occasionally form coalitions with these other interests.

In part because of its interest in liberalisation, BEUC is the European consumer group that most often finds itself in accord with at least some producers' preferences. In such circumstances, BEUC is willing to cooperate with the pertinent trade associations, but it resists losing its identity or autonomy to collaborative exercises. The closest such collaboration has been in response to the Commission's proposals for extending intellectual property protection, particularly on car spare parts. In its opposition to the proposals, BEUC cooperates with the representatives of independent producers and suppliers of car spare parts, insurance companies, and small and medium sized enterprises within the loose association ECAR. The participating organisations share information, coordinate activities, and occasionally make joint representations.

EURO COOP, not surprisingly given its role of representing both consumers and retailers, also sometimes finds common ground with more traditional business groups. With regard to agricultural policy, it has quite sustained common interests with some groups, while with others positions only coincide on particular issues. Recently, for example, it worked with the European Union of the Fruit and Vegetable, Wholesale, Import and Export Trade to resist, successfully, proposals for a protectionist regime on Mediterranean fruit.

Consumer organisations also, on occasion, coordinate their activities with other civic interest organisations. In September 1995, for example, BEUC joined the Euro Citizen Action Service (ECAS), the European Environmental Bureau (EEB), the European Federation for Transport and Environment (T&E) and the European Public Health Alliance (EPHA) in forming the European Campaign for Clean Air (ECCA).[11] COFACE joined the campaign shortly thereafter. The campaign was organised in an attempt to counter the close consultations between the Commission and the automobile and oil industries in preparing proposals for the next round of automobile emissions limits (ECCA 1995).[12] The campaign has subsequently issued numerous joint press releases, some of which have been on behalf of only some of the participating members, and it has organised two conferences involving Commission and member government officials.

COOPERATION BEYOND EUROPE

Increasingly Europe's consumers are affected by decisions taken not only beyond their national borders, but also beyond the boundaries of the EU. As noted earlier, many of the European consumer groups were founded by international organisations. Most of these organisations, however, are largely concerned with sharing information among national members, coordinating responses to common problems and promoting best practice. This is due in part to the weakness of governance structures at the global level, which means that there is relatively little policy for consumers to try to influence.

The two most significant exceptions to this generalisation concern food quality and technical standards. These are two areas in which consumer interest is significant and in which global forums play an important role. Consequently, as at the European level, it is in these areas that consumer cooperation at the global level is most developed. In both cases, Consumers International (CI), which is composed of more than 215 independent consumer organisations from eighty-seven countries, is the primary representative of consumer interests. Because BEUC's members are also, for the most part, members of CI the two organisations cooperate closely on issues of particular relevance to European consumers. The two organisations, for example, 'speak with one voice' on trade issues (BEUC, 1995: 33).

The Codex Alimentarius Commission, which is comprised of 146 countries, is the crucial body regulating foodstuffs at the global level. It sets standards in areas such as food hygiene and regulates the use of food additives, pesticides and veterinary drugs. The CI has been lobbying for improved consumer access to the Codex Alimentarius Commission itself and for greater consultation with consumers at the national level. Its proposals were discussed at the meeting of the Codex Committee on General Principles in November 1996 and at the 1997 session of the Codex Alimentarius Commission. In July 1995 the Codex Alimentarius Commission agreed that consumer representatives should be able to join expert committees. BEUC and CI work together on food issues through a joint Food Working Group.

Consumer participation in standard setting at the international level is better established and also benefits from consumer representation in the national delegations. In 1995 there were CI observers in nine International Standards Organisation (ISO) and International Electro-technical Committee (IEC) working groups and committees in addition to 143 (European) national consumer representatives on sixty-six committees and working groups (ANEC, 1995a and b). Participation in the international standards bodies is important for European consumers as a significant proportion of European standards, particularly in the electro-technical sphere, originate at the international level. According to CENELEC, in 1991 90 per cent of draft European technical standards in the electro-technical sector originated at the international level (Nicolas, 1995). The Secretary General of ANEC estimates that the equivalent figure for CEN is 40 per cent. The international standard setting is sufficiently important to Europe's consumers that ANEC finances consumer representation in some of the key international committees and working groups.

At its 1994 world congress, CI (then still IOCU) adopted technical standards as one of its six priority areas. This will involve launching global campaigns, establishing a policy committee to direct its efforts and setting up a network among national groups, similar to ANEC, in order to exchange information and expertise between members at a technical level. CI is also active in the United Nations Economic Commission for Europe (UN-ECE), which is an international forum for regulatory alignment. CI focuses on regulations concerning automobiles, particularly those to do with vehicle safety. Decisions taken there are often used as the foundations for EU regulations.

Although international associations initially set up a number of the European consumer organisations, the structure of consumer organisation at the international level currently has little impact on consumer collective action at the European level. In large part this is because only CI, representing just one tradition of consumer association, is active on consumer issues at the international level.

CONCLUDING REMARKS

Consumer groups have used a variety of incentives to organise consumers at the national level. These different traditions are echoed at the European level and influence how each European organisation functions. The particular interests of the different types of member organisations are also reflected in the policy priorities of the Euro groups and influence their ability and willingness to cooperate with each other and with non consumer interest groups.

Although the traditions of national organisation are reflected at the European level, the techniques largely are not. While their national members provide selective benefits to encourage participation, neither BEUC nor EURO COOP do so. Rather the pursuit of collective benefits is the principal motivation for cooperation between national consumer groups at the European and global levels.

This is because the national consumer organisations were formed in order to pursue political aims collectively. The creation of a level of governance that affects the attainment of these objectives almost naturally produced a new level of cooperation. This cooperation is facilitated by the commitment of the national groups' leaders, the externalisation of ideological differences and the EU's policy style, which makes it relatively easy to reconcile different preferences.

Cooperation is also encouraged by the sense that it is necessary in order to defend hard won gains. Both COFACE and EURO COOP were initially created in order to identify and respond to potential problems emerging from the creation of the EEC. The heightened activity of the consumer organisations in the late 1980s and early 1990s was prompted by concerns that the SEM's liberalising agenda would undermine consumer protection at the national level. Further, the national consumer organisations lack the resources, both financial and moral, necessary to realise objectives individually, so cooperation was and is the only way forward. Nonetheless, the Commission has played an important role in promoting and supporting consumer cooperation at the European level.

Just as consumer cooperation at the European level has been induced by the importance of EU policies for consumers, so too has collective action at the international level. As at the European level, this cooperation is most highly developed in the policy areas that are both important to consumers and have significant levels of activity at the targeted level of governance.

Although they have quite substantial resources in absolute terms, consumer associations tend to be more poorly resourced than trade associations relative to the breadth of their policy remit. Further, organisation and participation should not be confused with influence. Just because consumer organisations participate quite actively in the policy process does not mean that their concerns are necessarily taken on board by policy makers. On the other hand, as I have argued elsewhere (Young, 1997b), the concerns of consumers can be and sometimes are injected into the policy process by other actors on the European stage, including member governments, the Commission and the European Parliament. Thus the extent and quality of cooperation between consumers is only part, albeit a significant one, of the story.

NOTES

1 This chapter is based on research funded by Phase II of the Economic and Social Research Council's Single European Market Initiative (Award L113251029). I am grateful to the other contributors to this volume for their comments during our ECPR workshop in Heidelberg and subsequently. For an analysis of the development of European consumer policy in general see Young (1997b).
2 Mazey and Richardson (1992) make a similar observation regarding European environmental organisations.
3 Now called Consumers International (CI), it is based in London with five regional offices.
4 In 1994 CEG had thirty-one member organisations, five of which belonged directly to European consumer organisations.
5 Until 1994 the CEG belonged to two of the European consumers organisations: the European Consumers' Organisation (BEUC) and the Confederation of Family Organisations in the European Community (COFACE). Following a cut in government support, it dropped its membership of COFACE.
6 For the sake of simplicity I will use CCC throughout even though it was disbanded on 13 June 1995 and replaced by the Consumers' Committee, which has a different composition, but essentially the same function. The members of the Consumers' Committee were appointed on 1 February 1996.
7 This section draws heavily on interviews and correspondence with current and former representatives of each of the European consumer organisations as well as national associations in the UK and Sweden conducted between April 1994 and May 1996.
8 In 1972 the Contact Committee lapsed and was replaced by the Consumer Consultative Committee in 1973. In 1989 representatives of national consumer organisations gained direct membership and the body was renamed

the Consumers Consultative Council. In 1994 BEUC's representation was doubled, ETUC's representation was restricted to consumer departments of trade unions or affiliated organisations and IEIC was admitted.

9 For a full account of this clash and its aftermath see Young (1997b).

10 In seven member states consumers are represented on the national standards bodies' boards and the standards bodies in eight member states have internal consumer committees. Only Belgium, Greece, Ireland, Italy and Spain rely on *ad hoc* consultations with consumers (ANEC 1995a).

11 For a full description of the coalition see Ruth Websters, Chapter 8 in this volume.

12 For a more detailed discussion of EU policy in this area see Young (1997a).

8 Environmental collective action

Stable patterns of cooperation and issue alliances at the European level

Ruth Webster

If we consider volume of legislation as the benchmark for a policy area's significance, the environment must be among the European Union's (EU) most important. The EU has gained considerable competence in environmental protection since the 1967 directive on the classification, packaging and labelling of dangerous substances. Besides legislation, research initiatives and EC environmental action programmes, the longer term aim of integrating environmental considerations within other policy areas indicates the scale and scope of European environmental policy.

Numerous environmental non governmental organisations (NGOs) act on the European stage, but there are seven core organisations. They are the European Environmental Bureau (EEB), Friends of the Earth Europe (FoEE), Greenpeace International, the World Wide Fund for Nature (WWF), Climate Network Europe (CNE), the European Federation for Transport and the Environment (T&E), and BirdLife International. Together these networks make up the Group of Seven and coordinate their activities on an informal basis. This chapter seeks to examine patterns of associability between these environmental networks, and also between them and other types of interests operating within the European environmental arena. Collaboration and coalition-type behaviour between interests raises similar collective action issues to those discussed in the literature on group formation, organisation and maintenance. Therefore, the chapter will consider the free rider problem and the role of incentives in organisational collective action.

ORGANISATIONS AND COLLECTIVE ACTION: THE LITERATURE

In his study of coalition formation in Washington, Hula (1995) compares and contrasts the formation of coalitions with the formation of interest groups. Drawing on the ideas and theories of Olson (1971) and Salisbury (1969), he examines the role of incentives in coalition formation. This chapter adopts a similar approach as a starting point for investigating environmental interest collaboration.

Hula suggests that incentives play a role in attracting organisational participation in collective actions in the same way as they attract individual participation. However, the type of incentives that encourage organisations to enter into coalitions are different from the incentives offered to individuals (Hula, 1995: 240). The collective action issues facing individuals and organisations diverge. In other words, the free rider problem has varying impacts upon individual and organisational collective action.

Hula examines why organisations join political coalitions. He defines political coalitions as 'groups of organizations united by a common political goal' (*ibid.*). Political coalitions act within the policy process and seek to influence policy outcomes. According to Olson's theory, policy outcomes lead to the supply of collective benefits. Just as Olson questions the idea that individuals, acting out of rational self-interest, will choose to bear the costs of group membership in return for collective benefits, Hula considers whether organisations will join political coalitions if collective benefits are the only reward. Does the logic of free riding apply to organisations too? Though Hula acknowledges that there will always be free riders, and that Olson's group size argument may account for organisational coalition formation, he considers the latter a partial explanation (*ibid.*: 241–2). He illustrates his argument by highlighting the contrasts between individuals participating in groups and organisations participating in political coalitions:

> Whereas the potential member of a coalition is, at least formally, an organization, the actual member is usually a staffer employed by the organization. This creates an important qualitative difference between the task confronting an interest group entrepreneur, who must mobilize potentially apolitical individuals, and the role of a coalition broker, who brings paid Washington representatives into a coalition.
>
> (*ibid.*: 242)

If individuals do not respond to political goals, then organisations' policy makers and public affairs personnel certainly do. For the environmental NGOs at the European level, staff from the Brussels offices often represent the organisations in collaborative ventures. These staff members are already politically active on the organisations' behalf, therefore mobilising them to participate in political coalitions compares favourably with the task of mobilising individuals to join groups. In essence, Hula contends that for organisations already pursuing political goals there are benefits from participating in collective action. Coalitions improve organisations' chances of influencing the policy process and reduces their workload (*ibid.*: 242). The idea that organisations may wish to work towards political goals via alliances and coalitions is echoed in the work of Knoke, Pappi, Broadbent and Tsujinaka (1996) and of Gray and Lowery (1995).

Hula cites three reasons why organisations join political coalitions: strategic or policy oriented reasons, selective benefits and symbolic gestures. Organisations may become coalition members in order to influence the policy process and achieve favourable policy outcomes, secure selective benefits such as information, or keep up appearances (Hula, 1995: 241). In keeping with the collective action literature, these three reasons can be translated as incentives for organisations participating in coalitions. Indeed, they are selective incentives that only benefit the organisations involved in collective action. Such incentives provide the starting point for examining the patterns of associability between the environmental NGOs and interests operating within the European environmental arena.

THE ENVIRONMENTAL NGOs – INTERNAL DYNAMICS AND ACTIVITIES AT THE EUROPEAN LEVEL

The European Environmental Bureau

Created in 1974, the European Environmental Bureau (EEB) was the first environmental organisation to be set up at the EU level. The impetus for its establishment came from European Community NGOs, which recognised the need for cooperation between environmental interests to raise the profile of the environment as one of the European Community's responsibilities (EEB, 1994: 3, 5). As a European federation representing some 132 organisations from twenty-four countries, including the fifteen EU member states (EEB, 1996: 28), the EEB boasts a geographically wide spread and socioeconomically varied membership base. Members range from heritage interests such as the UK's National Trust to national environmental NGOs including the Dutch organisation Stichting Natuur en Milieu. Several national-level organisations of the international NGOs, namely WWF, BirdLife International and FoE International (FoEI) are also EEB members.

The EEB's internal structure is made up of various tiers. The members are organised into national conferences. A representative from each national conference sits on the EEB Executive Committee. There is one representative for each EU member state plus a representative from Norway. An annual general assembly is held in Brussels and has the task of defining the programme of activities. The secretariat, permanently based in Brussels, consists of eleven staff members including the Secretary General, scientific advisor and specific campaign and programme coordinators (EEB, 1996: 30). With regard to financial matters the EEB receives core funding from the European Commission and contributions from EU countries.

The EEB is active on a range of issues including the European eco label, the Eco-Management and Audit Scheme (EMAS), air quality and water management. More generally, the Bureau works towards the creation of a fully integrated environmental policy at the European level. Its good relations with the European institutions, in particular with the Commission Services Directorate-General DG XI responsible for the environment, nuclear safety and civil protection, have been remarked upon (Mazey and Richardson, 1993c; Rucht, 1993). There are regular meetings between the EEB executive committee and EU institutions. The EEB is the environmental representative on a number of Commission advisory committees, for example, the Motor Vehicle Emissions Group.

Friends of the Earth Europe

In 1986, FoEI marked its arrival in Brussels with the opening of a policy coordination office. Friends of the Earth Europe (FoEE) is a regional (Europe) association of FoEI. It therefore shares the same membership as the international network. There are currently some twenty-nine FoE organisations in twenty-eight European countries (The EU Committee of the American Chamber of Commerce, 1995: 245). Originally intended as a policy coordinating or facilitating office, the Brussels base is increasingly active in interest representation activities at the EU level and also works on a number of topics of its own. The member organisations have a dominant position within FoEE, which means the activities of the Brussels office are determined by the members and FoEE's work proceeds on the basis of membership consensus. Member groups are independent organisations pursuing environmental campaigns at all levels (international to local). They assume leading roles in campaign issues according to their particular interests and expertise. For example, Friends of the Earth England,

Wales and Northern Ireland is active on a lot of transport related issues at the national and European level. In addition, the member organisations retain political responsibility for campaigns. Member organisations also contribute to the funding of FoEE along with EU sources. FoEE coordinates member activities in areas such as biotechnology and transport (The EU Committee of the American Chamber of Commerce, 1995: 245). It is also working on issues related to a sustainable Europe.[1]

Greenpeace International

Greenpeace International established a European unit in Brussels in 1988. In structural terms the European unit is subsumed within Greenpeace International's political unit. Its main task is to help Greenpeace International execute various international campaigns. The personnel in the Brussels office advise Greenpeace International on developments at the EU level and work on campaign strategies. At present there are two European advisors dedicated to activities at the EU. On the EU stage the European unit represents Greenpeace International. Since Greenpeace International has member organisations throughout Europe, the European unit also represents them at this level. Greenpeace International is the funding source for the European unit. Consequently, money from the national Greenpeace organisations (for example, Greenpeace UK, Greenpeace Germany) finances the international organisation's Brussels office as well as other departments such as the economic unit and scientific laboratories. In contrast with the other environmental NGOs at the EU, the European unit does not receive funding from the European Commission. This corresponds with Greenpeace's policy of maintaining financial and political independence.[2]

World Wide Fund for Nature

In 1989 the World Wide Fund for Nature (WWF) European Policy Office opened in Brussels. In 1995 there were eight members of staff in the policy office with a further seven in the European field programme office in the organisation's Geneva headquarters. The fourteen national WWF organisations (twelve in the EU member state countries) are a source of funding for the European office but they are not involved in its day-to-day management. Rather they are organised into different thematic teams on subjects such as agriculture or climate issues. As its name suggests the European office is focused on policy.

It participates in lobbying activities at the EU level and is also involved in communications, information collection and dissemination and fund raising. At the European level WWF has been very active on the structural funds, agriculture and rural development policy and overseas development. The European Commission is a further funding source for the WWF European policy office.[3]

Climate Network Europe

Climate Network Europe (CNE) is one of eight regional focal points for NGO members of the international Climate Action Network. Established in 1989, CNE's aim is 'to promote action to limit human induced climate change to ecologically sustainable levels' (Climate Network Europe pamphlet).[4] There are some sixty European environmental NGO members of CNE. They include several national branches of WWF and Friends of the Earth. Within Europe there is an advisory board with representatives from the most active member organisations. The board decides upon the main subjects for CNE to address. The network's list of responsibilities includes coordinating the membership's climate related activities; cooperating with the other regional focal points of Climate Action Network; providing an information service on climate related topics; and monitoring policy developments at the European Union. Working with the other environmental NGOs in Brussels is also mentioned (*ibid.*).

BirdLife International

BirdLife International (as it is now named) was founded in 1922. The European Community Office (ECO) opened in 1993 following the partners' (that is, members') decision that an office in Brussels would enable the organisation to act efficiently on matters at the European level. There are twenty-nine European partners in BirdLife International. The UK's Royal Society for the Protection of Birds (RSPB) is one of the largest member organisations. BirdLife has a common European programme, which is drawn up by the organisation's secretariat based at BirdLife International's headquarters in Cambridge. The programme is agreed by the partners at BirdLife's European conference and coordinated by the European Community Office. The European office is also responsible for following and analysing policy developments, maintaining contacts with the European Union institutions and engaging in lobbying activities on policies that relate to birds and their habitats. Indeed, 'ECO acts as the first point of contact through which the European institutions can access BirdLife's world-wide network of expertise' (BirdLife pamphlet).[5] The Common Agricultural Policy, the birds directive, strategic environmental impact assessment, the structural funds and trans European networks are examples of the issues that attract the European office's attention. Funding comes from two main sources, namely the BirdLife partners and the European Commission, which contributes to the office's core funding.

The European Federation for Transport and the Environment

T&E was founded in 1989 and set up the Brussels office in 1992. T&E is an umbrella organisation with twenty-nine members in eighteen countries within the European Union, European Free Trade Area (EFTA) and Eastern Europe. The majority of its members are NGOs operating at the national level. They fall into the following categories: environmental NGOs, environmental transport associations and public transport users' groups. International NGOs such as WWF and the International Union for Public Transport have associate memberships. At the European level T&E's activities focus on air and road transport. Public transport, trans European networks, motor vehicle emissions and air quality are examples of the type of subjects addressed. T&E also commissions research and publishes widely on transport and environment issues. Sources of funding include the members and the European Commission.[6]

Summary: points of departure

The EEB was the only Brussels based environmental NGO until the others followed in the 1980s and 1990s. Prior to their move to Brussels, the other environmental NGOs had access to the EEB working groups and, through the Bureau, the European policy process. However, as Tony Long, Director of the WWF European Policy Office, points out, the time came for the other environmental NGOs to establish a Brussels presence in order to deal effectively with environmental activities at the EU level (Long, 1995: 673). Long cites two reasons for the NGOs setting up in Brussels: environmental policy's coming of age at the European level following the Single European Act in 1986 and the resulting increase in legislative and other measures to protect and promote Europe's environment; and the NGOs' eagerness to pursue funding opportunities at the European level (Long, 1995: 673–4).

There are important differences between the seven NGOs operating at the EU. In Rucht's (1993) analysis of cross national cooperation between environmental groups the EEB and FoEE are described as stable trans national alliances and Greenpeace International and WWF are characterised as supranational non governmental organisations (Rucht, 1993: 82–6). These categories are indicative of the distinctive organisational and operational dynamics of these NGOs and the more recent additions to the Brussels scene. Whereas the Brussels office of the EEB is the organisation's apex, the Brussels office of Greenpeace is one aspect of the NGO's global structure. Likewise WWF, Friends of the Earth International and BirdLife International have headquarters elsewhere. Relations between member organisations and the NGOs' EU-level representations are not equally transparent. For the EEB the link between the 132 members and the secretariat is quite clear – groups join the Bureau in order to become members and benefit from the organisation's membership services (EEB, 1996: 11). For T&E the link appears to be similar although there are different types of membership, namely full or associate. In contrast, the relationship between Greenpeace International's European unit and the Greenpeace national organisations is more opaque. As part of Greenpeace's political unit, the Brussels office represents Greenpeace International at the EU level. This includes the national organisations as part of the overall structure but does not extend to representing the European national organisations individually. Consequently, the member link can only be considered as an indirect one.

Turning to operational dynamics, the relationship between member organisations and the NGOs' EU base may impact upon the seven's collective actions at the European level. Decision making procedures vary. For example, FoEE requires the unanimous agreement of the members prior to presenting its position to the European institutions. Yet, the T&E secretariat is not bound by this principle.

A degree of overlap exists between the members of the seven NGOs. For example, several national-level WWF organisations are members of the EEB and CNE. The same is true for Friends of the Earth International. The RSPB is a member of BirdLife International, the EEB and CNE. Transport 2000 is a member of CNE and T&E. Contact between the NGOs through the members may shape their patterns of interaction at the European level.

ENVIRONMENTAL NGOs AND COLLECTIVE ACTION

The seven environmental NGOs participate in different types of collective action. Several factors shape collective action, including the number and nature of the organisations involved, the duration of the venture, and the events and activities undertaken by the participants. The terms single issue alliances, informal collaborations, semi permanent coalitions and formal cooperation can be used to describe the many patterns of interaction between interests operating at the European level, be they business and industry associations, consumer and citizen organisations or environmental NGOs. The range of collective action involving the environmental NGOs is best illustrated with examples. The first involves only environmental organisations at the EU level, the second groups together environmental, public health, citizen and consumer interests.

STABLE PATTERNS OF COOPERATION: THE GROUP OF SEVEN

There is considerable contact between the NGOs within the European environmental arena. They interact regularly as the Group of Seven to coordinate their activities at the European level. The Group of Seven started off as the Group of Four – comprising the EEB, WWF, Greenpeace and FoEE. Cooperation between these organisations began with two purposes in mind. First, to work together on the revision of the Treaty of Rome leading up to the Maastricht Treaty. Second, to establish contact with DG XI on a more regular basis so that the NGOs could receive feedback from the Commission.[7] The numbers increased as the specialist environmental organisations established themselves in Brussels. One of the criteria for membership is the maintenance of some sort of presence in Brussels. A further criterion is that organisations must operate throughout Europe. This tends to exclude national-level NGOs and keep the membership numbers manageable.

It may be easier to characterise the Group of Seven and outline its internal structure by beginning with a description of what it is not. It is not a formal organisation with a written constitution or legal statutes; there is no separate organisational structure or group secretariat. Rather it is a mechanism, an informal arrangement between the NGOs which enables them to coordinate their activities and act sometimes as a single lobby within the European environmental arena. The group has operated for several years. Therefore an established collaborative structure exists with regular meetings. The meetings are held internally with the NGOs taking turns to act as the host. The informal nature of the group encourages flexibility. If one or more NGOs do not want to act on a particular subject they are not bound to proceed as part of the group. For example, the collective publication, *Greening the Treaty II: Sustainable Development in a Democratic Union. Proposals for the 1996 Intergovernmental Conference* (Climate Network Europe *et al.*, 1995) does not have BirdLife's name or logo on the cover.

It is clear from NGO activities and projects, not to mention the specialist environmental networks, that they each have areas of expertise (Long, 1995). Their individual campaigns are not restricted by their participation in the group. Because it is an informal cooperative arrangement the NGOs are free to continue with their own work programmes.

The type of subjects that involve collaboration are those of common interest; in other words, horizontal issues. The review of the Fifth Environmental Action Programme and the revision of the Maastricht Treaty are examples of the type of subjects on which the environmental interests work together. There are several forms of collective action by the group. One is the coauthorship of publications and press releases bearing the seven NGO logos. Another is interacting with the EU institutions. The environmental NGOs also participate in the policy process and lobby collectively.

The maintenance of regular contact between the seven environmental NGOs in Brussels appears to be relatively simple. Apart from the telephone and fax, two of the seven organisations share the same building. With only seven main interests with offices in Brussels the environmental lobby is small enough to encourage collective action. According to Olson (1971) collective actions involving a limited number of participants are more readily organised than larger groups. The potential members are more susceptible to face-to-face pressure and are more likely to participate if the provision of a collective good seems to depend on their contribution.

Incentives for participating in the Group of Seven

As noted above, the NGOs initially worked together on the revisions of the Treaty of Rome in 1992. Collaboration continued as a means of gaining more regular contact with DG XI and acting as a single focal point for the Commission. Since then the environmental organisations have continued to coordinate their activities and launch collective actions via the group. There are a number of incentives for the participants, who regard the Group of Seven as their central collaborative forum, namely access to information and expertise, greater influence or lobbying capabilities, and practical benefits as a result of sharing responsibilities.

The importance of exchanging information and drawing on others' expertise should not be underestimated. The seven NGOs have established positions within the EU environmental arena in their own right. They can boast about the numbers of individuals and groups they represent and present a record of past campaign successes. Moreover, they can bring knowledge and experience gained from previous campaigns at the international, national and local levels to their collaborative efforts at the European level. Some of the NGOs, notably the EEB, WWF and T&E, have access to the Commission via advisory committee and working groups. In turn the information and contacts made through advisory group membership can benefit the entire group. Applying the typology of incentives outlined in Chapter 1, information can be a material or social selective incentive depending upon the type of information gained through participating in a group or coalition. Greenwood and Aspinwall in Chapter 1 refer to 'hard' and 'soft' information in the incentives typology.

Hula suggests that 'some organizations are motivated to participate in coalitions by strategic policy concerns ... they select coalition strategies because they view them as the most effective way to shape policy outcomes' (Hula, 1995: 241). Several selective incentives for joining coalitions may appeal to the environmental NGOs, which are seeking to enhance their influencing capabilities over policy outcomes at the European level. These incentives include securing additional access to the EU institutions and opportunities to shape policy demands. During an interview one environmentalist noted that the Group of Seven helps the flow of information between the NGOs and the institutions. If DG XI wishes to discuss a matter with the environmental organisations the Group of Seven acts as a 'one stop shop'. Often the meetings between the NGOs and senior officials and political figures from the institutions are group initiatives. Participating in the Group of Seven also enables the NGOs to contribute towards and develop policy demands. As well as having an additional lobbying platform through the group, the environmental organisations have the opportunity to influence the group's message.

Undoubtedly from a strategic, policy oriented angle, the environmental lobby acting as one can add weight to an argument and achieve more than separate actions. However, it is important to remember a collective approach may not be the most appropriate influencing strategy for every issue. One environmentalist remarked during an interview that it is sometimes important to act separately but send similar messages to the institutions in order to match the volume of papers from other, opposing lobbies.[8] Even when the environmental NGOs act separately their actions can be coordinated. Choosing to act together or alone according to the issue is built into the group's flexible operational and organisational structure.

Further incentives for joining the group are practical ones for the NGOs' Brussels based personnel, namely saving resources (in particular, time) and a reduction of their workloads. Sharing responsibilities for issues that are dealt with via the group can alleviate the pressures on individual members' resources. For example, if one NGO is concentrating on the Commission while another is contacting the European Parliament, activities can be divided between the organisations. Since many environmental NGOs have small secretariats in Brussels the opportunity to share the burden is most welcome. These selective incentives for participating in the Group of Seven are largely material.

Another selective incentive for coalition formation is Hula's suggestion that organisations participate as a symbolic gesture – keeping up appearances in front of one's peers, other EU-level actors (including the institutions) or the organisations' membership (Hula, 1995: 248–9). Turning to the Group of Seven, this incentive seems to be less relevant to the participating NGOs. Although the group is a stable collaborative forum with public evidence of organisational collective action through publications and statements, the seven participants are established, independent political actors with considerable, individual campaign commitments. In this context, it seems unlikely that the NGOs use the Group of Seven to enhance their image. The incentives for belonging to the group seem to be more firmly based on the benefits gained from coordinating activities and working together on matters of common interest. Nevertheless it is impossible to identify every motivation for associating and symbolic gestures may form part of the picture.

This discussion suggests that the ideas from the collective action literature can be applied to the Group of Seven. In particular, a range of selective incentives to encourage environmental participation can be identified. There may be other factors influencing collective action by the environmental NGOs, either from particular attributes of the group (for example, organisational and operational dynamics) or from further ideas advanced in the literature.

Other factors influencing NGO participation in the Group of Seven

The global aspect of environmental protection and the common bond between environmental NGOs may help to explain collective action via the Group of Seven at the European level. Comments emphasising how pollution fails to respect borders or how environmental problems transcend national boundaries may be clichéd, yet they emphasise the need to address environmental issues beyond the national level. Having set up operations at the European level the environmental NGOs may be more able to engage in, and sustain, collective action than other types of NGO because of their shared commitment to protecting and enhancing the environment. Cross sectoral collaboration between business and industry interests is often a short term phenomenon based on a particular event or issue. The Group of Seven environmental NGOs share fundamental ideas and principles about the environment which may encourage and maintain collaboration at a deeper level. As one environmentalist suggested during a recent research interview with the author, collaboration between the environmental NGOs can go beyond the lowest common denominator. The concept of shared belief systems among political actors forms part of the advocacy coalition framework (Jenkins-Smith and Sabatier, 1994; Sabatier, 1988). For the actors within Sabatier's advocacy coalitions there are three categories of shared belief – deep core beliefs, policy core beliefs and secondary beliefs. The NGOs' environmental beliefs fall within the deep core category. This category is the strongest and more resistant to change than the others. Although the Group of Seven members may have common principles about environmental protection they may not share the same operational ideas and practical steps to promote protection and solve environmental problems. Different methods of achieving goals distinguish the NGOs. However, the variations in approach do not detract from the common beliefs and commitments towards environmental protection.

Turning to operational dynamics, the type of issues and subjects dealt with collectively may also feature in an explanation of the Group of Seven. The environmental organisations collaborate on horizontal issues, that is matters that affect the entire sector. Operating in this step-by-step manner contributes to the maintenance of the Group as well as its formation.

The organisational aspects of the Group of Seven may help to explain its longevity. The flexible internal structure accommodates the members' needs and wishes by coordinating activities on matters that interest all seven and by allowing members to participate only when it suits. Undoubtedly, the informal nature of the group encourages flexible working practices.

As noted, overlapping membership is a feature of the environmental NGOs operating at the EU level. Evidence from the business sector suggests that organisations which share members may be inclined to enter into collaborative arrangements (Greenwood, 1995a – on biotechnology interests). This could be regarded as a bottom-up approach with member interaction stimulating organisational interaction. In this way any anxiety that the membership may have about collaboration can be alleviated if the potential coalition partner means more to them than just another European association. Moreover, groups with dual membership may be more committed to any alliances between their organisations. These dual members could also play an important role within collaborative structures by increasing understanding between organisations and furthering their common agendas and collective actions at the EU level.

Does dual membership foster collective action between the environmental NGOs at the EU? Although it seems plausible that member groups and associations can promote organisational collaboration, the extent to which this is possible must partly depend on how influential the members are within the organisations. Who makes the decisions to form alliances? The seven NGOs are represented in the Group of Seven by Brussels based secretariats and some of the international NGOs merely have policy offices at the European level. Therefore the decision to participate in alliances and coalitions is not taken at the same level in each NGO. While the secretariats of some organisations have to consult the members, others do not. Since the relationships between members and staff are not uniform, it cannot be assumed that overlapping membership automatically improves collective action prospects between the seven environmental organisations.

Ideas from the literature and organisational and operational aspects of the Group of Seven enable us to gain some insight into what collective action has to offer the seven environmental NGOs. There are membership benefits for these political actors including information and enhanced lobbying capabilities, all of which enable the seven to pursue their aims within the European policy process. The flexible organisational structure and operational basis recommend the Group of Seven to the environmental networks. They may also contribute to sustaining the group. Perhaps collective action is also maintained by the common guiding principles (shared values) of the environmental organisations and the global nature of environmental protection.

If stable patterns of cooperation between the environmental NGOs are illustrated by the Group of Seven, issue based alliances between the environmental NGOs and other types of organisations at the European level are illustrated by the European Campaign for Clean Air.

ISSUE ALLIANCES: THE EUROPEAN CAMPAIGN FOR CLEAN AIR

As the name suggests, the campaign centres around the EU's existing and proposed legislation on air quality and motor vehicle emissions standards. Six European-level associations form the European core of the campaign, namely the European Bureau of Consumer Unions (BEUC), the European Citizen Action Service (ECAS), the EEB, the European Public Health Alliance (EPHA), T&E, and the Confederation of Family Organisations in the European Community (COFACE). ECAS assembled the associational core. After several meetings, the six issued a campaign document entitled *Memorandum By: The European Campaign for Clean Air. New EU Pollution Standards For Motor Vehicles and Air Quality Directives.*[9]

The memorandum outlines three reasons behind the campaign. First, the public's right to know about the levels of pollution affecting them. Second, the need to bring the public health and environmental aspects of air quality to the attention of the EU institutions. In particular, to ensure that all the stakeholder interests are brought into the consultation process, not just the oil and automobile industries, which were included under the framework of the European Auto Oil Programme. Third, the need to bring together different categories of interest (environmental, consumer, public health) in acknowledgement of the global scale and scope of air quality and pollution problems and EU policy and legislation. Whereas, the EEB and BEUC collaborated during the 1980s over the lead content in petrol, the larger coalition of interests is required in the 1990s to deal effectively with the myriad aspects of the proposed legislation.

The campaign seeks 'more recognition by governments and the EU Institutions that air pollution from motor vehicles causes premature deaths and exacerbates diseases among children and other groups in society as well as damages the environment'. In addition, 'EU legislation for the year 2000 should be based on the highest international standards, and best available technologies' (The European Campaign for Clean Air: 8).

The intention is to involve interests at the local and national levels in addition to the European, thereby presenting a truly Europe-wide campaign to the EU institutions. On the European side, the partner associations organise seminars to which they invite Commission officials and members of the European Parliament as well as representatives from the oil and automobile industries, national and international environmental and health experts and NGOs representing environmental, consumer and health interests at local, national and trans national levels. Press releases, letters to the Commissioners and Commission President are other examples of these European associations' collective actions.

When comparing the Group of Seven with the European Campaign for Clean Air two contrasting point are obvious. Whereas the Group of Seven is exclusive to environmental NGOs, the campaign amalgamates environmental and other types of interest group. While the Group of Seven collaborates on several subjects, the campaign focuses on one multifaceted issue.

Incentives for participating in the European Campaign for Clean Air

Is it possible to explain the involvement of environmental, citizen and consumer NGOs in this campaign by identifying possible selective incentives for participation? The strategic, policy oriented incentive for joining the coalition is quite evident. The campaign has an explicit influencing aim within the EU policy process. One of the reasons behind the campaign is the NGOs' wish to achieve equal recognition within the policy making process *vis-à-vis* emission standards for motor vehicles. This is an issue of access to the other policy actors, in particular the Commission services responsible for drafting legislative proposals. In this respect the Campaign for Clean Air can be viewed as the NGOs' reaction to the Commission's technical research initiative, the European Auto Oil Programme. This programme brought together the oil and automobile industries in an attempt to assess the most cost effective measures to achieve lower emissions from road transport to meet the EU's air quality objectives. By forming a coalition, the NGOs hope to have more access to, and a greater impact on, the institutions.

Information exchange and knowledge sharing may also feature as an incentive for joining the campaign. In common with the Group of Seven environmental NGOs, the organisations in the clean air coalition boast different areas of expertise and experiences of the European policy process. The coalition can draw on the European member associations' relations with the EU institutions including the Commission services and European Parliament standing committees. Since different types of NGOs are involved in the campaign their combined links to the institutions are quite comprehensive.

Sharing tasks and reducing organisations' (or more accurately their secretariats') workloads is a further incentive. In common with the Group of Seven, the campaign enables member NGOs to conserve resources while remaining active on the air quality issues.

Other factors influencing NGO participation in the European Campaign for Clean Air

As in the case of the Group of Seven, there may be reasons in addition to selective incentives for the creation and membership of the clean air campaign. They include the campaign's issue base, the role of the coalition organiser (entrepreneur), and other actors within the EU policy process. Because the campaign focuses on a particular issue, the subject of air quality standards and pollution from motor vehicles is the catalyst for collaboration between the six European-level NGOs. The organisations' shared interest in the issue and common goals are the coalition's galvanising factor.

From the outset of the clean air campaign, ECAS acted as a coalition broker (Hula, 1995). In other words ECAS fostered collaboration between the six organisations. ECAS's brokering role (to create coalitions between interest groups) is not exclusive to this campaign. In addition to the clean air campaign, ECAS has taken the lead in forming European-level coalitions such as the European Public Health Alliance (EPHA), the European Forum for the Arts and Heritage (EFAH) and the European Third Sector Training Network (REEN) (European Citizen Action Service, pamphlet).[10] Consequently, the role of ECAS as a coalition organiser/entrepreneur must feature in an examination of the clean air campaign. In the group formation literature the entrepreneur is the focus of exchange theory. Salisbury (1969: 25–6) examines how an entrepreneur may bear the start up costs for a group in exchange for a salaried position once the group is up and running. Macleod and McCulloch suggest that if the entrepreneur is responsible for group formation, 'this implies that the establishment of the group would owe more to the personal ambition of one or more individuals than to a commitment to influencing policy' (Macleod and McCulloch, 1996: 10). Since coalition formation is part of ECAS's remit and the Campaign for Clean Air has an explicit policy oriented aim, Salisbury's entrepreneur does not appear to be an accurate description of that organisation. Entrepreneurs pursuing collective goods or policy goals rather than self- advancement are included in subsequent developments of exchange theory (Sabatier, 1992: 107–9). The policy oriented aspect of the expanded theory provides a more appropriate description of ECAS's reason for organising the campaign. However, exchanging initial costs for a position within the coalition remains less convincing because within ECAS there is no formal secretariat organising the activities of the campaign. Instead the member NGOs assume this responsibility.

It is possible to view the campaign for clean air as a reaction to events and the actions of other organisations and institutions within the European policy process, namely the Commission and the two industry associations (the European Association of Automobile Manufacturers and the European Petroleum Industry Association) involved in the European Auto Oil Programme. The campaign memorandum states one of the reasons for forming the coalition as the NGOs' concern 'about the extent to which this process has become institutionalised in a Tripartite Commission and the two industries concerned' (The European Campaign for Clean Air: 1). If this interpretation is accepted, pluralist references to interest articulation and the ideas of countervailing sources of power should be considered as part of the explanation of the clean air campaign.

Once again, ideas and issues raised in the literature suggest several reasons for NGO participation in the European Campaign for Clean Air. In addition to selective incentives, the campaign's issue base for these political organisations stands out along with the NGOs' response to events in the policy process and the actions of the Commission and the oil and car industries. Organisational details, namely the role of ECAS as coalition broker, should also be considered as a factor in a possible explanation.

THE EU POLICY MAKING ENVIRONMENT AND ENVIRONMENTAL COLLECTIVE ACTION

The examination of collective action by environmental NGOs through the Group of Seven or in the European Campaign for Clean Air has made few references to the EU or any features in the policy process which may help or hinder environmental NGOs' collaborative activities. Several factors attracted the majority of environmental organisations to Brussels in the 1980s and early 1990s. Tony Long (1995) identifies financial incentives as funding is available to the NGOs via the structural funds and other EU programmes. The important role of EU financial support to the environmental movement is discussed by Marks and McAdam (1996). Their study of 'social movements and the changing structure of political opportunity in the European Union' examines the impact of European integration and the consequent institutional and political developments on social movements. They argue that the environmental movement has benefited from the integration process to a greater extent than other new social movements (Marks and McAdam, 1996: 113). In addition to the financial support (to the organisations directly and via programmes and grants) they consider the Commission and European Parliament 'attitudinally sympathetic and structurally open to the interests of the movement' (*ibid*.: 114). There is even a suggestion that the Commission provides financial assistance to the NGOs in order to make the EU more environmentally aware and reactive to the campaigns and lobbying activities of the environmental organisations (*ibid*.). This positive setting has enabled the NGOs to establish themselves at the European level and pursue their goals within the policy process.

The EU's activities in the environmental arena are another encouraging element. The EU has gained considerable competence in environmental protection since the 1967 directive on the classification, packaging and labelling of dangerous substances. Besides legislation and research initiatives, the scale and scope of the environmental action programmes has increased since their introduction in 1973. Marks and McAdam comment on the way in which the environmental movement has had considerable success in transferring strategies employed at the national level to the European level (*ibid*.: 115). If the agreeable climate created by institutional attitudes and actions (with the exception of the Council of Ministers) encourages the environmental NGOs' participation in the EU policy process, it could be argued that it also benefits their collaborative ventures. Perhaps it would be misleading to imply that the institutions directly promote organisational alliances. However, it seems fair to suggest that the EU is 'attitudinally sympathetic and structurally open' to the EEB or WWF when they act alone and when they act collectively with the Group of Seven or other types of interests in issue based alliances.

CONCLUDING REMARKS

Environmental NGOs participate in various types of collective action at the European level. The Group of Seven and the European Campaign for Clean Air are indicative of the more stable (though informal) patterns of cooperation and issue based alliances that exist between the main environmental networks and other types of interest operating within the EU environmental arena. Hula's (1995) argument that political coalitions comprising organisations already active in the policy process are more readily mobilised than groups of individuals is appropriate for the above discussion of collective action involving the environmental NGOs. These NGOs are routine actors, pursuing political goals, within the EU policy process. Although collective goods, in the form of policy outcomes, may fail to mobilise individual participation, they are an important motivating factor for these environmental organisations. There may also be a role for selective incentives in organisational collective action and coalition formation by the environmental NGOs. Indeed, information, greater influence within the policy process and resource savings are significant, exclusive benefits from membership of stable collective forums and issue alliances. Other factors, including organisational and operational aspects of collaborative structures such as the Group of Seven and the European Campaign for Clean Air, seem to be conducive to participation.

Of course, the Group of Seven and the European Campaign for Clean Air are merely indicative of environmental collective action at the European level. More permanent cooperation exists between environmental and other organisations (business and labour) in the form of European Partners for the Environment (EPE) and other issue based alliances exist, for example environmental NGOs at the national and European level coordinated their activities over the trans European transport network. Further investigation of these collective actions may reveal the extent to which the selective incentives and other factors discussed above encourage environmental NGOs, to coordinate their activities and collaborate at the EU level.

NOTES

1 Information from interview with the author, July 1996.
2 Information from telephone conversation with the author, August 1996.
3 Information from interview with author, June 1995.
4 This undated pamphlet describes the organisational structure and activities of Climate Network Europe and was obtained from the organisation's Brussels office.
5 This undated pamphlet describes the organisational structure and activities of BirdLife International and the European Community Office and was obtained from the organisation's Brussels office.
6 Information from interview with the author, July 1995, and from NGO pamphlets.
7 Information from an interview with a representative from an environmental NGO, June 1995.
8 Information from an interview with a representative from an environmental NGO, July 1996.
9 This undated document was obtained from one of the participating NGOs.
10 This undated document describes the aims and activities of the European Citizen Action Service and was obtained from the organisation's Brussels office.

9 Collective attraction – the new political game in Brussels

Mark Aspinwall

The introduction to this volume referred to Alexis de Tocqueville and his well-known views on civic associability in the United States: 'Americans of all ages, all conditions, and all dispositions constantly form associations.... religious, moral, serious, futile, extensive or restricted, enormous or diminutive' (de Tocqueville, 1946: 376). Somewhat less well-known is his concurrent observation that a 'virtuous materialism' is the principal motivating force behind Americans' actions, such that 'the desire of acquiring the good things of this world is the prevailing passion of the American people' (*ibid.*: 403). De Tocqueville effectively anticipated the debate that developed more than 130 years later over the reasons for collective action. Do individuals and other actors collaborate because of a rationally determined opportunity to improve their lot materially? Or are socially derived impulses behind their decisions? This question, one of the most basic in the social sciences, remains unresolved.

In this study, the only one to assess systematically the causes of trans national collective action among non state interests, the striking conclusion is that collective action is far more complex than conventional theories allow. In the tug of war with national advocacy systems, EU-level groups are using increasingly sophisticated means to attract allegiance, including group specialisation, diversification of political objectives, and temporary alliances. In addition, both the groups themselves and the EU institutions are socialising private interests to the efficacy of Euro representation.

EU politics is an untidy system, and its complexity makes collective action problematic but also increases its urgency. An intricate enmeshing of supranational policies has ushered in a cooperative federalism without a state (Mény *et al.*, 1996: 17), in which authority is held simultaneously in Brussels, nation states, and to some extent substate regions. This means that the locus of power is ambiguous and changing. At the same time, greater economic openness is permitting, encouraging, and even forcing more trans national activity. How are non state actors to understand, never mind influence, such a system without international collaboration?

The argument that 'rational, self-interested individuals will not act to achieve their common or group interests' (Olson, 1971: 2) could hardly have anticipated EU politics at the end of the century. The nationally based actors who are making decisions about whether to join Euro groups are themselves organised in order to achieve common or group interests. These political actors very often are choosing between the best options for achieving their existing aims, and they have shown themselves capable of overcoming the cultural, linguistic, and political transaction costs involved in collective action in a multinational setting. Yet material gain – at least among economic interests – is never far from the surface. As Grant Jordan explains in Chapter 2, the reality is that firms' selfish objectives 'are perhaps not obtainable at all without collective action and can only be provided through collective means'. The growth and complexity of regulation has a profound influence upon economic interests. They must be in a position to influence regulators, and this makes lobbying a far more important objective of collective action in the late twentieth century than it has ever been previously. The paradox of rational choice collective action theory is that without collective action, selfish material aims may never be maximised; but collective action would appear to be impossible because of the difficulty of fairly sharing (and knowing) costs.

In addition to the complexity of motivations behind collective action in the European Union, the contributors to this volume have highlighted the growing importance of interest groups for the operation of the European institutions, as well as the reverse – the growing importance of the institutions for interest groups. The ongoing development of the EU comprises a positive sum game for European interest groups. The technical nature and interrelatedness of regulatory issues, and the role of the member states in its formulation and subsequent administration, mean they have more input at both the European and national levels. Moreover, in the advocacy void created by the absence of strong EU-level political parties, interests have been able – and encouraged – to express views on issues of relevance. The partial shift of power away from the Council of Ministers since 1986, and the growth of policy competence at the supranational level, have increased the vacuum effect of the void. It is this juxtaposition of supranational interest group pluralism and national statism that makes the new politics of the EU so fascinating and unpredictable. In this sense, EU politics is a major departure in Europe and indeed more closely resembles American politics, where strong parties representing class or religious groups, and an aloof civil service acting in the national interest are both anathema.

The chapters in this book have focused attention not just on theoretical issues and business groups, but also under-studied groups such as consumers and the professions. While these remain in the minority (63 per cent of all Euro groups represent businesses), they are becoming more numerous and more important in the policy process. This can be attributed to the completion of the Single European Act (since when 69 per cent of EU-level public interest groups have come into existence) and the opportunities presented by the European institutions to become involved in the policy process.

This final chapter draws out some themes common to the contributions, which come under the broad headings of the changing nature of interest representation, the complexity of incentives, the endurance of national distinctions, and the role of institutions. What becomes strikingly apparent from a reading of these contributions is that the role and structure of European interests have fractured dramatically, to embrace a wide array of group types organised for many different purposes. Moreover, the European institutions, especially the Commission, are actively involved in the creation and maintenance of these groups. At the same time, national differences remain potent, and interests retain both cultural and economic allegiances to member states.

THE CHANGING NATURE OF EUROPEAN INTEREST GROUPS

A key theme uniting the chapters in this book is that European interest representation has become increasingly diversified and specialised. More than ever, Euro groups are protagonists, seeking to influence policy rather than simply monitor events (though data presented in Chapter 1 show that information is still very important). They have evolved into a multitude of groups, targeted at specific issues, some only for a limited amount of time. Euro groups have also responded to the group shopping tendency of national interests by evolving a wide range of groups, distinguished by ideology or by other characteristics of the interests they wish to attract.

This suggests that representative forums have matured, developing for particular purposes, often competing for members and presenting actors with a choice. As Maria Green Cowles points out in Chapter 5, for big firms, the choice has increasingly been to join direct firm organisations (which comprise 30 per cent of all Euro business groups). Initially acting to supplement industry federations, direct firm membership groups have become an alternative to them. Early groups like the Ravenstein Group, the European Enterprise Group, and the Groupe des Présidents had attempted to transform existing organisations. Later groups, like the EU Committee of the American Chamber of Commerce and the European Round Table of Industrialists, were forces in their own right, competing with industry federations for members and influence.

However, the picture is complicated – survey results show that, over time, the number of business direct firm organisations has not grown relative to federations; this would suggest that the shift has primarily been one of a greater reliance on existing direct firm organisations (although new big business direct firm organisations have been created as well). An important and as yet unresolved question is whether federations of national associations increasingly present the most viable advocacy option for smaller firms.

In addition to a more specialised form of organisation, the role of big business groups has evolved as well. Initially established as select social clubs, they transformed into a series of intra-industry sectoral associations, then inter-sectoral associations, and finally, to (often) temporary groups rallying round a particular policy issue. The tendency has been toward greater focus on particular problems, first within sectors, then in cross sectoral cooperation, and finally on specific issues. Moreover, whereas business interests used to be more clublike, responsive, and monitoring in their aims, the evolution of business representation shows a growing determination to influence events in Brussels, rather than simply monitor them.

While business representation appears to be fragmenting along a large–small functional differentiation, consumer representation has fragmented along ideological lines, where the specialisation of Euro groups corresponds to nationally rooted divisions over conceptions of the public interest (see Young, Chapter 7). This is treated in more detail below, but one of the most important results of this division of labour is that it removes ideological conflict from intra-Euro group deliberations. The fracturing of environmental interest representation is due not to functional or ideological specialisation but to the increased competence of the EU, funding opportunities, and encouraging signals sent by Brussels, all of which caused a rapid proliferation of European offices in the 1980s. The EEB was the only environmental group in Brussels until the 1980s, when several others followed suit. Prior to establishing themselves as separate European groups, these others used the EEB to stay connected to the policy process in Brussels.

Unlike consumers, environmental groups share ideological precepts, as Ruth Webster points out in her discussion of the seven principal groups (see Chapter 8). Because of the trans-boundary nature of the issue, they are global in scope and outlook, and even the self-consciously European environmental groups usually have members from well beyond the EU's borders. Moreover, they are made up of various sorts of members – environmental NGOs, national environmental associations, and others. While these groups are politically active in the EU policy making process, they also collect information, raise funds, and participate in various other tasks.

Nevertheless, the idiosyncratic organisational structure of the groups leads to important differences in effectiveness. Some are highly centralised, with authority in international offices; others leave important decision making to member associations. Indeed, the Brussels office is not the peak office in most cases – international environmental organisations such as Greenpeace and Friends of the Earth predated their Brussels offices and keep important decision making power at the international level. In the case of Greenpeace, this means that the Brussels office performs a perfunctory agency role. The same was initially true of Friends of the Earth Europe, although it has evolved into an actor in its own right.

A comparison can be made with the associations of the professions, whose Brussels offices are also quite weak (see Chapter 6). The most important distinction between the Euro groups in the professions occurs along sectoral lines, while the pan sectoral groups are weak and divided. But in contrast to environmental groups, the reason for the weakness of the associations of the professions is the power of national groups, not the power of international groups. Therefore, the history of policy making in a particular sphere, and the relationship between the state and the relevant groups at the national level, is an important determinant of the structure and power of Euro groups.

Further evidence of specialisation among Euro groups is their occasional spin-off of new groups in order to capitalise on a perceived new 'market' or to respond to a demand for new representation. The European Trade Union Confederation (ETUC), for example, generated both the EURO-C consumer group and the professional association EUROCADRES. EURO-C was formed in 1994 to represent trade union consumer concerns, and was partly in response to changes in the eligibility of trade union representatives to participate in the Commission's Consumers Consultative Council (Young, Chapter 7). EUROCADRES was formed in 1993 to represent salaried, unionised professional and managerial staff (Chapter 6).

One of the most significant ways European interests have become more specialised is to make increasing use of *ad hoc* collaboration, a sort of disposable collective action. Nowhere is this tendency more striking than in the environmental field, where a sort of regularised '*ad hoc*ism' takes place under the Group of Seven rubric. One or more of the NGOs may decline to participate on particular issues if they so desire, lending the group an atmosphere of à la carte flexibility. However, as Webster points out (Chapter 8), they 'share fundamental ideas and principles about the environment'. Referring to Sabatier's typology, she suggests that these deep core beliefs ensure the continuity of the group over the long term.

The same is true of the business community, where a new tendency among business groups has been to form *ad hoc* alliances to address specific problems or policy challenges, many of which have come in the aftermath of the single market. In addition, *ad hoc* coalitions have formed across the business–consumer–environmental divides, as issues are interpreted as having an impact on a wide range of interests. The chapters by Young, Webster, and Cowles (7, 8 and 5) offer numerous examples of these *ad hoc* groups. Pollution, for example, transcends not only physical boundaries but also social groups, and so in 1995 BEUC joined with a number of citizen, environmental, and other groups to form the European Campaign for Clean Air. In addition, BEUC has collaborated with a loose alliance of firms known as ECAR on the Commission's proposals to extend intellectual property protection to car spare parts, and COFACE, EURO-C, and EURO COOP jointly tackled the question of hormone use in food products. Business groups have also blurred the distinction between producer and consumer interests, as the example of ENER-G8 shows. ENER-G8 is a coalition of eight major firms in energy-intensive industry, whose purpose is to represent the firms' interests as energy consumers. Firms also represent their interests as transport consumers (in the trucking, aviation, and maritime modes), though this is done through federations of national associations.

Part of the reason for this evolution of Euro groups is that their objectives have changed. They have become more determined to exert political influence, as the next section shows. In addition, nationally based groups have a choice of methods for exercising voice. The increased availability of information on European affairs and technological advancement in its delivery remove the need to be in Brussels. The evidence from Denmark shows that 'Euro group membership is but one among several routes to policy making in Brussels' (see Chapter 4). Once they have decided to engage in lobbying, national associations consciously choose a variety of routes to influence European political events. They may join Euro groups, take action in Brussels by themselves, or lobby the Danish government, depending on the type of organisation and the issue.

THE MIXED BAG OF INCENTIVES

Most of the contributions to this volume point to the difficulty of corralling incentives into discrete categories such as material and social, collective and selective. Actors are motivated in numerous ways, and different actors may join the same group for different reasons. A plurality of rationalities exists, depending not only on the member but on the type of representative organisation (see Chapter 2). Jordan rejects the strictly utilitarian basis for business mobilisation, and with it Offe's distinction between the utilitarian incentives underlying business mobilisation and the redefinition of interests necessary to bring organised labour together. He sees both a utilitarian and social rationality in business associability: 'membership of business organisations is distinguished by its lack of immediate self-interest'; and he raises a number of potential motivating factors that are not utility maximising but that plausibly invoke collective action among firms nonetheless. One of the conclusions is that firms do not seem to be concerned with particular outcomes. Doing the right thing, hedging bets, dealing with uncertainty, and similar motivations figure prominently in the rational firm's calculation.

The empirical chapters bear out the multitude of incentives drawing interests to Europe. Business, consumers, environmentalists, and professional interests are drawn (to a greater or lesser degree) by the possibility of influencing new policies, gaining information, the entrepreneurial role of group leaders, funding, to counter the influence of competing groups, social interaction, a normative feeling that contribution is good, the signals from the Commission, and many other factors. Jordan allows for material motives in his array of incentives attracting business to Brussels, and Sidenius demonstrates empirically that collective material incentives do motivate business (and other) groups. Moreover, big business, now more politically attuned to Brussels than ever, is arguably in search of policies that will materially improve their competitive position. Though there is little hard data, uncertainty also appears to play a role. The ambiguous nature of incentives – leading to a perception that issues and agendas might not be fully known, much less influenced, until the member has joined – seems to impel membership.

We see evidence, particularly in the business realm (see Chapters 4 and 5) that a gradual change has taken place in the attractiveness of Euro groups. Members have become more alert to the possibilities of policy change in Brussels, and as such are demanding that Euro groups provide influence. Groups want to see specific policies adopted (or rejected, as the case may be). Therefore, in a relative sense, collective benefits (public goods) have become more important than selective benefits. Where selective benefits are important, they are both socially oriented (as in the satisfaction of having contributed to a cause) and material – where market information and policy influence are made available to members.

Though many groups seek to influence policy, the transition to political influence is especially marked in the business realm. Cowles points out that the incentives attracting big business changed from social interaction and information gathering to economic gain and political lobbying from the 1960s to the 1990s. This occurred as business leaders became aware of what was at stake in Brussels, as the competence of the European Community grew, and as Commission officials made conscious efforts to involve business leaders in decision making. Cram and Young (in Chapters 3 and 7) demonstrate how the swelling of activity in Brussels is due in no small measure to the active creation by Eurocrats of an environment conducive to dialogue and joint problem-solving. Consistent with what the survey data showed us in Chapter 1, big business responded in a positive way to the growing authority of the European institutions. Interestingly, however, the survey also suggested that business groups believe information remains nearly as important to their members as influence. This apparent contradiction deserves further research, but could plausibly be explained in a number of ways: first, that group leaders are unaware of their members' preferences; second, that a distinction exists between big business (politically motivated) and small firms (information motivated); third, that the shift in incentives has been relatively small.

The Danish case illustrates this paradox. Whereas Cowles demonstrates the new activism of big business, taking initiatives with the premeditated intent of influencing policy, Sidenius shows in his survey results that influence was less important to Danish associations than either information gathering or liaison creation (this was the case for every type of association, including business), although policy influence has increased in importance since 1985.[1] It is possible that the difference is due to a distinction between associations and firms as actors, with associations acting principally as information conduits in the first instance, while direct firm organisations are geared more toward policy action, particularly the ones representing large firms with a track record of lobbying. Alternatively, the difference may be due to the fact that having an impact at EU level has not traditionally been important to many Danish business associations.[2] At any rate, it is a potentially important finding (and deserves further research), because of the prevalence of both types of organisation in Brussels.

An equally important conclusion of the Danish research is the holistic view of incentives taken by national associations. The evidence suggests that incentives are not viewed in isolation from one another by associations, but as a package. When Euro groups are valued highly by national associations, it is for many reasons, not just a few, and 'the more important one task is considered to be, the more importance is attached to other tasks as well. The extent and diversity of political activity – and the socialisation of members – creates a demand for various services supplied by Euro groups' (Chapter 4). A circular and mutually reinforcing demand creation system emanates from the interest groups themselves.

This circular and mutually reinforcing demand creation system may have its genesis in individual policy entrepreneurship. For example, the professional group SEPLIS was created by a former Commission official (Chapter 6); likewise, M. Von Geldern, a senior director of Euratom, organised the Groupe des Présidents to increase interaction between the business community and the Commission (Chapter 5). Though most of the business community did not share his desire for greater European integration, he was able to draw them in with the promise of information about Commission activities. However, as the Danish case shows, incentives are not isolated services, but are socially derived. They are learned, and cognitive connections are made between the various benefits – perceived and real – stemming from Euro group membership. As Jane Mansbridge argues (1992), interest groups change the preferences of members by bringing new information to light and by creating a deliberative environment within which actors' views on various challenges and opportunities are conditioned.

This socialisation tendency is supported by another – paradoxical – finding from Sidenius's study. Among national associations that have established themselves in Brussels, there is greater appreciation of the role of Euro groups than among those associations still located in Denmark. Therefore, the attitudes of associations toward Euro groups appear to be polarised – the more involved national associations become, the more important they perceive membership to be. Jordan also draws our attention to the role business groups play in socialising members. Drawing on Plotke, he notes the apparent need for business to interpret economic events in a normatively similar fashion, which in turn helps firms make a commitment to achieve a collective goal.

Socialisation comes not simply from a learning process engendered by presence in Brussels, but also from overlapping membership, as Webster points out in this volume. WWF International, for example, is an associate member of the European Federation for Transport and Environment, and various transport groups are also members. Promiscuous joining mitigates uncertainty about coalition partners, but whether it also stimulates collective action depends on other factors, such as the decision making power of the European groups.

Most incentives have come from some combination of perceived or real benefits emanating from the European level, but in several cases, the external world provided a rationale for groups to form and members to join. The environmental area is an especially potent example of this. The trans-boundary nature of pollution brought about international collective action among environmental groups several decades ago, and at the European level from 1974. But environmental groups are unusual among European interests, precisely because they are so internationalised – organising across borders well in advance of European stimuli. Though they were also profoundly influenced by external events, big business groups were closely tied to member states until the 1980s, when a combination of events, such as recession and increased competition, forced a rethink of their strategies and undermined their 'national champion' status (Chapter 5). They also had to deal with new standards coming from international bodies, such as the code of conduct for multinationals proposed by the OECD. Likewise, consumer interests are affected by global forums, albeit in the limited areas of food quality and technical standards. Most groups involved in consumer advocacy at the EU level were created more or less directly by groups operating at the international level (Chapter 7).

We have been presented with many collective action success stories in these chapters. Has the collective action problem – brought to our attention more than thirty years ago by Mancur Olson – been solved? Earlier I described the void in EU politics in which interest groups have new incentives to organise in Brussels. The cases presented in the preceding chapters seem to confirm this growing Euro-enthusiasm, and for certain types of actors under certain conditions, collective action does not appear to be problematic. The relatively small number of national consumer associations, for example, limits the latent population and mitigates the potential free rider problem. Furthermore, they are in the business of political advocacy; their avenues are limited by scarce resources and the consequent inability to take direct action, as firms do. Thus, political realities can limit options and encourage membership of European-level interest groups. As Grant Jordan explains, 'if an organisation seeks to attain some important end then it is likely to enter with some enthusiasm into any alliance that helps it secure this. . . . [We] are dealing with a how rather than a why matter' (Chapter 2)

In these cases, selective incentives are rarely necessary to motivate actors. Instead, Euro groups are created and joined by determined political actors who tend to share a culture of associability, at least in certain countries. Even actors from non EU countries are commonly to be found in Euro groups. Nowhere is this dynamic more obvious than in the collaboration between environmental NGOs. Driven by their commitment and chronic activism, their experience in the rest of the world, and their cross pollination of various NGOs, environmental groups seem to have very little trouble acting together on European political issues. The Group of Seven anticipated the Maastricht Treaty, and organised in order to help influence it as well as to increase contact with DG XI (Chapter 8).

Thus, the evidence compiled seems to justify the view that collective action at the EU level comes as a near automatic response to the desire to achieve some primordial objective. However, we need to exercise some caution. For a start the numbers should make us suspicious. While some 693 European level groups are now in existence, in Denmark alone there are an estimated 1,900 organised groups. In the United States there are roughly 23,000 non profit membership organisations of national scope (Burek, 1993). Counting only trade, business, commercial, environmental, and agricultural organisations there are 4,934 established national groups. Many of these are not politically active and most are not located near Washington, but the sheer scale of associability is a salutary reminder of the under-development of Euro representation. It is true that the European Union does not have anything like the competence over policy enjoyed by the member states or the US federal government. Moreover, the member states retain important roles in implementation, administration, and enforcement, even in those areas where the EU does have competence. But the explanation for the relatively low number does not lie simply with the lack of EU authority. Rather it has to do with the rootedness of national politics: interests remain tied in important ways to the politics of their home countries.

THE IMPORTANCE OF NATIONAL POLITICS

In truth we know much more about the successful cases of European collective action than we do about the failures, although we have evidence in this volume from Danish politics, consumer advocacy, and the professions that Euro groups are not all they could be. Is it possible to surmise whence these problems in Euro associability arise? The historical institutionalist approach employed by Laura Cram (Chapter 3) in discussing the EU institutions also speaks in important ways to the experience of some interests who remain doggedly bound to national-level political systems. If the 40-year history of the European Union and its institutional predecessors creates a certain path dependency, we might expect the far longer history of European states to influence interest advocacy as well.

Indeed, policy making at the national level has a great deal of momentum behind it. Cultural and historical links between the state and domestic social groups have impressive force, impeding European participation of national associations of the professions and some national consumer groups. As Peter Hall (1986: 18) noted, there are 'structural consistencies behind the persistence of distinctive national patterns of policy'. The evidence for the relevance of national context abounds in this volume. But the obstacles manifest themselves in different ways. In the professions, they have stymied European collaboration; among consumer interests they have encouraged it, mainly to ensure the viability of distinctive ideological approaches.

In the professions, the lack of mobility across national frontiers, 'extreme differences in the relationship between the state and the professions between member states' and different national traditions of interest organisation helped impede effective EU organisation (see Chapter 6). One of the implications of these persistent national cleavages is that members of the Euro groups that do exist to represent the professions demand far different behaviour, than do members of more active associations. SEPLIS members, for instance, 'sought to limit its role to that of a listening post and information provider' because they wanted to take political action themselves (Chapter 6). Moreover, the three peak-level associations are all weak (with the possible exception of EUROCADRES because of its parent ETUC) and rarely even speak to each other. The growth of *ad hoc* collaboration that is a rapidly evolving feature of the Euro group landscape has not touched the Jurassic Park of professional interest representation.

In addition to these cross sectoral groups, sectoral professional associations exist at the European level, but these are also marked by bottom heaviness: that is, the national elements are far stronger than the European offices which nominally tie them together. All in all:

> the extent of associational fragmentation, locations outside Brussels, undivided (into European) international associations, sectoral associations not affiliated to peak associations, parallel national associations with Brussels offices, and 'empty shell' groups in professional fields is indicative of weak and problematic patterns of collective action.
>
> (Greenwood, Chapter 6 this volume)

This weakness is due to two factors – one is the dearth of European competence over areas of interest to these associations; the other is the strong link many professions have to national regulatory regimes. These national regimes are tenacious not simply because of the historical weight behind them, but because they are tied to normative social and economic questions such as the proper level of regulation, public access to services, and the degree of state control of services. In the UK, for instance, the professions tend to be self-regulating, exercising social closure; in France by contrast, the regulation of professions is controlled by the state. Even the 1984 agreement at the Fontainebleau summit to take a catholic, cross sectoral approach to mutual recognition of professional qualifications, and the ensuing General Systems Directives of 1988 and 1991, failed to promote effective and powerful Euro groups in the field of the professions. Such is the power and inertia of national regulation.

Consumer groups are also affected by national context. Consumers from the northern/core states show a much greater aptitude for organisation at both the national and European levels than consumers from the southern/peripheral states. The latter fail to join some Euro groups; lower dues are used to encourage them to join (see Chapter 7), which arguably represents a form of selective incentive. However, the important point is that cultural variation between member states has produced a much different pattern of European collective action in the consumer field than in the field of the professions. In the

consumer field, it has *encouraged* Euro groups to form in order to
ensure the continued vitality of distinct national objectives, cultural
orientations, and traditions of representation amid the evolution of
EU institutions. In consumer representation, five principal groups
exist in Brussels, but they range in emphasis from the European
Consumers' Organisation (BEUC), which is the most liberal and is
built upon product monitoring groups in some member states; to the
Confederation of Family Organisations in the European Community
(COFACE), which is primarily concerned with the health, education,
and justice aspects of consumer affairs (Chapter 7). European collective action in this sense can be seen as motivated not simply by
incentives coming from the European level, but also by a desire to
replicate national styles in Brussels. It suggests that the ideological
and cultural divisions between member states have been transmitted
upwards to the advocacy community in Brussels.

The same trend exists in business advocacy, but it is more developed. While UNICE – a federation of national associations – was
created in the mould of the continental style of representation, direct
firm membership is more clearly a British-driven style. This direct firm
membership style took hold long after the federation UNICE was
created, partly because the national champion status of big business
prevented them from taking part in European-level advocacy in the
early years of the EC. Moreover, continental custom did not welcome
direct lobbying by firms, which raised suspicions of political manipulation (Chapter 5).

Therefore, one of the most important implications of the growth in
direct representation of big business was that it signalled an erosion of
obstacles to cross border collective action at the national level.
National champions were on the decline, facing greater competition
within Europe and from beyond Europe; the continental cultural
taboo against firms directly engaging in political lobbying also
seemed to be eroding. The hierarchical relationship between continental firms and their local and national associations was undermined by the presence of big companies in Brussels. It was in this
context that the direct firm membership organisations began to
assume the role (mentioned earlier) of a relative shift in emphasis
towards representing big business. In short, the distinction in representation styles is no longer rooted in territorial differences. As Cowles pointed out, the Brussels experience has even begun to transform
national political representation (a reversal of early experience) as
organisational patterns in Brussels are grafted onto national industry
federations.

The experience in Denmark also demonstrates how supranational collective action is limited by entrenched state-based institutions. Even in a country long noted for its culture of political activity and associability 'not all politically active interest associations actually join a Euro group' (Chapter 4), even where there is EU political activity that affects their interests. Although there are significant differences between the propensities of national associations to join Euro groups, depending on their characteristics, the way they are affected by the EU, their objectives, and the incentives before them, more than one-third of Danish groups which are influenced by EU activity do not join Euro groups. Labour organisations are more likely than any other type of actor – including business – to join Euro groups, to engage in political activity in Brussels on their own account, and to lobby on EU affairs within Denmark. This finding undermines assumptions of business interest predominance in EU advocacy, at least from the Danish perspective. Moreover, some national organisations have even considered exiting Euro groups, and according to Sidenius's findings some form of rational analysis over costs and benefits usually lies behind this deliberation (see also Chapter 2 on the exit option).

THE ROLE OF THE INSTITUTIONS

One of the most significant conclusions to be drawn from virtually all the authors in this volume is that the role of the European institutions is crucial to understanding how incentives for collective action are produced, disseminated, and interpreted. Participation in the policy process, initiating research, funding group development, and promoting ideas are especially important institutional roles. In addition, as Cram points out in Chapter 3, propagating the symbols and myths of 'European-hood' are a less tangible but equally powerful means of attracting interests. Thus, the socialisation effort that groups undertake to condition members to the efficacy of the group is practised by the Commission as well.

Like Jordan, Cram stresses the social aspects of membership. Both authors are deeply suspicious of the notion that collective action is motivated by material self-interest. Whether it is to reduce uncertainty, behave in a socially acceptable way, or to be part of a glorious new endeavour, group memebers respond to the social aspect of European collective action. It is this sense that something important is going on in Brussels – which produces a desire for belonging, unclear and intangible though the final result may be – that seems to draw interest groups in greater numbers than ever before. This magnetism is in no small measure a product of the deliberate actions of the European institutions.

Cram argues that interests follow authority, but also points to the importance of learning, of structure, of purposive agency on the part of the EU institutions, and of the creation and replication of the idea of Europe as forces impelling collective action. These act in a powerful way to attract interests even before authority is located in Brussels; moreover, the initial attraction builds momentum toward greater European legitimacy as cognitive links are established between group formation and political outcomes. Interests 'shoot where the ducks are' but also shoot where the decoys are, and a mutually reinforcing process is set in motion: interests are attracted by authority, but authority is partly created by the legitimacy of a constituency. 'The development of particular norms and standard operating procedures does not come about purely by chance but may actively have been encouraged by the semi autonomous EU institutions' (Cram, Chapter 3).

Empirical evidence for the importance of the institutions can be found in the business, environmental, labour, consumer, and social spheres. As the institutions developed, interests followed: UNICE was created in the wake of the establishment of the European Economic Community, and it was Commission entrepreneurship that brought business leaders to Brussels as early as the 1960s. Consumer organisations, which predated the SEA, increased their activity afterwards. The proliferation of environmental groups in the 1980s was partly due to expanded European-level competence.

But there is more to this story. The Commission actively sought the participation of existing interests in the integration process before new policies were in existence, and also sought to create new interests which would represent segments of society unrepresented in Brussels. For example, the Commission made a conscious decision in advance of the Single European Act to involve the business community in its decision making process. Moreover, the creation of the consumer group BEUC was promoted by the Commission, which also helped to develop COFACE and EURO COOP through a series of study days in Brussels. It continues to provide about one-third of the operating budgets of the consumer organisations in Brussels and provides funding for EUROCADRES indirectly through ETUC. It also contributes to the funding needs of all environmental organisations except Greenpeace. Interests have begun to aggregate in the areas of homelessness, poverty, family policy, old age, and disability, due to the intervention of the Commission and despite the lack of binding legislation in these fields.

Though the Commission is not the only European institution to which interests are attracted and by which they are affected, it is the most important. Of course the Council of Ministers – including its attendant working parties and COREPER offices – provides a focus for interest groups once they get to Brussels. The Court of Justice is also having an increasing impact on European integration. Likewise the European Parliament has greater power in limited areas and has seen an increase in lobbying groups at its doors. But unlike the Court of Justice, which sits in judgement of past events; unlike the Council, which represents national interests; and unlike the Parliament, which does not have enough coherence to speak with one voice, it is primarily the Commission which is able to generate the ideas necessary to involve new interests in its efforts. It is able to do this because it is responsible for drafting policy proposals, which need expert input, and because it has an overtly pan European outlook. Moreover, whereas conflict resolution is weighted toward territorial issues in the Council, and ideological issues in the Parliament, the Commission is the institution where functional conflict is resolved. Thus, the incentives that socialise interests to European solutions come from the Commission most importantly.

TOWARD A EURO POLITY?

The contributors to this volume have explored the growth of interests, the changing nature of Euro groups, the diversity of motives behind their membership decisions, the important interaction between member state and European politics, and the complex pattern of institutional incentives. The importance of the European level for interest groups is now beyond question; they in turn are contributing to the process of European integration. Collective action between interests, like collective action between states, helps to knit together formerly disparate networks of actors, and futher the process of European integration. But it is unlikely that Euro politics will lead to a breakdown of the national model of state–society relations in favour of a new European polity. Rather, it appears that a positive sum game is emerging in which interests have a greater say in Brussels while also retaining their historically specific roles in the member states.

Many unanswered questions remain. The interaction and mutual effect of national and EU systems of interest representation has only been touched on briefly in this volume, and needs a great deal of exploration. In particular, the transformation of national politics should be treated in a comparative manner to determine how the emerging political system in Brussels affects long-standing relationships between the state and society in the member states. How widespread is the practice of emulation – where national associations adapt to the organisational style of either EU federations or other national associations? Do EU federations join national associations as a means of influencing national politics?

We would benefit from further work in all these areas and we also need to know why groups fail to form, why they go bust, and why they lose members. Even if it is true that collective action is unproblematic once a common political objective is found, it does not necessarily follow that the lack of more groups is due to the lack of common political objectives. A further issue is the distinction between the logic of membership and the logic of influence: an examination of group behaviour would yield important insights into how group creation and growth is translated into concrete achievement.

NOTES

1 However, it is important to note that business associations in particular seek specific information, which is more relevant to policy influence than general information.
2 I thank Niels Sidenius for this point.

Bibliography

Alter, K. and Meunier-Aitsahalia, S. (1994) 'Judicial Politics in the European Union: European Integration and the Pathbreaking Cassis de Dijon Decision', *Comparative Political Studies*, 26, 4: 536–61.

Andersen, S. and Eliassen, K. (eds) (1993) *Making Policy in Europe: The Europeification of National Policy-Making*, London: Sage.

——(1993) 'Complex Policy-Making: Lobbying the EC', in S. Andersen and K. Eliassen (eds), *Making Policy in Europe: The Europeification of National Policy-Making*, London: Sage.

ANEC (1995a) European Association for the Coordination of Consumer Representation in Standardisation: *Consumer participation in standardisation*, ANEC 95/GA/56, Brussels: ANEC.

——(1995b) 'Directory of national and European consumer representatives in standardisation', ANEC 95/GA/60, Brussels: ANEC.

Aspinwall, M. (1995a) *Moveable Feast: Pressure Group Conflict and the European Community Shipping Policy*, Aldershot: Avebury.

——(1995b) 'International Integration or Internal Politics? Anatomy of a Single Market Measure', *Journal of Common Market Studies*, 33, 4: 475–99.

Averyt, W. (1975) 'Eurogroups, Clientela, and the European Community', *International Organization* 29, 4: 949–972.

Axelrod, R. (1984) *The Evolution of Co-operation*, New York: Basic Books.

BEUC (1995) The European Consumers' Organisation: *Annual Report 1994*, BEUC/55/95, Brussels: BEUC.

Boleat, M. (1994) 'The Role of Trade Associations', *Public Policy Review*, 43–6.

Bredima-Savopolou, A. and Tzoannos, J. (1990) *The Common Shipping Policy of the EC*, Amsterdam: Elsevier.

Bregnsbo, H. and Sidenius, N. C. (1993) 'Denmark: The National Lobby Orchestra', in M. P. C. M. van Schendelen (ed.) *National Public and Private EC Lobbying*, Aldershot: Dartmouth.

Bressand, A. (1990) 'Beyond Interdependence: 1992 as a Global Challenge', *International Affairs*, 66, 1: 47–65.

Bulmer, S. (1994a) 'The Governance of the European Union: A New Institutionalist Approach', *Journal of Public Policy*, 13, 4: 351–80.

——(1994b) 'Institutions and Policy Change in the European Communities: The Case of Merger Control' *Public Administration*, 72: 423–44.

Burek, D. (ed.) (1993) *Encyclopedia of Associations*, Detroit, Gale Research, Vol. 1. (National Organizations of the United States).

Burley, A. and Mattli, W. (1993) 'Europe Before the Court: A Political Theory of Legal Integration', *International Organisation*, 47: 41–76.

Butt Philip, A. (1985) *Pressure Groups in the European Community*, UACES Occasional Paper No. 2, London: UACES.

Butt Philip, A. and Gray, O. (eds) (1996) *Directory of Pressure Groups in the EU*, 2nd edn, London: Cartermill.

Button, K. and Fleming, M. (1992) 'The Changing Regulatory Regime Confronting the Professions in Europe', *The Antitrust Bulletin*, 37, Summer: 429–52.

Camerra-Rowe, P. (1994) 'Lobbying in the New Europe: Firms and Politics in the New Europe', Ph.D. thesis, Duke University, North Carolina, USA.

——(1995) 'Exit and the Collective Representation of Business in the European Union', Paper presented to ECSA Annual Conference, Charleston South Carolina, USA, May 11th, 1995.

Cawson, A. (1992) 'Interests, Groups and Public Policy-Making: the Case of the European Consumer Electronics Industry', in J. Greenwood, J. R. Grote and K. Ronit (eds) *Organised Interests and the European Community*, London: Sage.

CEG (1995) Consumers in Europe Group, *Annual Report 1994*, London: CEG.

Cerney, P. (1988) 'The Process of Personal Leadership: The Case of De Gaulle', *International Political Science Review*, 9: 2, 131–42.

——(1995) 'Globalization and the Changing Logic of Collective Action', *International Organization*, 49, 4: 595–625.

Clark, P. B. and Wilson J. (1961) 'Incentive Systems: A Theory of Organization', *Administrative Science Quarterly*, 6: 129–66.

Climate Action Network (1994) *International NGO Directory*, Brussels: CAN.

Climate Network Europe et al. (1995) *Greening the Treaty II: Sustainable Development in a Democratic Union. Proposals for the 1996 Intergovernmental Conference*, Utrecht, The Netherlands: Climate Network Europe.

Coen, D. (1995) 'The Firms' Political Action in the European Union', Paper prepared for presentation to the fourth biennial conference of the European Community Studies Association, Charleston, South Carolina, May 11–14.

——(1997) 'The Evolution of the Large Firm as a Political Actor in the European Union', *Journal of European Public Policy*, 4: 1, 91–108.

COFACE (April 1995) Confederation of Family Organisations in the European Community, 'List of member organisations', Brussels: COFACE.

Collie, L. (1993) 'Business Lobbying in the European Community: The Union of Industrial and Employers' Confederations of Europe', in S. Mazey and J. Richardson (eds) *Lobbying in the European Community*, Oxford: Oxford University Press.

Connelly, P. (1992) *Dealing With Whitehall*, London: Century Business.

Confédération Européenne des Cadres (1995) Presentation of the CEC, Brussels: CEC.

Cowles, M. G. (1994) *The Politics of Big Business in the European Community: Setting the Agenda for a New Europe*, Ph.D. thesis, The American University, Washington DC.

——(1995a) 'Setting the Agenda for a New Europe: The ERT and EC 1992', *Journal of Common Market Studies*, 33, 4: 501–26.

Cowles, M. G. (1995b) 'The European Round Table of Industrialists: The Strategic Player in European Affairs', in J. Greenwood (ed.) *European Casebook on Business Alliances*, Hemel Hempstead: Prentice-Hall.

—— (1996a) 'The EU Committee of AmCham: The Powerful Voice of American Firms in Brussels,' *Journal of European Public Policy*, 3, 3: 339–58.

—— (1996b) 'German Big Business: Learning to Play the European Game', *German Politics and Society*, 14, 3: 73–107.

—— (1996c) 'Business Means Europe – Who Built the Market?' in M. Bond, J. Smith and W. Wallace (eds) *Eminent Europeans*, London: Greycoat Press.

—— (1996d) 'Emerging Forms of State–Society Relations in the EU: The Case of Industry,' paper presented at the Conference of Europeanists, 14 March, Chicago.

—— (1997) *The TransAtlantic Business Dialogue*, working paper, Center for German and European Studies, Georgetown University, DC, USA: Center for German and European studies.

—— (forthcoming) 'Organising Industrial Coalitions', in H. Wallace and A. R. Young, (eds) *Participation and Policy-Making in the European Union*, London: Oxford University Press.

Cram, L. (1993) Calling the Tune Without Paying the Piper? Social Policy Regulation: The Role of the Commission in European Union Social Policy', *Policy and Politics*, 21: 135–46.

—— (1994) 'The European Commission as a Multi-Organization: Social Policy and IT Policy in the EU', *Journal of European Public Policy* 1, 2: 195–217.

—— (1995a) 'Business Alliances in the Information Technology Sector', in J. Greenwood (ed.) *European Casebook on Business Alliances*, Hemel Hempstead: Prentice-Hall.

—— (1995b) 'Policy Making and the Integration Process: Implications for Integration Theory', paper prepared for presentation to the European Community Studies Association biennial conference, Charleston, South Carolina, May 11–14.

—— (1996a) 'Integration Theory and the Study of the European Policy Process', in J. Richardson (ed.) *European Union: Power and Policy-making*, London: Routledge.

—— (1996b) 'Providing the Catalyst for Collective Action? The EU Institutions and Euro-Interests in EU Social Policy', in D. Fink Hafner and T. Cox (eds) *Into Europe? Perspectives from the UK and Slovenia*, Lubljana: Academic Press.

—— (1997) *Policy-Making and the European Union: Conceptual Lenses and the Integration Process*, London: Routledge.

Cyert, R. and March, J. (1963), *A Behavioural Theory of the Firm*, New Jersey: Prentice-Hall.

Dankelman, S. (1996) 'Diploma Diplomatics: The Europeanisation and Transformation of National Professional Institutions', paper prepared for presentation to the 1996 joint sessions of the European Consortium for Political Research, Oslo, 29 March–3 April.

Dehousse, R. (1993) 'Integration v Regulation: On the Dynamics of Regulation in the European Community', *Journal of Common Market Studies*, 330, 4: 383–402.

de Tocqueville, A. (1946) *Democracy in America*, London: Oxford University Press.

Deutsch, K. (1953, 1966) *Nationalism and Social Communication*, 2nd edn, Cambridge, Mass.: MIT Press.

—— (1968) *The Analysis of International Relations*, London: Prentice-Hall.

Di Maggio P. J. and Powell, W. W. (eds) (1991) *The New Institutionalism and Organizational Analysis*, London: University of Chicago Press.

Dunleavy, P. (1991) *Democracy, Bureaucracy, and Public Choice*, Hemel Hempstead: Harvester Wheatsheaf.

ECCA (1995) European Campaign for Clean Air, 'Memorandum on new EU pollution standards for motor vehicles and air quality directives', Brussels: ECCA.

Edelman, M. (1967, 1985) *The Symbolic Uses of Politics*, Chicago: University of Illinois Press.

Ehrmann, H. W. (1957) *Organized Business in France*, Princeton, NJ: Princeton University Press.

Elder, C. D. and Cobb, R. W. (1983) *The Political Use of Symbols*, New York: Longman.

EURO-C (1994) '*EURO-C' the ETUC's voice on behalf of consumers*', Brussels: EURO-C.

EUROCADRES (1994) 'Report on Activities: February 1993 to July 1994', 504/94/E/b, Brussels: EUROCADRES.

EUROCADRES (1995) 'Report on the Employment and Unemployment Situation of Professional and Managerial Staff in Europe', December 1995, 1671/E, Brussels: Eurocadres.

Euroconfidentiel (1996) *The Directory of EU Trade and Professional Associations and Their Information*, 2nd rev. edn, Geneva: Euroconfidentiel.

EURO COOP (1993) European Community of Consumer Cooperatives, 'Consumer cooperatives and their activities at national and European level', Brussels: EURO COOP, October.

European Commission (1990) 'Commission communication on the development of European standardisation: Action for faster technological integration in Europe', COM(90) 456 Final, 16 October, Luxembourg: Office for Official Publications of the European Communities.

—— (1991a) *Directory of EC Trade and Professional Associations 1992*, Editions Delta, Brussels/Luxembourg.

—— (1991b) *Consumer Policy in the Single Market*, Luxembourg: Office for Official Publications of the European Communities.

—— (1992) *Directory of Trade Associations and Pressure Groups in the European Community*, Brussels and Luxembourg: Office of Official Publications of the European Communities.

—— (1993) 'Communication concerning the application of the Agreement on social policy presented by the Commission to the Council and the European Parliament', COM(93)600 Final, 14 December 1993, Luxembourg: Office for Official Publications of the European Communities.

European Environmental Bureau (1994) *EEB Twentieth Anniversary*, Brussels: EEB.

—— (1996) *Activity Report 1995, Programme of Activities 1996*, Brussels: EEB.

The EU Committee of the American Chamber of Commerce (1995) *EU Environment Guide 1996*, Brussels: The EU Committee of the American Chamber of Commerce.

Evetts, J. (1995) 'International Professional Associations: The New Context for Professional Projects', *Work, Employment and Society*, 9, 4: 763–72.

Friedland, R. and Alford, R. (1991) 'Bringing Society Back In: Symbols, Practices, and Institutional Contradictions', in P. J. Di Maggio and W. W. Powell (eds) *The New Institutionalism and Organizational Analysis*, London: University of Chicago Press.

Friedson, E. (1986) *Professional Powers*, Chicago: University of Chicago Press.

Feld, W. J. (1966) 'National Economic Interest Groups and Policy Formation in the EEC', *Political Science Quarterly*, 91, 3: 392–411.

Galtung, J. (1973) *The European Community: A Superpower in the Making*, Oslo: Universitetsforlaget.

Garrett, G. (1992) 'International Cooperation and Institutional Choice: The European Community's Internal Market', *International Organisation* 46, 2: 533–60.

Garrett, G. and Weingast, B. (1993) 'Ideas, Interests and Institutions: Constructing the European Community's Internal Market', in J. Goldstein and R. Keohane (eds) *Ideas and Foreign Policy: Beliefs, Institutions and Political Change*, London: Cornell University Press.

Grant, W. (1993) 'Pressure Groups in the European Community: An Overview', in S. Mazey and J. Richardson (eds) *Lobbying in the European Community*, Oxford: Oxford University Press.

Grant, W. and Marsh, D. (1977) *The CBI*, London: Hodder & Stoughton.

Gray, V. and Lowery, D. (1995) 'Reconceptualizing PAC formation: It's not a collective action problem, and it may be an arms race', Paper presented at the American Political Science Association Conference, Chicago, August 30–September 3.

Gray, V. and Lowery, D. (1997) 'Reconceptualizing PAC formation: It's not a collective action problem, and it may be an arms race', *American Politics Quarterly* 25, 3.

Green, D. and Shapiro, I. (1994) *Pathologies of Rational Choice Theory*, Yale, Conn.: Yale University Press.

Greenwood, E. (1965) 'Attributes of a Profession', in M. Zald (ed.) *Social Welfare Institutions*, London: John Wiley.

——(1995a) (ed.) *European Casebook on Business Alliances*, Hemel Hempstead: Prentice-Hall.

Greenwood, J. (1995b) 'The Pharmaceutical Industry: A European Business Alliance That Works', in J. Greenwood (ed.) *European Casebook on Business Alliances*, Hemel Hempstead: Prentice-Hall.

——(1997) *Representing Interests in the European Union*, London: Macmillan.

Greenwood, J. and Cram, L. (1996) 'European Level Business Collective Action: The Study Agenda Ahead', *Journal of Common Market Studies*, 34, 3: 449–63.

Greenwood, J., Grote, J. and Ronit, K. (1992) *Organised Interests and the European Community*, London: Sage.

Greenwood, J., Levy, R. and Stewart, R. (1995) 'The European Union Structural Fund Allocations: "Lobbying to Win" or Recycling the Budget?' *European Urban and Regional Studies*, 2, 4: 317–38.

Greenwood, J. and Ronit, K. (1995) 'European Bioindustry', in J. Greenwood (ed.) *European Casebook on Business Alliances*, Hemel Hempstead: Prentice-Hall.

Greenwood, J. and Ronit, K. (1992) 'Established and Emergent Sectors: Organized Interests at the European Level in the Pharmaceutical Industry and the New Biotechnologies', in J. Greenwood, J. R. Grote and K. Ronit (eds) *Organized Interests and the European Community*, London: Sage.

Grunert, T. (1987) 'Decision Making Processes in the Steel Crisis Policy of the EEC: Neocorporatist or Integrationist Tendencies', in Y. Meny and V. Wright (eds) *The Politics of Steel: Western Europe and the Steel Industry in the Crisis Years (1974–1984)*, New York: De Gruyter.

Haas, E. (1958) *The Uniting of Europe: Political, Social, and Economical Forces 1950–1957*, Stanford, Stanford University Press.

—— (1970) 'The Study of Regional Integration: Reflections on the Joys and Anguish of Pre-Theorising', *International Organisation*, 4: 607–46.

—— (1975) *The Obsolescence of Regional Integration Theory*, Berkeley, Calif.: Institute of International Studies.

Hall, P. A. (1986) *Governing the Economy: The Politics of States Intervention in Britain and France*, Cambridge: Polity Press.

—— (1989) *The Political Power of Economic Ideas*, Princeton, NJ: Princeton University Press.

Hammerich, K.E. (1969) *L'Union des Industries de la Communauté Européenne du Marché Commun*, Stockholm: Fédération des Industries Suédoises.

Hardin R. (1982) *Collective Action*, Baltimore, Md.: Johns Hopkins University Press.

Harris, R. and Lavan, A. (1992) 'Professional Mobility in the New Europe: The Case of Social Work', *Journal of European Social Policy*, 2, 1: 1–15.

Harvey, B. (1995, 2nd edn) *Networking in Europe*, London: National Council of Voluntary Organisations.

Hirschman, A. O. (1970) *Exit, Voice, and Loyalty. Responses to Decline in Firms, Organizations, and States*, Cambridge, Mass.: Harvard University Press.

—— (1982) *Shifting Involvements*, Oxford: Martin Robertson.

Holmes, P. and McGowan, F. (1997) 'The Changing Dynamic of EU–Industry Relations: Lessons from the Liberalization of European Car and Airline Markets', in H. Wallace and A. R. Young (eds) *Participation and Policy-Making in the European Union*, Oxford: Clarendon Press.

Hula, K. (1995) 'Rounding up the Usual Suspects: Forging Interest Group Coalitions in Washington', in A. Cigler and B. Loomis (eds) *Interest Group Politics*, 4th edn, Washington, DC: CQ Press.

Jachtenfuchs, M. and Kohler-Koch, B. (Hrsg.) (1996) *Europäische Integration*, Opladen: Leske und Budrich.

Jacquemin, A. and Wright, D. (1994) 'Corporate Strategies and European Challenges Post 1992', in S. Bulmer and A. Scott (eds) *Economic and Political Integration in Europe: Internal Dynamics and Global Context*, Oxford: Blackwell.

Jenkins-Smith, H C. and Sabatier, P. (1994) 'Evaluating the Advocacy Coalition Framework', *Journal of Public Policy*, 14, 2: 175–203.

Jordan, A.G. (1994) 'A Conceptual Analysis of "Interest Groups": Identifying the Field of Interest', paper prepared for presentation at the IPSA World Congress, Berlin.

Jordan, A. G., and Maloney, W. A. (1994) 'How Bumblebees Fly: Accounting for Public Interest Representation', British Interest Group Project, working paper series no. 6, Aberdeen: University of Aberdeen.

Jordan, A. G., and Maloney, W. A. (1996) 'How Bumblebees Fly: Accounting for Public Interest Participation', *Political Studies*, 44, 4: 668–85.

——(1997) *The Protest Business*, Manchester University Press.

Josselin, D. (1996) 'Domestic Policy Networks and European Negotiations: Evidence from British and French Financial Services', *Journal of European Public Policy*, 3, 3: 297–317.

Kassim, H. (1995) 'The Development of the Common Air Transport Policy: The Implications for Existing Theory and Future Theorising', unpublished paper, Birkbeck College, London.

Kingdon, J. W. (1984) *Agendas, Alternatives and Public Policies*, New York: HarperCollins.

Kramnick, I. (ed.) (1987) *The Federalist*, London: Penguin.

Kirchner, E. J. (1978) *Trade Unions as a Pressure Group in the European Community*, Westmead: Saxon House.

Knoke, D. (1988) 'Incentives in Collective Action Organizations', *American Sociological Review*, 53, June: 311–29.

Knoke, D., Pappi, F. U., Broadbent, J. and Tsujinaka, Y. (1996) *Comparing Policy Networks: Labor Politics in the US, Germany, and Japan*, Cambridge: Cambridge University Press.

Kohler-Koch, B. (1993) 'Germany: Fragmented but Strong Lobbying,' in M. P. C. M. Van Schendelen (ed.) *National Public and Private EC Lobbying*, Aldershot: Dartmouth.

Kosmidis, M. (1996) 'A Comparative Analysis of EU Telecom's Policy in Southern Europe: Greece, Spain and Portugal', paper presented at the Joint Sessions of the ECPR, Oslo, March.

Landmarks Publications (1995, 5th edn) *European Public Affairs Directory 1995*, Brussels: Landmarks.

Laslett, J. (1991) 'The Mutual Recognition of Diplomas, Certificates, and Other Evidence of Formal Qualifications in the European Community', *Legal Issues of European Integration*, 1990/1: 1–66.

Leone, R. A. (1986) *Winners, Losers, and Government Regulation*, New York: Basic Books.

Lindberg, L. and Campbell, J. (1991) 'The State and the Organization of Economic Activity', in J. Campbell, R. Hollingsworth and L. Lindberg (eds) *Governance of the American Economy*, Cambridge: Cambridge University Press.

Lindberg, L. and Scheingold, S. (1970) *Europe's Would-Be Polity: Patterns of Change in the European Community*, Englewood Cliffs, NJ: Prentice-Hall.

Lindblom, C. E. (1965) *The Intelligence of Democracy*, Toronto: Collier-Macmillan.

Long, T. (1995) 'Shaping Public Policy in the European Union: A Case Study of the Structural Funds', *Journal of European Public Policy*, 2, 4: 672–9.

Lovecy, J. (1993) 'Regulating Professional Services in the Single European Market: The Cases of Legal and Medical Services in France and the United Kingdom', paper prepared for presentation to the European Community Studies Association Third Biennial International Conference, Washington, DC, May 1993.

Macleod, C. and McCulloch, A. (1996) 'Coordination of interest: government and the voluntary environmental sector', paper presented at the American Political Science Association, San Francisco, August 29–September 1.

Majone, G. (1989) 'Regulating Europe: Problems and Prospects', *Jarbuch zur Staats-und Verwaltungswissenschaft*, Baden-Baden: Nomos Verlags gesel-leschaft.

—— (1991a) 'Cross-National Sources of Regulatory Policy-Making in Europe and the United States,' *Journal of Public Policy*, 11,1: 79–106.

—— (1991b) 'Market Integration and Regulation: Europe after 1992', *European University Institute Working Papers*, SPS No. 91/10, Florence.

—— (1992a) 'Regulatory Federalism in the European Union', *Government and Policy*, 10: 299–316.

—— (1992b) 'Market Integration and Regulation: Europe after 1992', *Metroeconomica*, 43: 131–156.

—— (1993) 'The European Community: Between Social Policy and Social Regulation', *Journal of Common Market Studies*, 31, 2: 153–69.

Mansbridge, J. (1992) 'A Deliberative Theory of Interest Representation,' in M. Petracca (ed.) *The Politics of Interests: Interest Groups Transformed*, Boulder, Colo.: Westview.

March, J. and Olsen, J. (1989) *Rediscovering Institutions: The Organizational Basis of Politics*, New York: The Free Press.

Marks, G. and McAdam, D. (1996) 'Social movements and the changing structure of political opportunity in the European Union', in G. Marks, F.W. Scharpf, P. C. Schmitter and W. Streeck (eds) *Governance in the European Union*, London: Sage.

Marwell, G. and Ames, R. E. (1979) 'Experiments on the Provision of Public Goods', *American Journal of Sociology*, 85: 926–37.

Marsh, D. (1976) 'On Joining Interest Groups: An Empirical Consideration of the Work of Mancur Olson', *British Journal of Political Science* 6: 257–71.

Mazey, S. and Richardson, J. (1992) 'Environmental Groups and the EC: Challenges and Opportunities', *Environmental Politics*, 1, 4: 109–28.

—— (1993a) (eds) *Lobbying in the European Community*, Oxford: Oxford University Press.

—— (1993b) *Policy Coordination in Brussels: Environmental and Regional Policy*, Brussels: European Public Policy Institute (EPPI), Occasional Papers 93/5.

—— (1993c) 'Environmental Groups and the EC: Challenges and Opportunities', in D. Judge (ed.) *A Green Dimension for the European Community: Political Issues and Processes*, London: Frank Cass.

—— (1994) 'The Commission and the Lobby', in G. Edwards and D. Spence (eds) *The European Commission*, London: Longman.

McLaughlin, A. and Jordan, G. (1993) 'The Rationality of Lobbying in Europe: Why Are Euro-Groups so Numerous and so Weak? Some Evidence From the Car Industry', in S. Mazey and J. Richardson (eds) *Lobbying in the European Community*, Oxford: Oxford University Press.

McLaughlin, A., Jordan, G. and Maloney, W. (1993) 'Corporate Lobbying in the EC', *Journal of Common Market Studies*, 31, 2: 191–212.

McLean, I. (1991, 2nd edn) *Public Choice: An Introduction*, Oxford: Blackwell.

Mény, Y., Muller, P. and Quermonne, J.-L. (1996) *Adjusting to Europe*, London: Routledge.

Metcalfe, L. (1992) 'After 1992: Can the Commission Manage Europe', *Australian Journal of Public Administration*, 51, 1: 117–30.

Meynaud, J. (1964) *Les Consommateurs et le Pouvoir*, Lausanne: Études de Science Politique.

Millman, T. (1994) 'The UK Engineering Profession: The Case for Unification', *Policy Studies*, 15, 1: 26–41.

Mitrany, D. (1943, 1966) *A Working Peace System*, Chicago: Quadrangle Books.

Moe, T. (1980) *The Organization of Interests: Incentives and the Internal Dynamics of Political Interest Groups*, Chicago: University of Chicago Press.

Moravcsik, A. (1993) 'Preferences and Power in the European Community: A Liberal Intergovernmentalist Approach', *Journal of Common Market Studies*, 31, 4: 473–524.

Murphy, R. (1988) *Social Closure*, Oxford: Clarendon Press.

Mytelka, L. and Delapierre, M. (1987) 'The Alliance Strategies of European Firms in the Information Technology Industry and the Role of ESPRIT', *Journal of Common Market Studies*, 26, 2: 231–53.

NCC (1988) National Consumer Council, *Consumers and the Common Agricultural Policy*, London: HMSO.

NCC (1995) *Agricultural Policy in the EU*, London: NCC.

Neale, P. (1994) 'Expert Interest Groups and the European Commission: Professional Influence on EC Legislation', *International Journal of Sociology and Social Policy*, 14, 6/7: 1–24.

Nicolas, F. (1995) *Common Standards for Enterprise*, Luxembourg: Office for Official Publications of the European Communities.

OECD (1983) Organisation for Economic Co-operation and Development, *Consumer Policy During the Past Ten Years: Main Developments and Prospects*, Paris: OECD.

Offe, C. (1985) *Disorganized Capitalism*, Cambridge, Polity Press.

Olsen, O. J. and Sidenius, N. C. (1991) 'The Politics of Private Business, Cooperative and Public Enterprise – Denmark', Roskilde: Roskilde University Center and University of Aarhus.

Olson, M. (1965) *The Logic of Collective Action*, Cambridge, Mass.: Harvard University Press.

——(1971) *The Logic of Collective Action: Public Goods and the Theory of Groups*, Cambridge, Mass.: Harvard University Press .

Orzack, L. (1991) 'The General Systems Directive and the Liberal Professions', in L. Hurwitz and C. Lequesne (eds) *The State of the European Community*, Boulder, Colo.: Lynne Rienner.

——(1992) 'International Authority and the Professions: The State Beyond the Nation State', Jean Monnet Chair Papers, European Policy Unit at the European University Institute, Florence: European Policy Unitat EUI.

Pagoulatos, G. (1996) 'Governing in a Constraining Environment', paper prepared for presentation to the 1996 Joint Workshops of the European Consortium for Political Research, Oslo, March 29–April 3.

Pedler, R. H. and van Schendelen, M. P. C. M. (eds) (1994) *Lobbying the European Union. Companies, Trade Associations and Issue Groups*, Aldershot: Dartmouth.

Peters, G. (1992) 'Bureaucratic Politics and the Institutions of the European Union' in A. Sbragia (ed.) *Euro-Politics: Institutions and Policy-Making in the 'New' European Union*, Washington, DC: The Brookings Institution.

Peterson, J. (1995) 'Decision-Making in the European Union: Towards a Framework for Analysis', *Journal of European Public Policy*, 2, 1: 69–93.

Petracca, M. P. (1992) (ed.) *The Politics of Interests: Interest Groups Transformed*, Boulder, Colo.: Westview Press.

Philip, A. B. (1991) *Directory of Pressure Groups in the European Community*, Harlow: Longman.

Pierson, P. (1993) 'When Effect Becomes Cause: Policy Feedback and Political Change', *World Politics* 45: 595–628.

—— (1996) 'The Path to European Integration: A Historical Institutionalist Analysis', *Comparative Political Studies*, 29: 2, 123–63.

Pijnenburg, B. (1996) 'EU Lobbying by *Ad Hoc* Coalitions: An Exploratory Case Study', paper prepared for presentation to the Annual Meeting of the Western Political Science Association, San Francisco, March 14–16, 1996.

Plotke, D. (1992) 'The Political Mobilization of Business', in M. P. Petracca (ed.) *The Politics of Interests. Interest Groups Transformed*, Boulder, Colo.: Westview Press.

Pollack, M. (1995) 'Creeping Competence: The Expanding Agenda of the European Community', *Journal of Public Policy*, 14: 97– 143.

Preston, J. (1995) 'EU Issue Emergence – The Case of Policy for Small and Medium Sized Enterprises', paper presented to UACES research conference 'Integration within a Wider Europe', University of Birmingham, 18–19 September 1995.

Pryce, R. (1973) *The Politics of the European Community*, London: Butterworth.

Putnam, R. (1993) *Making Democracy Work: Civic Traditions in Modern Italy*, Princeton, NJ: Princeton University Press.

—— (1995), 'Tuning In, Tuning Out: The Strange Disappearance of Social Capital in America', *PS: Political Science and Politics*, 28, 4: 664–83.

Rowley, A. (1974) *The Barons of European Industry*, New York: Holmes and Meier.

Rucht, D. (1993) 'Think Globally, Act Locally? Needs, Forms and Problems of Cross-National Cooperation Among Environmental Groups', in J. D. Liefferink, P. D. Lowe and A. J. P. Mol (eds) *European Integration and Environmental Policy*, London: Belhaven Press.

Sabatier, P. (1988) 'An Advocacy Coalition Framework of Policy Change and the Role of Policy-Oriented Learning Therein', *Policy Sciences*, 21: 129–68.

—— (1992) 'Interest Group Membership and Organization: Multiple Theories', in M. Petracca (ed.) *The Politics of Interests: Interest Groups Transformed*, Boulder, Colo.: Westview Press.

Sabatier, P. and McLaughlin, S. (1990) 'Belief Congruence Between Interest Group Leaders and Members: An Empirical Analysis of Three Theories and a Suggested Synthesis', *Journal of Politics*, 52, 3: 914–35.

Salisbury, R. H. (1969) 'An Exchange Theory of Interest Groups', *Midwest Journal of Political Science*, 13, 1: 1–32.

Sandholtz, W. (1992a) *High-Tech Europe: The Politics of International Cooperation*, Berkeley: University of California Press.

—— (1992b) 'ESPRIT and the Politics of International Collective Action', *Journal of Common Market Studies*, 30: 1–21.

—— (1993a) 'Choosing Union: Monetary Politics and Maastricht', *International Organisation*, 47, 1: 1–39.

Sandholtz, W. (1993b) 'Institutions and Collective Action: The New Telecommunications in Western Europe', *World Politics*, 45, 2: 242–70.

—— (1996) 'Membership Matters: Limits of the Functional Approach to European Institutions', *Journal of Common Market Studies*, 34, 3: 403–29.

Sandholtz, W. and Zysman, J. (1989) '1992: Recasting the European Bargain', *World Politics*, 42, 1: 95–28.

Savary, J. (1984) *French Multinationals*, New York: St Martin's Press.

Sbragia, A. (1992) 'Introduction', in Sbragia, A (ed.) *Euro-Politics: Institutions and Policy-Making in the 'New' European Union*, Washington, DC: The Brookings Institution.

—— (1994) 'From "Nation-State" to "Member-State": The Evolution of the European Community', in P. M. Lutzeler (ed.) *Europe After Maastricht*, Oxford: Berghahn Books, 69–87.

Schlozman, K. and Tierney, J. (1986) *Organized Interests and American Democracy*, New York: Harper and Row.

Schlozman, K., Verba, S. and Brady, H. (1995) 'Participation's Not a Paradox: The View from American Activists', *British Journal of Political Science*, 25: 1–36.

Schmidt, V. (1996) 'Loosening the Ties that Bind: The Impact of European Integration on French Government and its Relationship to Business,' *Journal of Common Market Studies*, 34, 2: 223–54.

Schmitter, P. and Streeck, W. (1981) 'The Organization of Business Interests: A Research Design to Study the Associative Action of Business in the Advanced Industrial Societies of Western Europe', Berlin: International Institute of Management.

Secretariat of the European Commission (1992) *An Open and Structured Dialogue Between the Commission and Special Interest Groups*, Brussels: Secretariat of the European Commission.

SEPLIS (1996) 'The Liberal Professions and Europe', Brussels: SEPLIS.

Shapiro, M. (1992) 'The European Court of Justice', in A. Sbragia (ed.) *Euro-Politics: Institutions and Policy-Making in the 'New' European Union*, Washington, DC: The Brookings Institution.

Sharp, M. (1990) 'The Single Market and Policies for Advanced Technologies' in C. Crouch and D. Marquand (eds) *The Politics of 1992*, Oxford: Basil Blackwell.

Sidenius, N. C. (1994) 'The Logic of Business Political Organization in Western Europe', paper prepared for presentation at the ECPR Joint Sessions of Workshops, Madrid.

Sidjanski, D. (1967) 'Pressure Groups and the European Community', *Government and Opposition*, 3: 397–416.

Sidjanski, D. (1989) 'South European Interest Groups and their Inclusion in the European Community', *Yapi Kredi Economic Review*, 3, 2: 159–93.

Steinmo, S; Thelen., K; and Longstreth, F. (eds) (1992) *Structuring Politics: Historical Institutionalism in Comparative Analysis*, Cambridge: Cambridge University Press.

Taylor, P. (1983) *The Limits of European Integration*, London: Croom Helm.

—— (1989) 'The New Dynamics of EC In Integration in the 1980s', in J. Lodge (ed.) *The European Community and the Challenge of the Future*, London: Pinter.

Thelen, K. and Steinmo, S. (1992) 'Historical Institutionalism in Comparative Politics', in K. Thelen, S. Steinmo and F. Longstreth (eds) *Structuring Politics: Historical Institutionalism in Comparative Analysis*, Cambridge: Cambridge University Press.

Truman, D. B. (1951) *The Governmental Process: Political Interests and Public Opinion*, New York: Alfred A. Knopf.

Tsebelis, G. (1994) 'The Power of the European Parliament as a Conditional Agenda Setter', *American Political Science Review*, 88, 1: 128–42.

Udehn, L. (1996) *The Limits of Public Choice*, London: Routledge.

van Schendelen, M. P. C. M. (ed.) (1993) *National Public and Private EC Lobbying*, Aldershot: Dartmouth.

Vickers, G. (1965) *The Art of Judgement*, London: Chapman & Hall.

Vipond, P. (1995) 'European Banking and Insurance: Business Alliances and Corporate Strategies', in J. Greenwood (ed.) *European Casebook on Business Alliances*, Hemel Hempstead: Prentice-Hall.

Vogel, D. (1989) *Fluctuating fortunes: The political power of business in America*, New York: Basic Books.

Walker, J. (1983) 'The Origins and Maintenance of Interest Groups in America', *American Political Science Review*, 77: 390– 406.

Weale, A. (1992) *The New Politics of Pollution*, Manchester: University of Manchester Press.

Weiler, J. (1991) 'The Transformation of Europe', *Yale Law Journal*, 100: 2, 403–83.

Weir, M. (1992) 'Ideas and the Politics of Bounded Innovation', in K. Thelen, S. Steinmo and F. Longstreth (eds) *Structuring Politics: Historical Institutionalism in Comparative Analysis*, Cambridge: Cambridge University Press.

Wilding, P. (1982) *Professional Power and Social Welfare*, London: Routledge and Kegan Paul.

Wilson, J. Q. (1973) *Political Organizations*, New York: Basic Books.

Wincott, D. (1994) 'Is The Treaty of Maastricht An Adequate "Constitution" for the European Union?' *Public Administration*, 72, 4: 573–90.

—— (1995) 'Institutional Interaction and European Integration: Towards an Everyday Critique of Liberal Intergovernmentalism', *Journal of Common Market Studies*, 33, 4: 597–609.

Yonsdorf, W. (1965) 'Monnet and the Action Committee: The Formative Period of the European Communities,' *International Organization*, 19, Autumn: 885–912.

Young, A. (1997a) 'Clean Air Versus Mobility: The Politics of Air Pollution from Road Traffic in the European Community', SEI Working Paper, Falmer: Sussex European Institute.

—— (1997b) 'Consumption without representation? Consumers in the Single Market', in H. Wallace and A. R. Young (eds) *Participation and Policy-Making in the European Union*, Oxford: Clarendon Press.

Young, O. (1991) 'Political Leadership and Regime Formation: On the Developments of Institutions in International Society', *International Organisation*, 45, 3: 281–308.

Index